Fiqh al-Imam

In the name of Allah, Most Gracious Most Merciful.
All praise be to Allah, Lord of the Worlds, and peace and blessings
be upon His Messenger Muhammad, the Mercy of the Worlds.

Fiqh al-Imam
Key Proofs in Hanafi Fiqh

On Taqlid
and the Hanafi Interpretation
of the Prophetic Statement
"Pray as you have observed me pray"
(*Sahih al-Bukhari*)

Foreword by
SHAYKH YUSUF MOTALA

ABDUR-RAHMAN IBN YUSUF

WHITE THREAD PRESS
SANTA BARBARA • CALIFORNIA • USA

First Edition January 1996
Second Revised and Extended Edition September 1996
Third Revised Edition First Printing June 2003
Second Printing May 2004 with indexes added

ISBN 0-9728358-0-6

Published by:
White Thread Press
California USA
www.whitethreadpress.com
info@whitethreadpress.com

Distributed in the UK by Azhar Academy Ltd. London
sales@azharacademy.org
Tel: +44 (208) 534 9191

Library of Congress Cataloging-in-Publication Data

Ibn Yusuf, Abdur-Rahman, 1974-
   Fiqh al-Imām : key proofs in Ḥanafī fiqh on taqlīd and the Ḥanafī interpretation of the prophetic statement "pray as you have observed me pray (Ṣaḥīḥ al-Bukhārī)" / by Abdur-Rahman Ibn Yusuf ; foreword by Shaykh Yusuf Motala.-- 3rd rev. ed., 2nd print.
      p. cm.
   Includes index.
   ISBN 0-9728358-0-6 (pbk. : alk. paper)
   1. Islamic law--Sources. 2. Hanafites. I. Title.
   KBP295.I236 2004
   340.5'9--dc22

                                    2004007912

Printed and bound in the United States of America on acid free paper

For Yusuf & Yusuf
My father Yusuf Mangera &
My shaykh Yusuf Motala

Contents

FIQH AL-IMAM

Contents

Foreword

In the name of Allah Most High.

My dear Abdur-Rahman (may Allah protect you).
In accordance with the Sunna, I send you greetings of peace.

It has been a great source of pleasure to learn of the publication of the new edition of *Fiqh al-Imam*. May Allah accept the book and grant it the honor of acceptance among the elect and laity.

If every worshipper studies this book once, he will experience a transformation in his prayer. Since he has until now been performing his prayer according to legal rulings [*fatawa*]; whereas after studying this book, he would increase in his conviction, that the way he stands, recites, bows, prostrates, and sits in the prayer is indeed in one hundred percent emulation of the Mercy of the Worlds, Muhammad, the Messenger of Allah ﷺ. He will sense a special kind of contentment and happiness.

May Allah grant us the ability to emulate the Messenger ﷺ in all our acts of worship and practice. May He maintain in us the love of the Messenger ﷺ and grant us death in that state.

[Shaykh] Yusuf [Motala]
Senior Hadith teacher and Rector
Dar al-ʿUloom al-ʿArabiyya al-Islamiyya
Holcombe, Bury, UK
May 6, 2003/Rabiʿ al-awwal 4, 1424

Introduction

Many Muslims nowadays are often confused by the appearance of variations in the way other Muslims pray. New Muslims who are unaware of the fact that there are four traditional schools of Islamic jurisprudence are especially liable to become confused as to why one of their fellow Muslims says *"amin"* silently after reciting Surat al-Fatiha, while another Muslim brother, three rows back, utters *"amin"* aloud. A curious worshipper might also wonder why some Muslims raise their hands before going into *ruku* [bowing], and others leave their arms and hands hanging to their sides.

Regardless of which method a person follows in his prayer, observing these types of differences can be quite confusing for one who is unaware of the different methods of prayer. This confusion, if increased or prolonged, can lead a person to begin criticizing all methods of prayer, not to mention his or her own way of praying. To add to this confusion, there are some people who officiously go about informing other worshippers that their method of prayer is wrong, and that the Messenger of Allah 鐌 never used to pray that way. They also regularly condemn anyone who follows a position other than their own.

So what are the reasons for the differences observed in the prayer? Are some of these methods incorrect and a deviation from the sacred teachings of Islam? Is there room for such differences in the way Muslims worship? Furthermore, if all the positions of the four traditional schools of Islamic law or *madhhabs* are valid, then is there one that is more superior to the others or are they all the same in the sight of Allah 鐌?

FIQH AL-IMAM

Gradual Changes in the Prophetic Example

The prayer went through various changes throughout the life of the Messenger ﷺ. For instance, in the early days of Islam, it was permissible to speak in prayer. It was also permissible to move about while praying. The hands were raised at nearly every posture, including when coming up from the first prostration [*sajda*]. Likewise, in fasting, a person had to begin his fast from the time he fell asleep, even if that happened to be just after sunset. One can find many examples of changes and transformations that took place in the various rituals of Islamic worship over the twenty-three years of prophethood.

Therefore, one possible source of why some narrations on prayer seem to apparently conflict with one another, is the gradual transformation of the *salat* that took place during the lifetime of the Messenger of Allah ﷺ. The presence of these apparently conflicting narrations is thus one of the reasons why there are scholarly differences of opinion today on prayer and other aspects of worship. It was the work of the *mujtahid* Imams to sift through these apparent contradictions and to select those narrations which would help to understand and formulate the Sunna in a systematic way.

Some scholars state that it is due to Allah's love for His Messenger ﷺ that He kept alive the various actions and postures he performed throughout his life—in the form of four *madhhabs* or schools of jurisprudence—the Hanafi, Maliki, Shafi'i and Hanbali schools.

One of the main intentions in the preparation of this book was to provide for all access to evidences of the Hanafi prayer in the English language. It was hoped that this would facilitate a deeper understanding of the Hanafi position regarding the method of prayer, and also engender greater confidence in those positions, especially for those who follow the Hanafi school. By gaining insight into the strength of evidences and the sound methodology through which a school derives its rulings, a person can feel more confident in his following of that school.

This book, while highlighting some of the differences of opinion between the various schools regarding certain aspects of *salat,* primarily focuses on presenting the prominent opinions of the Hanafi school on those issues. By the grace of Allah ﷻ, much of the confusion that people had concerning such issues (either through seeing others pray differently or from being influenced by those who do not follow one of the four traditional schools of jurisprudence) has been removed by earlier editions of this book and other similar publications.

The Legality of the Four Schools

It must be remembered that the intent of this work has not been to, in any way, discredit the opinions of any of the other three traditional schools of jurisprudence (Maliki, Shafi'i and Hanbali). Each of the four schools has its sources in the Qur'an and hadith, and they differ only in the interpretation, application, and scholarly analysis of those sources. Therefore, it is very possible that if one finds the arguments and evidences presented in the works on Hanafi jurisprudence to be strong and convincing, he may feel the same way when reading literature from the other three schools. It is for this reason that the great Imams had a deep and mutual respect for one another's legal positions. Consequently, accepting as valid the opinions of all four legal schools would become a cornerstone of Sunni jurisprudence. However, the etiquette that was and is still observed by each of the four schools is:

> Our opinion is correct with the possibility of being incorrect, and their opinion is incorrect with the possibility of being correct.

Hence, the scholars of one school do not criticize the scholars of another school, but rather understand that each is following an interpretation of the same sources of *Shari'a* (the Qur'an and hadith) as propounded by their Imams—all of whom possessed the ability to infer rulings directly from the Qur'an and the hadiths of the Messenger ﷺ. These four schools have been accepted century after century by the People of the Sunna and Community [*Ahl al-Sunna wa 'l-Jama'a*]. Although there are those who do not follow a school of jurisprudence and claim to rely only on the hadiths, what they are in fact claiming is a place alongside the four Sunni Imams. These same people also follow the interpretations of scholars they trust, which is similar to following one of the four schools of Islamic jurisprudence. The difference however is that they replace the opinions of the righteous Imams of earlier centuries with the opinions of scholars of latter times.

It is important to note that when enumerating the opinions on the various aspects of prayer in this book, only the names of those Imams have been mentioned who hold the same opinion as the Hanafis on a particular issue, since the main purpose of this book is to demonstrate the strength of the Hanafi position and not of the other valid schools of jurisprudence. Therefore, terms such as "group one" or "group two" have been employed when referring to those conflicting views. Also, whenever a consensus of the four Imams on an issue is being discussed, the opinion that conflicts with the consensus would be the opinion of those who do not follow one of the traditional schools of jurisprudence.

The Format of This Book

This book covers twelve of the most important aspects of prayer in which there are differences of opinion. Each chapter begins with an introduction and thereafter mentions the various scholarly opinions on the particular aspect of prayer being discussed. Evidences from the Qur'an, hadiths, statements of the Companions, and logical reasoning, are then presented under their respective subheadings; and finally, those hadiths which appear to contradict the Hanafi opinion are analyzed and explained. The discussion is then summarized with a conclusion.

Four chapters have been added to the beginning of the book. They discuss the importance of *taqlid* or "following a school in Islamic law;" the status of 'Abdullah ibn Mas'ud ﷺ; the position of Imam Abu Hanifa as a Follower [*tabi'i*], scholar, and narrator of hadith; and the question of which opinion is correct in the sight of Allah ﷻ. It is hoped that these chapters will provide further insight into the methodology of the Hanafi school in particular and into traditional scholarship in general.

Another important point to remember here is that it is sufficient for a Muslim to rely on the legal opinions of any one of the four schools of Islamic law without specifically knowing the evidence behind their opinion, since *taqlid* means to follow an Imam while trusting that he has correctly interpreted the sacred texts to the best of his ability. However, in view of the oft-repeated claim made by those who do not practice *taqlid* of a *madhhab*—that the traditional schools of jurisprudence base their opinions and rulings on mere conjecture and analogy rather than sound evidences—it was necessary to compile the evidences of the Hanafi school. Presenting the evidences and highlighting some of the methodology of the Hanafi school will demonstrate to the layman how the school goes about deriving rulings from the Qur'an, hadith and other sources of *Shari'a* [Sacred Law].

The task of compiling, studying, analyzing, and inferring rulings from the sacred sources is a difficult task to undertake and is certainly not the job of a student of the sacred sciences, like the compiler of this book. Such work has already been ably accomplished by the great scholars of the past, like 'Allama Badr al-din al-'Ayni, Jamal al-Din al-Zayla'i, Murtada al-Zabidi, Muhammad Nimawi, Zafar Ahmad 'Uthmani, and Anwar Shah Kashmiri, to mention a few from among the renowned Hanafi scholars in this field. The *Umma* is greatly indebted to these and other scholars for the studies they undertook and the works they produced that are shining lamps in the darkness of ignorance. This is part of the true heritage of the Muslim *Umma* in the form of traditional scholarship.

The first edition of this work was published approximately eight years ago, in January 1996, while the author was in his fifth year of study at the Darul Uloom al-Arabiyya al-Islamiyya in Bury, North England. By the grace of Allah ﷻ, it met with great approval and acceptance; hence, a second edition (revised and extended) was prepared and published in September of the same year along with three extra chapters. The second edition was also quickly exhausted off the shelves, after which it remained out of print for several years. By the mercy and grace of Allah Most High, this third edition of *Fiqh al-Imam* has been developed. Changes specific to this edition are as follows:

(1) Each chapter has been thoroughly revised and many changes have been made in language and sentence structure.

(2) The page layout and formatting of the chapters have been changed to facilitate easier reading and comprehension.

(3) The transliteration of Arabic terms has been refined, as can be observed from the title itself, originally published as *"Fiqhul Imaam,"* now *"Fiqh al-Imam."*

(4) Several new scholarly points and arguments have been added throughout the discussions in the various chapters.

(5) Many Arabic terms used in previous editions have been replaced with their English equivalents, with the Arabic in brackets where deemed necessary.

(6) *The Chicago Manual of Style* has been followed as closely as possible, though with some exceptions, in the presentation of this book. For instance, common Arabic terms such as hadith, *salam, madhhab,* and *rak'a,* have been pluralized in English simply by adding an "s," but in the case of *rak'a,* a "t" has also been inserted for clarity.

It would also be beneficial to mention at this point the primary sources of reference for this work. Most of the discussions in this book are based on the popular works of *fiqh* and Hadith, in Arabic and

Urdu, of prominent Hanafi scholars. The following works constitute the primary source material for this book:

1. *Ma'arif al-sunan* [Knowledge of the Ways], a partial commentary of *Sunan al-Tirmidhi* in Arabic, by the late Hanafi hadith scholar 'Allama Yusuf Binnori of Pakistan.

2. *Darse Tirmidhi* [Lessons on *Tirmidhi*], an explanation of the chapters on worship [*'ibadat*] of *Sunan al-Tirmidhi* in Urdu by the renowned contemporary scholar Mufti Taqi 'Uthmani.

3. *Tanzim al-ashtat* [Arrangement of the Scattered], a complete and comprehensive (yet concise) Urdu commentary on the *Mishkat al-Masabih* [Niche of the Lamps] by Maulana Abu 'l-Hasan, a teacher of hadith and other religious sciences in Bangladesh.

4. *Fath al-Mulhim* [Victory of the Inspirer], a three volume commentary in Arabic of the first portion of *Sahih Muslim* by the great exegete and hadith scholar Maulana Shabbir Ahmad 'Uthmani, which was subsequently completed by Mufti Taqi 'Uthmani in a further five volumes known as the *Takmila* [Completion].

5. *Awjaz al-masalik* [Most Concise of Paths], an expansive Arabic commentary on the *Muwatta* [The Trodden Path] of Imam Malik by the renowned Hadith scholar of the Indian subcontinent, Shaykh Zakariyya Khandelwi.

6. *Ikhtilafe Ummat owr Sirate Mustaqim* [Differences in the *Umma* and the Straight Path], a work in Urdu by the late scholar of hadith, *fiqh* and *tasawwuf,* Shaykh Yusuf Ludhyanwi of Pakistan.

7. *Ashraf al-tawdih* [The Most Noble Clarification], an explanation in Urdu of the *Mishkat al-Masabih* [Niche of the Lamps] by Maulana Nazir Ahmad, a senior teacher of hadith in Pakistan.

Other works consulted have been provided in the Bibliography.

The majority of hadiths and quoted texts in the books listed above have been verified from their original sources by the compiler of this book. Those that have not been verified (mainly due to the unavailability of the original source texts to the compiler) have been distinguished by a "U" in the reference.

Finally, in accordance with the hadith of the Messenger of Allah ﷺ, which states that "The one who is not grateful to people is not grateful to Allah," I end this introduction by fulfilling the pleasant task of expressing gratitude to all those who have assisted in anyway, shape, or form throughout the various editions of this book. I wish especially to thank my teachers, who were great channels of inspiration, knowledge, and guidance for me, as well as my family, friends, and colleagues, without whom this work would have proved very difficult. Allah is well aware of their contributions, however insignificant they may have seemed. May Allah reward them all abundantly in this world and the next, and accept this humble offering on behalf of myself, my family, teachers, and friends. *Amin.*

Abdur-Rahman ibn Yusuf
May 11, 2003/Rabi' al-awwal 9, 1424

PART ONE

1

Taqlid: Following a School in Islamic Law

THE MAIN OBJECTIVE of this book is to provide in-depth discussions on those aspects of a Muslim's prayer which are subject to differences of opinion in the four *madhhabs* or "schools of Islamic law," giving special attention to the Hanafi opinion on each issue. However, since even the concept of *taqlid* or "following a school in Islamic law" is unfamiliar to many Muslims, a discussion on this subject is necessary at the outset.

In this regard, *taqlid* will be discussed under the following three headings in this chapter: (1) *What is Taqlid;* (2) *Taqlid:* Following an Imam in the Matters of *Shari'a;* (3) Following One Particular Imam in Every Juristic Issue. This will hopefully remove any confusion regarding the issue of *taqlid,* and comfort those who seek clarification on the subject.

1. WHAT IS TAQLID?

Definition of Taqlid

Literal: *Taqlid* is the verbal noun derived from the Arabic root *q-l-d,* which means to place, gird, or adorn with a necklace.

Technical: The acceptance of another's statement without demanding proof or evidence, on the belief that the statement is being made in accordance with fact and proof.

3

FIQH AL-IMAM

Taqlid in General

The faculty of *taqlid* is inherently existent in us. If we had refrained from the *taqlid* of our parents and teachers, then today we would be deprived of even the basic and preliminary needs of humanity. By nature, man is endowed with the ability to imitate and follow others. If this was not the case, we would not have been able to learn our mother tongue. If we had refused to accept unquestioningly (without demanding proof) every command, beck, and call of our teachers, we would have been ignorant of even the alphabet of the languages we speak, let alone the study and writing of books in those languages. Our whole life—every facet of it: eating, drinking, wearing garments, walking, earning, and so forth—is connected with this very concept of *taqlid*. Our intellectual and cultural development is the result of *taqlid* of our parents, teachers, and others.

If the technical terminology of every branch of knowledge were not acquired on the basis of *taqlid* (i.e. without questioning the authority of that terminology), then proficiency in such knowledge could not have been attained. If the meanings of words and their idiomatic usages were not acquired through *taqlid* of linguists and the norms of our linguistic discourses, we would not become conversant in any language.

Sometimes man learns the harmful effect of poison as well as the remedial effects of medicines by virtue of *taqlid*. In war, if an army does not accept unquestioningly every order of its commander, victory may not be attained. If the various agencies of government do not obey the laws promulgated by the law makers, then law and order cannot be maintained in the land. In short, the progress and perfection of our physical, spiritual, intellectual, academic, moral and social life is firmly rooted in *taqlid*—to accept and obey professional authority.

The Necessity of Taqlid

There are two types of *wujub* [the compulsory nature of something] in jurisprudence: *wujub bi 'l-dhat* and *wujub bi 'l-ghayr*.

4

Wujub bi 'l-dhat means "compulsory in itself"—in other words, acts ordered or prohibited by Islamic law due to something in their intrinsic nature, like the command of prayer and the prohibition of polytheism.

Wujub bi 'l-ghayr means "compulsory due to an external factor"—in other words, acts that are not compulsory or prohibited in themselves, but constitute the basis for other actions that are specifically commanded or prohibited in the Qur'an and hadiths; or let us say that such acts which take on the obligatory nature of the actions that they form the basis of.

An example of this is the writing of the Holy Qur'an and hadiths. The Messenger of Allah ﷺ is reported by 'Abdullah ibn 'Umar ؓ as saying, "We are a nation that neither writes nor calculates" (*Sahih al-Bukhari, Muslim*). This hadith, by way of implication (since it was said concerning the observation of the moon), negates the transcribing of the Qur'an and hadiths. However, it has been found necessary to record the Qur'an and hadith in writing to preserve their authenticity and make both more widely available. Therefore, such writing is not considered to be in conflict with the above hadith, and no one questions the necessity of such writing nor does anybody demand proof for it.

The preservation of the Qur'an and hadith is an act categorically commanded (thus *wujub bi 'l-dhat*) and emphasized by *Shari'a*. Experience tells us that such preservation is not normally possible without recording the Qur'an and hadith in writing. It is for this reason that the writing of the Qur'an and hadith has also been decreed as *wajib*. Consensus of the entire *Umma* [Muslim Community] regarding the recording of the Qur'an and hadith in writing has been reported through the ages in an unbroken chain of transmission. The need for this recording is thus classified as *wujub bi 'l-ghayr*. In exactly the same way, *taqlid* or "following someone in matters of Islamic law," is also decreed as essential or *wajib*, falling within the classifications of *wujub bi 'l-ghayr.* We find ample evidence for the necessity of *taqlid* in light of the above explanation.

Taqlid is especially important in this age in which the vast majority of Muslims are ignorant of basic Islamic sciences. Thus, without *taqlid,* following the clear and definite commandments of the *Shari'a* would be virtually impossible. For those who have not acquired even a basic knowledge of the sources of *Shari'a* and methods of deriving rulings [*ijtihad*] from the sacred texts, *taqlid* becomes both essential and compulsory.

Evidence from Hadiths

Aswad ibn Yazid narrates:

> Mu'adh came to us in Yemen as a teacher (or as a leader). We asked him concerning a person who had died leaving [as his heirs] a daughter and sister. He decreed half the estate for the daughter and half for the sister (*Sahih al-Bukhari* 2:297).

This was during the lifetime of the Messenger ﷺ. From this hadith a number of points are established:

(1) *Taqlid* was in practice during the time of the Messenger of Allah ﷺ. The questioner (in the hadith) did not demand proof or a basis for the decree. He accepted the ruling, relying on the integrity, piety, and righteousness of Mu'adh ﷺ. This is a precise example of *taqlid* in practice.

(2) The Messenger ﷺ did not criticize the people of his time who followed Mu'adh ﷺ, nor did the Messenger ﷺ have any objection on the issue.

(3) This hadith furnishes proof for the validity of *taqlid shakhsi* or "following one particular person in the affairs of Islamic law." The Messenger of Allah ﷺ had appointed Mu'adh ﷺ to provide religious instruction to the people of Yemen. It is evident that the Messenger of Allah ﷺ granted the people of Yemen the right and permission to

refer to Mu'adh ☙ in all affairs of the *Din* [religion]. The permissibility and validity of *taqlid* is therefore evident from this, especially because of its prevalence in the glorious time of the Messenger ☙.

Evils of Discarding Taqlid

It is well known that many, if not a vast majority of people in this age, do not model their lives after the example of Allah's Messenger ☙. As a result they are governed by selfishness, corrupt motives, lust, insincerity, mischief, strife, anarchy, and opposition to the consensus of the rightly-guided scholars. This inevitably leads to the subjection of the *Din* to human desires. The hadiths on *fitan* [strife, trials, and tribulations] have forewarned us of the rise of these corrupt traits in man, and the scholars of this *Din* have been aware of this problem.

The absence of *taqlid shakhsi* will cause great harm and corruption in the *Din*. One of the destructive evils which will raise its ugly head in the absence of *taqlid shakhsi* is the appearance of self-appointed *mujtahids*. Some people will consider themselves to be capable of inferring religious rulings, and embark on the process of juristic [*shar'i*] analogical reasoning [*qiyas*]. They will consider themselves to be of equal or greater rank than the illustrious *mujtahids* of the early ages of Islam.

For example, the previous *mujtahids* have reliably stated that many laws are based on particular causes [*mu'allal*] and not definite causes. Citing this, some modernists might claim that even the command of *wudu'* for prayer is based on a particular cause [*mu'allal*]. According to them, this command could have been for the early Arabs, whose occupation of tending animals exposed them constantly to impurities, which could have called for ritual purification in the form of *wudu'*. They might claim, on this basis, that since people of the present time live in conditions of greater hygiene, *wudu'* is no longer necessary for prayer. [From the opening chapters of *Taqlid and Ijtihad* by Shaykh Masihullah Jalalabadi]

2. *TAQLID*: FOLLOWING AN IMAM IN THE MATTERS OF *SHARI'A*

Question

Some people say that *taqlid* [following the school of an Imam] is unlawful in *Shari'a*. They insist that a true Muslim should only follow the Holy Qur'an and Sunna, and they say it is equivalent to *shirk* [polytheism] to follow an Imam in the matters of *Shari'a*. They also claim that the Hanafi, Shafi'i, Maliki and Hanbali schools were formed some two hundred years after the Messenger's ﷺ death, and therefore, these schools are a reprehensible innovation [*bid'a*]. Some also stress that a Muslim should seek guidance directly from the Qur'an and Sunna and no intervention of an Imam is needed to practice upon the *Shari'a*. Please explain how far this view is correct.

Answer of Mufti Taqi 'Uthmani

This view is based on certain misunderstandings arising from unnecessary treatment of the complicated issues involved. The full clarification of this mistaken view requires a detailed article. However, I will try to explain the basic points as briefly as possible.

It is true that obedience, in its true sense, belongs to Allah ﷻ alone. We do not obey anyone other than Him. This is the logical requirement of the doctrine of *tawhid* [belief in the oneness of Allah ﷻ]. The obedience of the Messenger of Allah ﷺ has been ordered upon us, only because he is the Messenger of Allah who conveyed to us the divine commandments, otherwise he has no divine status deserving our obedience. By obeying and acting according to the teachings of the Messenger ﷺ, we obtain the pleasure of Allah ﷻ.

However, the crux of the matter is that the interpretation of the Qur'an and the Sunna is not a simple one. It requires an intensive and extensive study of the sacred sources of *Shari'a*, which cannot be undertaken by a person unqualified in the field. If every Muslim was obligated to consult the Holy Qur'an and Sunna on each and every problem arising before him, it would burden him with a responsibility that would be almost impossible to fulfill. This is because the derivation of the rules of *Shari'a* from the Qur'an and Sunna requires a thorough knowledge of the Arabic language and all the relevant sciences—a combination which every person is not known to have. The only solution to this problem is that a few people should equip themselves with the required knowledge of *Shari'a* and others should ask them about the rulings in their day-to-day affairs. This is exactly what Allah ﷻ has ordained for the Muslims in the following words:

> "Of every troop of them, a party only should go forth, that they [who are left behind] may get instructions in religion, and that they may warn their people when they return to them, so that they may beware [of evil]" (*al-Qur'an* 9:122).

This verse of the Holy Qur'an indicates in clear terms that a group of Muslims should devote themselves to acquiring the knowledge of *Shari'a* and all others should consult them for their rulings. Now, if a person asks a reliable scholar ['*alim*] about the juridical [*shar'i*] ruling in a specific matter and acts upon his advice, can any reasonable person accuse him of committing *shirk* on the ground that he has followed the advice of a human being instead of the Qur'an and Sunna? Certainly not.

The reason is obvious, because he has not abandoned obedience to Allah ﷻ and His Messenger ﷺ. Rather, he is in search of a way to obey them. However, being unaware of the *shar'i* commands, he has consulted a scholar in order to know what he is required to do by Allah. He has not taken that scholar as the subject of his obedience, but rather as an interpreter of the divine commands. Nobody can accuse him of committing *shirk*.

This is *taqlid* in essence: a person who is not able to understand the Holy Qur'an and Sunna, and so consults a Muslim jurist, often termed an Imam, and acts according to his interpretation of the *Shari'a*. The person never considers the Imam worthy of obedience, but seeks his guidance in order to know the requirements of *Shari'a* due to not having direct access to the Holy Qur'an and Sunna or not having adequate knowledge for deriving the rules of *Shari'a* from these sources. This behavior is called *taqlid* of that jurist or Imam. Thus, how can it be said that *taqlid* is equivalent to *shirk?*

The qualified Muslim jurists or Imams, who have devoted their lives to *ijtihad,* have collected the rules of *Shari'a* according to their respective interpretations of its sources in an almost codified form. This collection of the rules of *Shari'a* according to the interpretation of a particular jurist is called the *madhhab* or "school" of that jurist.

Thus, the school of an Imam is not something parallel to the *Shari'a* or something alien to it. In fact, it is a particular interpretation of the *Shari'a* and a collection of the major *shar'i* rules derived from the Holy Qur'an and Sunna by a reliable jurist, and arranged subject-wise for the convenience of the followers of the *Shari'a.* So, the one who follows a particular school actually follows the Holy Qur'an and Sunna according to the interpretation of a particular reliable jurist, whom he or she believes to be the most trustworthy and most well-versed in the matters of *Shari'a.*

As for the differences in the schools, they have emerged through the different possible interpretations of the rules mentioned in or derived from the Holy Qur'an and Sunna. In order to understand this point properly, it will be relevant to know that the rules mentioned in the Holy Qur'an and Sunna are of two different types.

The first type of rules are those which are stated in these sacred sources in such clear words that they allow only one interpretation. No other interpretation is possible thereof, such as the obligation of prayer, *zakat,* fasting and pilgrimage; and the prohibition of pork and adultery. With regard to this set of rules, no difference of opinion has ever taken place. All the schools of jurists are unanimous in their interpretation; hence there is no room for *ijtihad* or *taqlid* in these matters. Also, since everyone can easily understand them from the Holy Qur'an and Sunna, there is no need for consulting an Imam or jurist.

On the other hand, there are some rules of *Shari'a* derived from the Holy Qur'an and Sunna where any of the following situations may arise:

(1) The wording used in the sacred sources may allow more than one interpretation. For example, while mentioning the duration of the waiting period [*'idda*] for a divorced woman, the Holy Qur'an has used the following expression:

"And divorced women shall wait [as regards their marriage] for three periods of *quru'*" (2 :228).

The word *quru'* used in the above verse has two meanings. It stands both for the "period of menstruation" and the "period of cleanliness" [i.e. *tuhr*]. Both meanings are possible in the verse and each of them has different legal consequences.

The question that requires jurisprudential efforts here is: "Which of the two meanings is intended here?" While answering the question, the juridical opinions may naturally differ, as is the case. Imam Shafi'i interprets the word *quru'* as the "period of cleanliness," while Imam Abu Hanifa interprets it as the "period of menstruation." Both of them have a number of reasons in support of their respective views, and neither can be completely rejected. This example highlights one of the causes for differences of opinion among different schools.

(2) Sometimes disparity appears between two hadiths of Allah's Messenger 	, and a jurist has to reconcile them or prefer one of them over the other. In this case also, the view points of the jurists may differ from one another. For example, there are two sets of traditions found in the books of hadiths narrating different behaviors of the Messenger 	 while bowing [*ruku'*] in prayer. The first set of hadiths mentions that he used to raise his hands before bowing, while the other hadiths mention that he did not raise his hands except at the beginning of prayer. The jurists, while accepting that both ways are correct, have expressed different views regarding the question: "Which

of the two ways is more preferable?" Thus, situations like these also cause differences of opinion between various schools.

(3) There are many issues which are not specifically addressed in the Holy Qur'an and Sunna. The solution to these issues is sought either through analogy or through examples, found in the sacred sources, that have an indirect bearing on the subject. Here again, the jurists may have different approaches to extracting the required solution from the Holy Qur'an and Sunna.

Such are the basic causes of differences of opinion between the schools. These differences are in no way a defect in *Shari'a*, rather they are a source of flexibility composing a vast field of academic research governed by the principles of *Shari'a* and settled by means of the Holy Qur'an and Sunna for all time to come.

A Muslim jurist who has all the necessary qualifications for *ijtihad* is supposed to attempt his utmost to extract the actual meaning of the Qur'an and Sunna. If he does this to the best of his ability and with sincerity, he will be rewarded for accomplishing his duty, and nobody can accuse him of disregarding the *Shari'a,* even though his view may seem to be weaker when compared to others. This is a natural and logical circumstance, certain to be found in every legal system.

The established laws in every legal framework do not cover every minute detail and possible situation. Also, these laws are often open to more than one interpretation, and different courts of law, while attempting to understand them, often disagree about their meanings. One court may interpret the law in a particular way while another court may understand it in quite a different sense. Thus, nobody can say that the jurists have disrespected the laws of Islam by arriving at different opinions. And since every court of law intends to apply the established law to the best of its ability, its duty towards the Lawmaker (Allah ﷻ) will be discharged, and its jurists will be rewarded for it.

For example, if one of the courts mentioned earlier were a high court, all the lower courts and the people living under its authority would be bound to follow judgements made by the high court, even though their personal opinion might not conform to the opinion of the high court. In such a case, if the lower courts follow the decision of the high court, nobody can say that they are not following the law or that they take the high court to be a legislator of the law. This is because, in actual fact, the lower courts are following the decision of the high court as a trustworthy interpreter of the law, and not as a legislator.

In exactly the same way, the school of a Muslim jurist provides nothing more than a reliable interpretation of the *Shari'a*. Another qualified jurist may disagree regarding the interpretation of that jurist, but neither can he be accused of disregarding the laws of *Shari'a*, nor can anyone accuse the followers of a particular school of following something other than the *Shari'a* or of committing *shirk*. The reason for this is that these Muslims are following the school as a trustworthy interpretation of *Shari'a*.

The next question which may arise here is: "What should a person do with regard to these different schools, and which one of them should he follow?" The answer to this question is very simple. All of these schools have been sincere in their efforts to infer the true meaning of the *Shari'a;* therefore they are all equally valid. A person should follow the school of any of the recognized Imams whom he believes to be most knowledgeable and most pious.

Although the Muslim jurists who have undertaken the exercise of *ijtihad* have been many in number, the schools of the four Imams—Imam Abu Hanifa, Imam Malik, Imam Shafi'i and Imam Ahmad—are found to be more comprehensive, well-arranged, and well-preserved up to the present day. The Muslim *Umma* as a whole has taken these four Imams as having the most reliable interpretations of *Shari'a*.

The four schools are known as the Hanafi, Shafi'i, Maliki, and Hanbali schools. The rest of the schools [*madhhabs*] are either not comprehensive enough, in the sense that they do not contain all aspects of *Shari'a,* or have not been preserved in a reliable form. For this reason, the majority of the Muslim *Umma* belongs to one of these four schools. If a person adopts a school of Islamic law as an interpretation of the *Shari'a*, his obligation to follow the *Shari'a* stands fulfilled.

This is the true picture of the term *taqlid* with reference to the jurisprudential schools. I hope this explanation will be sufficient to show that *taqlid* has nothing to do with *shirk* or "ascribing partners to Allah," but is in fact a simple and easy way of following the *Shari'a.*

3. Following one Particular Imam in Every Juristic Issue

Question

It is generally believed by Sunni Muslims that each one of the four schools (Hanafi, Shafi'i, Maliki and Hanbali)—all being possible interpretations of the *Shari'a*—are correct and none of them can be held as something in contradiction with the *Shari'a*. But at the same time, we can see that the followers of the Hanafi school do not depart from the Hanafi view and do not adopt the Shafi'i or Maliki view in juristic matters. Rather, they deem it impermissible to follow the view of another jurist in any particular issue. How can this approach be reconciled with the belief that all the four schools are considered correct? It would seem that if they are all correct then there should be no harm in the Hanafis following Shafi'i, Maliki, or Hanbali views in some matters.

Answer of Mufti Taqi 'Uthmani

It is true that all the four schools are on the truth, and following any one of them is permissible in order to follow the *Shari'a*. However, a nonprofessional who lacks the ability to compare between the arguments of each school cannot pick and mix between different views to satisfy his personal desires. The reason for this approach is twofold.

Allah ﷻ has empathically ordered in a number of verses of the Holy Qur'an to follow the guidance of the *Shari'a*, and has made it strictly prohibited for one to follow one's desires vis-à-vis the rules of the *Shari'a*. The Muslim jurists, when interpreting the sources of the *Shari'a*, attempt never to satisfy their personal desires. They attempt to make their best effort to discover the spirit of *Shari'a*, and they base their opinions on the force of evidence and not merely on the search for convenience. They do not choose an interpretation on the basis of its suitability to their personal fancies; they choose it only on the basis of the strength of the evidence before them.

Now, if someone who has not studied Islamic law is allowed to choose any juristic view without consulting the arguments pertaining to those views, he will be at liberty to select only those views which seem to be more fulfilling to his personal requirements. This attitude will lead him to follow his own *desires* and not the *guidance*—a practice totally condemned in the Holy Qur'an.

For example, Imam Abu Hanifa is of the opinion that bleeding from any part of the body breaks the *wudu'*, while Imam Shafi'i believes that bleeding does not break the *wudu'*. On the other hand, Imam Shafi'i says that if a man touches a woman, his *wudu'* stands broken and he is obligated to make fresh *wudu'* before offering prayer, while Imam Abu Hanifa insists that merely touching a woman does not break the *wudu'*.

How can the practice of "pick-and-mix" be allowed? A layman may well choose the Hanafi opinion in the matter of touching a woman and the Shafi'i view in the matter of bleeding. Consequently, he will deem his *wudu'* unbroken even when experiencing both situations together (i.e. he has bled and happened to touch a women) even though his *wudu'* stands broken now according to both Hanafi and Shafi'i opinions.

Similarly, according to the Shafi'i view, a traveller can combine the two prayers of Zuhr and 'Asr. However, at the same time, if a traveller makes up his mind to stay in a town for four days, he is no longer regarded as a traveller in the Shafi'i view. Hence, he cannot avail himself of the concession of shortening the prayers [*qasr*] nor of combining two prayers. On the other hand, the period of travel, according to the Hanafi view, is fourteen days, and a person can continue to shorten his prayers as long as he does not resolve to stay in a town for fourteen days or more.

A traveler who has entered a city to stay there for five days, cannot combine two prayers, according to both Imam Shafi'i and Imam Abu Hanifa. This is because, by staying for five days, he cannot use the two concessions of *qasr* and of combining two prayers according to Imam Shafi'i, and because combining two prayers is not allowed according to Imam Abu Hanifa. Nevertheless, the approach of "pick and mix" still leads some people to adopt the Shafi'i view in the matter of combining prayers and the Hanafi view in the matter of the period of journey.

It is evident from these examples that the selection of different views in different cases is not based on the force of arguments leading to them, but on the facility provided by each. Obviously this practice is tantamount to following one's desires, which is totally prohibited by the Holy Qur'an. If such an attitude is permitted, it will render the *Shari'a* a plaything in the hands of the ignorant, and no rule of *Shari'a* will remain immune to distortion. This is why the practice of "pick-and-mix" has been condemned by all the renowned scholars of *Shari'a*. Imam Ibn Taymiya, the famous hadith scholar and jurist, says in his *Fatawa*:

> Some people follow at one time an Imam who holds marriage invalid, and at another time they follow an Imam who holds it valid. They do so only to serve their individual purpose and satisfy their desires. Such a practice is impermissible according to the consensus of all the Imams (*Fatawa Ibn Taymiya* 2: 285–286).

This was the basic cause for the policy adopted by the later jurists, who made it necessary for the common people to adopt a particular school in its totality. If one prefers the *madhhab* of Imam Abu Hanifa, then one should adopt it in all matters and with all its details. However, if one prefers another *madhhab* one should adopt that one in full. One should not pick and mix between the different views of the schools for one's own benefit.

The benefit of the validity of the *madhhabs,* according to the jurists, is that a person can elect to follow any one of them. But once a person has adopted a particular *madhhab,* then he should not follow any other *madhhab* in any matter, whether it be to seek convenience or to satisfy his personal choices, both of which are based on his desires and not on the force of argument. Thus, the policy of "allegiance to a particular school" was a preventive measure adopted by the jurists to preclude anarchy in the matter of the *Shari'a.*

However, this policy is meant for those who cannot carry out *ijtihad* themselves or cannot evaluate the arguments advanced by all the *madhhabs* in support of their views. For such people, the best approach is to follow one particular school as a credible interpretation of the *Shari'a.*

Nevertheless, those equipped with the necessary qualifications of *ijtihad* need not follow a particular school [*madhhab*]. They can derive the rules of *Shari'a* directly from the original sources. Similarly, those who are not fully qualified for the exercise of deriving rulings [*ijtihad*], but are so well-versed in the Islamic disciplines that they can evaluate the different juristic views on purely academic grounds (i.e. without being motivated by their personal desires), are not forbidden from preferring one school over the other in a particular matter. There are many Hanafi jurists who, despite their allegiance to Imam Abu Hanifa, have adopted the view of some other jurist in some juristic issues. Nevertheless, they are considered Hanafis.

This partial departure from the view of Imam Abu Hanifa could be based on either of the following grounds: sometimes jurists, after an honest and comprehensive study of the relevant material, come to the conclusion that the view of another Imam is stronger. Jurists may also find that the view of Imam Abu Hanifa, although based on analogy, does not conform to an authentic hadith, which is usually due to its not having been conveyed to the Imam; otherwise he most probably would have adopted a view in conformance with that hadith also.

Another case in which jurists have departed from the view of their Imam is when they have felt it a necessity for the collective good of the *Umma*. These jurists would follow another Imam not in pursuance of their personal desires, but to meet the collective needs of the *Umma* and in view of the changed circumstances prevailing in their time.

These examples are sufficient to show that the followers of a particular school do not take their school as a substitute for the *Shari'a* or as its sole version to the exclusion of every other *madhhab*. Followers of a *madhhab* do not give any *madhhab* a higher place than it actually deserves within the framework of *Shari'a*.

Before parting with this question, I would like to clarify another point which is extremely important in this context. Some people who have no systematic knowledge of Islamic disciplines often become deluded by their superficial knowledge based on self-study (in many cases, it being only through the translation of the Holy Qur'an and hadiths). Following this kind of cursory study, they assume themselves to be masters of Islamic learning and begin criticizing the former Muslim jurists. This attitude is based on ignorance and has no justification.

The extraction of juridical rules from the Holy Qur'an and Sunna is a very meticulous process that cannot be carried out on the basis of sketchy study. While studying a particular juristic subject, one has to collect all the relevant material from the Qur'an and hadiths found in the various chapters and books and undertake a combined study of the scattered material. One must examine the veracity of the relevant hadiths in light of the well-established principles of the science of hadith [*usul al-hadith*]. One must study the historical background of the relevant verses and traditions. In short, one has to first resolve a number of complicated issues involved. This whole exercise requires very intensive and extensive knowledge which is seldom found in the contemporary scholars who have specialized themselves in the subject, let alone the common people who have no direct access to the original sources of *Shari'a*.

The conclusion of the above discussion is that since all the four schools are based on solid grounds, it is permissible for a competent scholar to adopt another school's juristic view, if he has the required knowledge and ability to understand the merits of each *madhhab* on the basis of adequate academic research, without being indulged in pursuing his personal desires. The people who do not fulfill these conditions should not dare to do so, because it could lead to anarchy in the matter of *Shari'a*.

2

Imam Aʿzam Abu Hanifa and Hadith

THE YEAR 80 A.H. witnessed the birth of a great personality—one who engaged himself in the study of the religious sciences under the great scholars of his time; one who proceeded to process and codify this knowledge, especially in the field of jurisprudence [*fiqh*], for the benefit of the *Umma* of Muhammad ﷺ. This person was none other than Abu Hanifa Nuʿman ibn Thabit of Kufa. The intelligence, wisdom, prudence, piety, devotion, generosity, and good conduct he exemplified made him unique in his time. He attained a very high status in the various fields of *sacred knowledge* [*ʿilm*] and was given the title al-Imam al-Aʿzam or "the Greatest Imam."

Since, this book pertains in particular to the Hanafi school of *fiqh*, it was only fitting that this chapter on the founder of the Hanafi school follow the chapter on *taqlid*. We recount here the life of this great personality, who is renowned all over the world for his services to Islam and who is accepted by consensus of this *Umma's* scholars as a reliable interpreter of the *sacred texts*. His school of *fiqh* [*madhhab*] has continued to be adopted and followed by the vast majority of the People of the Sunna and Community [*Ahl al-Sunna wa 'l-Jamaʿa*] to this day.

Unfortunately, there are some who have considered themselves at liberty to raise objections to the Imam and slander him. They attempt to lower his status and show him to be deficient in the field of hadith.

21

However, anyone who studies the pages of history objectively will surely be impressed by his scholarship in the various fields of Islamic learning, especially his insight in hadith—the knowledge of which is indispensable for any jurist, let alone for someone regarded as "al-Imam al-A'zam."

An entire biography of the great Imam is beyond the scope of this work, so this chapter will focus mainly on a few aspects of his life: that of his position as a Follower [*tabi'i*], the most knowledgeable person of his time, and a narrator and hadith master [*hafiz*]. Only the statements of scholars of hadith [*muhaddithin*], prominent jurists [*fuqaha'*], elucidators of the Qur'an [*mufassirin*], and other religious experts will be presented in this regard. May Allah allow an authentic picture to emerge of the Imam's true position and scholarship in the fields of sacred learning, especially in the field of hadith.

IMAM ABU HANIFA: A FOLLOWER [*TABI'I*]

According to the majority of hadith scholars, a *tabi'i* or "Follower" is someone who met a Companion of the Messenger 🌸 or merely saw one while in the state of faith [*iman*]. It is not necessary for him to have remained in his company or to have narrated from him. Hafiz ibn Hajar al-'Asqalani has stated this definition to be the most preferred one (*I'la' al-sunan* 19:306). 'Allama 'Iraqi, Ibn al-Salah, Nawawi, and Hakim, among others, also agree on this definition.

According to this widely accepted opinion, Imam Abu Hanifa is considered to be a *tabi'i,* and this has been confirmed by many biographers and historians. This is a unique position held by him, since the same cannot be said regarding the other great Imams, Shafi'i, Malik, and Ahmad ibn Hanbal (may Allah be pleased with them all).

'Allama Dhahabi writes in his *Tadhkirat al-huffaz* that Abu Hanifa was born in 80 A.H. He saw Anas ibn Malik 🌸 more than once (every time Anas 🌸 visited Kufa). Hafiz 'Abd al-Ghani al-Maqdisi states:

Abu Hanifa saw Anas 🌸 (*Tadhkirat al-Rashid* 427).

Ibn Hajar al-Makki writes:

> It is true, as Dhahabi has stated, that Abu Hanifa saw Anas ibn Malik ﷺ when he was young (*al-Khayrat al-hisan*).

Khatib al-Baghdadi confirms in his *Tarikh al-Baghdad*:

> Abu Hanifa saw Anas ibn Malik ﷺ (*Tadhkirat al-Rashid* 281).

Hamza al-Sahami states:

> I heard Daraqutni say, "Abu Hanifa did not meet any Companion of the Messenger ﷺ except Anas ibn Malik ﷺ" (*Tabyid al-sahifa* 502).

Therefore, as many scholars have confirmed, Imam Abu Hanifa was most certainly a *tabi'i*.

Imam Abu Hanifa Narrated from the Companions

Imam 'Abd al-Qadir al-Misri states:

> The Companions from who, Abu Hanifa related [hadiths] were 'Abdullah ibn Unays, 'Abdullah ibn Jaz'a al-Zabidi, Anas ibn Malik, Jabir ibn 'Abdillah, Ma'qil ibn Yasar, Wathila ibn al-Asqa', and 'A'isha bint 'l-Ajrad ﷺ (*al-Fawa'id al-ba hiyya* 42).

'Abdullah ibn Ja'far al-Razi relates that Abu Yusuf said:

> I heard Abu Hanifa say to us, "I performed Haj with my father in 93 A.H. when I was 16 years old. There was a teacher [*shaykh*] present with many people around him, and I asked my father who it was. He informed me that it was a Companion of the Messenger of Allah ﷺ known as 'Abdullah ibn al-Harith ibn Jaz'a. 'What does he possess [that makes the people gather around him]?' I enquired from my father. He replied, 'Hadiths he has heard from the Messenger ﷺ.' Hence, I requested my father to take me closer so I could listen [to him]. He led me through the masses until I was close enough to listen. I heard him report that the Messenger ﷺ said, 'Whoever acquires an understanding of the religion of Allah, Allah suffices him in his matters of concern and provides him with sustenance from sources which he could not expect.'"

The great Maliki scholar Abu 'Umar Ibn 'Abd al-Barr, has also related the same incident (*al-Jawahir al-mudi'a* 1:273). 'Allama Khwarizmi states:

> Among the merits and virtues that are not shared by anyone after him was that Abu Hanifa narrated [directly] from the Companions of the Messenger ﷺ. Scholars are agreed upon this fact, although there is some dispute concerning the exact number of Companions (*Jami' al-masanid* 1:22).

The above statements make it clear that not only did Imam Abu Hanifa see some of the Companions, he also narrated from them.

Imam Abu Hanifa: Most Learned Person of His Time

Hafiz al-Sam'ani writes:

> Imam Abu Hanifa engaged himself in the acquisition of knowledge and exerted himself until he achieved what others did not. Once he visited Mansur [the Abbasid caliph] and found 'Isa ibn Musa with him. 'Isa said to Mansur, "This is the scholar of the world today" (*al-Ansab* 247).

Makki ibn Ibrahim once remembered Imam Abu Hanifa and said,

> He was the greatest scholar of his time (*I'la' al-sunan* 18:308).

Makki ibn Ibrahim was the Shaykh of Imam Bukhari through whom Imam Bukhari has transmitted most of his narrations whose chains reach the Messenger of Allah ﷺ through only three transmitters [*thulathiyyat*]. 'Abdullah ibn al-Mubarak relates:

> I entered Kufa and enquired from the scholars as to who was the most learned person in the city? They told me it was Abu Hanifa. Then I enquired from them as to who was the most devout worshipper and the one most occupied in acquiring sacred knowledge? Again they told me it was Abu Hanifa. Every good characteristic I enquired about, they answered, "We do not know of anyone who that characteristic could be attributed to except Abu Hanifa" (*al-Mizan* 58).

Muhammad ibn al-Bishr said,

> I would visit Abu Hanifa and Sufyan al-Thawri. When visiting Sufyan

he would ask me where I had come from. I would inform him from Abu Hanifa and he would remark, "You have just come from the greatest jurist in the world."

Abu Wahb Muhammad ibn Muzahin said,

I heard Ibn al-Mubarak say, "The greatest jurist is Abu Hanifa. I have not seen anyone like him in the field of jurisprudence."

Imam Shafi'i reports that Imam Malik was asked if he had met Abu Hanifa? His reply was:

Yes, I have seen a person who, if he says he could turn this pillar into gold, would be able to provide evidence for it (*Tabyid al-sahifa* 16).

Imam Shafi'i himself once said:

People are dependent on Abu Hanifa in the field of jurisprudence (*Tahdhib al-Tahdhib* 10:450).

'Allama Sha'rani writes:

Imam Shafi'i happened to visit Abu Hanifa's grave during the time of Fajr. He performed the prayer without reciting *qunut* [a special *du'a'*] and remarked, "How could I recite *qunut* in the presence of this Imam when it was his opinion not to recite it" (*al-Mizan*).

Imam Abu Hanifa's opinion was to recite the *qunut* for forty days in Fajr at the time of calamities only.

When the news of Imam Abu Hanifa's death reached Shu'ba, he exclaimed: "Truly to Allah we belong and truly to Him we shall return" [*Inna lillahi wa inna ilayhi raji'un*]. He then said,

The light of sacred knowledge has been extinguished from Kufa. They will never find anyone like him again (*al-Khayrat al-hisan* 71).

Imam Dhahabi writes:

Logic, debate, and wisdom acquired from the forbearers were not, by Allah, the areas of learning pursued by the Companions and the Followers [*tabi'in*]; Imam Awza'i, Thawri, Malik, and Abu Hanifa. Their fields of study were the Qur'an and hadiths (*Tadhkirat al-huffaz* 192).

FIQH AL-IMAM

Hence, this establishes that it was the science of Qur'an and hadith that Imam Abu Hanifa excelled in, and not just other subjects.

Imam Abu Hanifa: A Hadith Master [*Hafiz*]

The great hadith scholar 'Abdullah ibn al-Mubarak said:

> If Allah had not benefited me through Abu Hanifa and Sufyan al-Thawri, I would have been just like any ordinary person (*Tabyid al-sahifa* 1617).

Ibn Ma'in has been reported saying:

> I would never place anyone above Waki'. He would issue his legal rulings [*fatawa*] according to the opinion of Abu Hanifa and would memorize all the hadiths from him. He has heard a great deal of hadiths from Abu Hanifa (*I'la' al-sunan* 19: 315).

The above two statements indicate that Imam Abu Hanifa was a narrator of many hadiths; not just a few, as some claim. Muhammad ibn Sama'a states:

> The Imam has mentioned more than seventy thousand hadiths in his books, and has selected the *Athar* from forty thousand hadiths.

The great hadith scholar Zafar 'Uthmani, after quoting this statement, writes that the trueness of it is indicated by what the Imam's students have narrated from him. For instance, Imam Muhammad narrated from him in his six books known as the *Zahir al-riwaya* and in the other books known as *al-Nawadir;* Abu Yusuf in his *Amali* and *Kitab al-kharaj;* 'Abdullah ibn al-Mubarak in his books; and Waki' and other students in their books.

These rulings [*masa'il*] are in such abundance that their numbers are uncountable and their limits unreachable. If those rulings which are either explicitly or implicitly in conformance with linked [*marfu'*] or unlinked [*mawquf*] narrations are summarized, they would certainly reach this great number [i.e. forty thousand]. This is without taking into consideration the rulings the Imam derived through his own inference [*ijtihad*].

'Allama Zafar 'Uthmani further states that all of these rulings [*masa'il*] are in actual fact "hadiths," which the Imam narrated in the form of legal rulings and not as "formal narrations." It is virtually impossible that his inference (effort to derive religious rulings—*ijtihad*) would conform so closely with such a large number of hadiths if he was said not to have any knowledge of them.

The 'Allama also states that there are many hadiths which Imam Abu Hanifa formally narrated through his personal chains. They are those which the hadith masters have compiled as his *Masanid,* and also those which his students have transmitted from him, like Imam Muhammad in his *Kitab al-athar, Muwatta, Hujaj* and other works; Abu Yusuf, Ibn al-Mubarak, Hasan ibn Ziyad in their works; Waki' ibn al-Jarrah in his *Musnad;* Ibn Abi Shayba and 'Abd al-Razzaq in their *Musannafs;* Hakim in his *Mustadrak* and other works; Ibn Hibban in his *Sahih, Thiqat,* and other works; Bayhaqi in his *Sunan* and other works; Tabarani in his three *Mu'jams;* Daraqutni in his works; and other hadith scholars in their collections. If we were to compile all these narrations together in one place, they would constitute a very large volume of hadiths [*see I'la' al-sunan* 18:316].

IMAM ABU HANIFA: AN AUTHORITY AND CRITIC OF HADITH

'Allama Dhahabi writes in the introduction to his *Tadhkirat al-huffaz:*

> This is a review of those personalities whom I have judged to be reliable and the possessors of prophetic knowledge [*al-'ilm al-nabawi*], and those who could be consulted for their expertise in determining the authenticity or weakness [of narrations] and the reliability or weakness [of narrators] (1:2).

'Allama Dhahabi includes Imam Abu Hanifa among them, which makes it clear that he was a bearer of prophetic knowledge, possessed many narrations, and was considered an authority in the field of hadith.

Suwayd ibn Sa'd reports that Sufyan ibn 'Uyayna said:

The first person to encourage me to relate hadiths was Abu Hanifa. When I arrived in Kufa, he declared that this person possesses the largest number of narrations from 'Amr ibn Dinar. [On hearing this] people began to gather around me, and I began to relate to them (*I'la' al-sunan* 19: 315).

In another report Sufyan ibn 'Uyayna said:

The first person to make me a hadith scholar was Abu Hanifa (*al-Jawahir al-mudi'a* 1:30).

Imam Abu Yusuf said,

I have never found anyone with more insight into the interpretation of hadiths than Abu Hanifa (*Jami' al-'ilm* 1:29).

This statement of Abu Yusuf can be further understood by the following report of Mulla 'Ali al-Qari:

Imam Abu Hanifa was [once] with A'mash, who asked him about something. Imam Abu Hanifa replied, "My opinion in this matter is such-and-such." Upon hearing this, A'mash asked as to how he had formed this [opinion]. Imam Abu Hanifa said, "You reported to us from Abu Salih who reported from Abu Hurayra; you reported to us from Abu Wa'il who reported from 'Abdullah; and you reported to us from Abu Ilyas who reported from Abu Mas'ud al-Ansari that the Messenger of Allah ﷺ said such and such. You also reported the same to us from Abu Mijlaz, who reported it from Hudhayfa, who from Abu 'l-Zubayr, who from Jabir and Yazid al-Raqqashi, and they from Anas ؓ."

A'mash exclaimed, "Enough! Enough! What took me a hundred days to narrate you repeated to me in just an instance. I was not aware that your practice was based on these hadiths." Then he exclaimed, "O group of jurists, you are the physicians, and we are merely the pharmacists; and you [addressing Abu Hanifa] are both" (*Manaqib al-Imam* 484).

Imam Abu Yusuf also said,

I have never opposed Abu Hanifa on any issue, then went back and pondered over it, except to find his opinion more superior [to mine] and more benefiting in terms of the hereafter. At times, I would hold on to a particular hadith, but he would prove to possess more insight concerning its authenticity. There were times when he would strongly defend a certain opinion, and I would visit the scholars of Kufa to see if I could find some [other] hadiths to support his opinion. Sometimes I would return with two or three hadiths, and he would remark concerning one of them, "This is not strong," or concerning another, "This one is not linked [*ma'ruf*]." I would exclaim in amazement, "How do you say this when they support your opinion?" He would reply, "I possess insight into the knowledge of Kufa" (*al-Khayrat al-hisan* 69).

Yahya al-Himmani states:

I heard Abu Hanifa saying, "I have never seen a greater liar than Jabir al-Ju'fi or anybody more superior to 'Ata!" (*Tahdhib al-Tahdhib* 2:48, *Kitab al-'Ilal li 'l-Tirmidhi* 13:309).

Abu Sa'id al-San'ani asked Abu Hanifa his opinion on narrating from Sufyan al-Thawri? He said,

Record his hadiths, for he is reliable [*thiqa*], except his narrations from Abu Ishaq from Harith; and [avoid] the narrations of Jabir al-Ju'fi (*al-Jawahir al-mudi'a* 1:30).

It is also reported that Imam Abu Hanifa said regarding Zayd ibn 'Ayash that "he is unknown" [*majhul*] (*Tahdhib al-Tahdhib* 3:424). Furthermore, the great Imam was not only aware of 'Amr ibn Dinar's name but was also aware of his agnomen [*kunya*]. Ibn al-Mahdi said,

I have never seen anyone possessing greater knowledge of the Sunna than Abu Hanifa. We only became aware of 'Amr ibn Dinar's agnomen through him.

These statements related from Imam Abu Hanifa concerning the status of various narrators make it clear that they could have only been stated by an expert in the scrutiny and criticism of narrators and hadiths.

The great historian and sociologist of the Muslim world Ibn Khaldun writes a conclusive report on the status of jurists in the field of Hadith. He says,

Some people who are of a resentful disposition hatefully claim that there are jurists who know only a few hadiths, and they argue that this is the reason why so few hadiths have been [narrated] from them. This cannot be possible, especially in the case of the great Imams, because Islamic law [*Shari'a*] can only be derived from the Qur'an and Sunna. If one were to possess only superficial knowledge in this field, it would become necessary for him to occupy himself in learning it, for only then would he be able to acquire the religion [its rulings] from the correct source, i.e. from the one [Muhammad ﷺ] who had been appointed to propagate it (*Muqaddima Ibn Khaldun* 371).

Hence, this proves that it is impossible that someone whom a vast majority of this *Umma* has accepted as a competent jurist possess only a superficial knowledge of hadiths. The reliance and trust placed on Imam Abu Hanifa's school by the People of the Sunna throughout the majority of Muslim history, and the high regard with which his opinions are held concerning the acceptance or rejection of hadiths and their narrators, all establish his greatness in the field of Hadith.

Conclusion

A number of points have come to light from the above discussion. We have learned that it is not possible to be a jurist and not possess sound knowledge of the Sunna. Imam Abu Hanifa possessed deep insight into the knowledge of hadith, and was ranked as an authority in the field. 'Allama Dhahabi listed him among the hadith masters [*huffaz*] in his book *Tadhkirat al-huffaz*, and many referred to him as the greatest scholar of his time.

Many jurists would narrate their hadiths in the form of "religious rulings," which meant that they had fewer "formal narrations." However, this cannot be used as a reason for criticism, since the task of the jurist is to process the hadiths and derive rulings from them, as was learned from the Imam's conversation with the great hadith scholar, A'mash. It is therefore incorrect to criticize any great jurist on the basis of his not being aware of hadiths, especially someone of Imam Abu Hanifa's caliber.

We now end this chapter by mentioning some of the noteworthy aspects of Imam Abu Hanifa's gatherings and how his school of jurisprudence was formulated:

Khatib al-Baghdadi relates through his chain that Ibn Karama said, "We were once in the company of Waki' ibn al-Jarrah when someone made a remark that Abu Hanifa has erred. Waki' said, 'How can Abu Hanifa err when he has in his company the likes of Abu Yusuf, Zufar, and Muhammad with their power of analogy [*qiyas*] and inference [*ijtihad*]; the likes of Yahya ibn Zakariyya ibn Abi Za'ida, Hafs ibn Ghiyath, and Hibban and Mandal, sons of 'Ali with their memorization and understanding of hadiths; Qasim ibn Ma'n with his understanding of the Arabic language; and Dawud ibn Nudayr al-Ta'i and Fudayl ibn 'Iyad with their abstinence [*zuhd*] and piety [*wara'*]. How is anyone who has such people as his companions and sitting partners able to make a mistake? Even if he was to make one, they would surely guide him to the truth'" (*Tarikh al-Baghdad* 14:247).

Furthermore, Imam Tahawi related that Asad ibn al-Furat said,

The companions of Abu Hanifa who compiled and recorded the works [of his school] were forty. Those in the forefront were Abu Yusuf, Zufar, Dawud al-Ta'i, Asad ibn 'Amr, Yusuf ibn Khalid al-Samti, Yahya ibn Abi Zakariyya ibn Abi Za'ida, who was their scribe for thirty years....

After quoting the above two statements, the great hadith scholar Zafar Ahmad 'Uthmani comments:

Whoever has hadith masters [*huffaz*] of this caliber as his main students, to whom the hadith scholars have bowed their heads in recognition of their memorization [of hadiths] and extensive knowledge, then how is it possible for that person to have narrated only a few hadiths? (*I'la' al-sunan* 19:331)

May Allah ﷻ remove the veils of ignorance and deceit which distort and obscure the truth, and may He reveal it in its true form and grant us the ability to follow it, *amin*.

3

ʿAbdullah Ibn Masʿud ﷺ

SAYYIDINA ʿABDULLAH IBN MASʿUD ﷺ is one of the many Companions [*sahaba*] from whom the great Imams of jurisprudence have related hadiths and after whom modelled their juridical opinions. He is one of the most revered Companions and is known for his deep understanding of the Holy Qurʾan and jurisprudence [*fiqh*]. Many of his narrations form the basis of numerous opinions in the Hanafi school. Therefore, in an attempt to discredit the Hanafi school, some have attacked this great Companion of Allah's Messenger ﷺ and hurled a great amount of criticism at him.

This chapter has been included to highlight the merits and virtues of this great Companion in the words of the Messenger ﷺ. It is hoped that the words of the Messenger ﷺ will provide an effective means of correcting misconceptions and establishing the true status of this great Companion.

THE COMPANIONS OF ALLAH'S MESSENGER ﷺ

The Companions of Allah's Messenger ﷺ are considered to be the most superior and exalted people after the Messenger ﷺ and the other Envoys of Allah (upon them be peace). The consensus among the People of the Sunna [*Ahl al-sunna*] is that no one after them can attain their status. Their closeness to Allah's Messenger ﷺ—in fact their having merely seen him while they were in a state of *iman* [faith]—elevated them to stages that would be impossible for anyone else to reach.

Many narrations have been reported on the elevated rank of the Companions. The Messenger of Allah ﷺ issued grave warnings against criticizing them in any way. He said,

> Fear Allah in every matter concerning my Companions. Do not make them the targets [of your criticism] after me. Whoever loves them loves them out of love for me, and whoever hates them hates them out of hate for me. Whoever troubles them has troubled me and whoever troubles me has troubled Allah; and whoever troubles Allah, it is imminent that Allah seize him (*Mishkat al-Masabih* from *Sunan al-Tirmidhi*, 554).

In another hadith the Messenger of Allah ﷺ said:

> The best of my *Umma* are the people of my era [the Companions], then those who are after them [the Followers], then those who are after them [Followers of the Followers]. Thereafter, will be such people who will bear testimony where their testimony will not be needed; they will be deceptive and untrustworthy; and they will make vows but will never fulfill them (*Mishkat al-Masabih* from *Sahih al-Bukhari* and *Muslim*, 553).

He also said:

> I asked Allah about the conflicts [that are to occur] between my Companions after my departure. Allah revealed to me, "O Muhammad! In My sight, your Companions are like the stars in the skies. Some are stronger than others but each possesses a light. Whoever adopts any opinion from among the various opinions they differ in will be considered guided in My sight" (*Mishkat al-Masabih* from Razin al-'Abdari, 554).

Furthermore, Allah ﷻ has clearly expressed his satisfaction and pleasure with all the Companions in the Qur'an:

> "Allah is well pleased with them and they pleased with Him. He has prepared for them Gardens under which rivers flow, to dwell therein forever. That is the supreme success" (9:100).

From the above, the elevated status of the Companions becomes very clear and the *Umma* is warned not to criticize them in any way. In fact the Messenger of Allah instructed:

> If you come across those who curse my Companions, say, "May Allah's curse be upon you for your evil" (*Mishkat al-Masabih* from *Sunan al-Tirmidhi*, 554).

These were the Companions, the group Allah had selected for the companionship [*suhba*] of His beloved Envoy . They fulfilled their promises to Allah and conveyed the teachings and practices of His Envoy to the *Umma*, and Allah expressed His pleasure with them. Among these great Companions was 'Abdullah ibn Mas'ud .

HADITHS ON THE VIRTUES OF 'ABDULLAH IBN MAS'UD

Most of the narrations quoted here have been taken from 'Allama Shawkani's *Durr al-Sahaba*.

It is related that 'Abdullah ibn Mas'ud was very close to the Messenger . He was permitted to enter his house frequently and was also his companion on many journeys. He benefited immensely from the Messenger . 'Abd al-Rahman ibn Zayd relates:

> I asked Hudhayfa to inform me about someone who closely resembled the Messenger in manner, conduct, and behavior, so that I could learn from him. He replied, "We are not aware of anyone who possesses a closer resemblance to the Messenger in manner, conduct, and habit than Ibn Ummi 'Abd. This is until he enters into his house [after which we are not aware]" (*Sahih al-Bukhari, Sunan al-Tirmidhi*).

Ibn Ummi 'Abd was the agnomen of 'Abdullah ibn Mas'ud , since Ummi 'Abd was his mother's name. Hudhayfa meant that although he was not aware of the life of 'Abdullah ibn Mas'ud at home, his social conduct surely resembled that of the Messenger of Allah . Abu Musa narrates:

> My brother and I arrived from Yemen and remained [in Madina] for some time. We were led to believe that 'Abdullah ibn Mas'ud and his mother

were part of the Messenger's 🌺 household due to their [frequent] visits to his home and his attachment to them (*Sahih al-Bukhari, Muslim*).

This shows the closeness of 'Abdullah ibn Mas'ud to the Messenger 🌺. Therefore, the claim that 'Abdullah ibn Mas'ud ⬥ was ignorant of the way and manner of the Messenger 🌺 is totally unfounded. 'Alqama reports:

> When I arrived in Syria [Sham], I performed two *rak'ats* and then prayed, "O Allah, facilitate for me a pious companion." I met a group of people and sat down with them. One of them came along and sat down by my side. I enquired as to who he was, and he replied that he was Abu'l-Darda'. I informed him that I had asked Allah to provide for me a pious sitting-companion, and [it seemed as if] He had fulfilled this request. He asked where I had arrived from so I told him I was from Kufa. Upon this he remarked, "Do you not have Ibn Ummi 'Abd among you, the keeper of the slippers and pillow of the Messenger 🌺 and the one in charge of his ablution water? Among you is also the one who Allah has protected from Satan, as revealed upon the tongue of His Envoy 🌺; and there is also among you the keeper of the Messenger's 🌺 secrets, those which nobody besides him has any knowledge of" (*al-Mustadrak*).

Later on 'Alqama came to be recognized as one of the greatest students and successors of 'Abdullah ibn Mas'ud ⬥.

Knowledge of the Qur'an

'Abdullah ibn Mas'ud possessed deep insight into the meaning of the Qur'an, its method of recitation, and the causes of revelation of its verses. He himself stated:

> By the One besides Whom there is no Lord, there is no chapter revealed in the Book of Allah, except that I am the most knowledgeable one regarding where it was revealed. There is no verse from the Book of Allah that has been revealed, except that I am the most knowledgeable one regarding the circumstances of its revelation. If I were to learn of anyone possessing more knowledge than me of the Book of Allah who was within reach of a camel's journey, I would mount it [to visit him] (*Sahih al-Bukhari, Muslim*).

'Umar ibn al-Khattab ✿ relates that once the Messenger ﷺ said,

> Whoever gains satisfaction from reciting the Qur'an as though it were freshly revealed should recite it according to the recitation of Ibn Mas'ud.

'Umar ✿ then says,

> I went to convey the glad tidings of this to him and found that Abu Bakr ✿ had reached him before me and had conveyed the glad tidings to him. I have never been able to outdo Abu Bakr ✿ in any good deed; he has always surpassed me (*Musnad Abi Ya'la, Ahmad, Bazzar*).

At another point 'Umar ibn al-Khattab ✿ said regarding Ibn Mas'ud,

> A small person brimming with [the knowledge of] jurisprudence (*Mu'jam al-Tabarani*).

'Umar ibn al-Khattab ✿ is known for his scrupulousness in matters of religion. Therefore, his statements regarding 'Abdullah ibn Mas'ud ✿ are ample evidence that Ibn Mas'ud ✿ held a very high position in the science of jurisprudence. 'Ali ✿ narrates that the Messenger of Allah ﷺ said:

> If I were to appoint someone as a leader without consulting [anyone], I would appoint Ibn Ummi 'Abd (*al-Mustadrak*).

For the Messenger ﷺ to be able to place so much trust in a person and appoint him to manage the affairs of the Muslims surely indicates that the person had to be of high character, knowledge, and insight into the religion. Concerning him the Messenger ﷺ also said:

> I am pleased for my *Umma* with whatever Ibn Ummi 'Abd ✿ is pleased with (*al-Mustadrak*).

It is further related that

> once the Messenger ﷺ ordered 'Abdullah ibn Mas'ud ✿ to deliver a sermon. He stood up and said, "O People! Allah Most Glorified and Exalted is our Lord, Islam is our religion [*Din*], the Qur'an is our guide

[*imam*], the House of Allah [*Ka'ba*] is the direction we face in prayer [*qibla*], and this is the Envoy [of Allah] sent to us (gesturing towards the Messenger 🌸)." He then concluded, "We are satisfied with what Allah and His Envoy are satisfied with for us." The Messenger 🌸 remarked, "Ibn Ummi 'Abd has spoken the truth. Ibn Ummi 'Abd has spoken the truth, and I am satisfied with what Allah is satisfied with for me, for my *Umma,* and for Ibn Ummi 'Abd" (*Mu'jam al-Tabarani*).

'Abdullah ibn Mas'ud 🌸 was well known for delivering brief but very comprehensive sermons. He was also known for his piety among the Companions. He relates:

When the verse was revealed: "On those who believe and do righteous good deeds, there is no sin for what they ate [in the past], if they fear Allah [by keeping away from His forbidden things] and believe and do righteous good deeds, and again fear Allah and believe, and once again fear Allah and do good deeds with perfection [*ihsan*]. And Allah loves the good-doers" (*al-Qur'an* 5:93), the Messenger 🌸 informed me, "You are from among them" (*Sahih Muslim, Sunan al-Tirmidhi*).

'Ali ibn Abi Talib 🌸 narrates:

Once the Messenger 🌸 ordered 'Abdullah ibn Mas'ud 🌸 to climb a tree to bring something [a toothstick] down for him. Some of the Companions of the Messenger 🌸 caught sight of his calves while he was climbing and began to laugh at their thinness. The Messenger 🌸 remarked, "What are you laughing at? One leg of 'Abdullah will be heavier in the scale [on the Day of Judgement] than mount Uhud" (*Musnad Ahmad, Abi Ya'la, Mu'jam al-Tabarani*).

'Amr ibn al-'As 🌸 relates:

The Messenger of Allah 🌸 passed away in the state that he loved 'Abdullah ibn Mas'ud and 'Ammar ibn Yasir 🌸 (*Mu'jam al-Tabarani*).

OTHER HADITHS REGARDING 'ABDULLAH IBN MAS'UD 🌸.

Hudhayfa 🌸 narrates that the Messenger of Allah 🌸 said,

Whatever 'Abdullah ibn Mas'ud 🌸 narrates to you, accept it (*Sunan al-Tirmidhi*).

This proves that ʿAbdullah ibn Masʿud ☙ was considered (as all Companions are) a competent and reliable narrator of hadiths. It is reported that when Muʿadh ibn Jabal ☙ was on his deathbed he advised:

> Take knowledge from four people: ʿUwaymir Abu ʾl-Dardaʾ; Salman the Persian; ʿAbdullah ibn Masʿud; and ʿAbdullah ibn Salam, who was once a Jew but later embraced Islam (*Sunan al-Tirmidhi*).

Similarly Hudhayfa ☙ relates:

> We asked the Messenger of Allah ☸, "O Messenger of Allah! If only you could appoint a caliph." He replied, "If I appoint a caliph over you and you disobey him then you would be punished, but whatever Hudhayfa relates to you, accept it, and however ʿAbdullah ibn Masʿud teaches you to recite, recite in that way" (*Sunan al-Tirmidhi*).

It is reported that the Messenger of Allah ☸ also said,

> Learn the from four people: ʿAbdullah ibn Masʿud, Salim the slave of Abu Hudhayfa, Ubay ibn Kaʿb, and Muʿadh ibn Jabal ☙ (*Sahih al-Bukhari, Sunan al-Tirmidhi*).

Hafiz ibn Hajar al-ʿAsqalani states that the mention of someone's name before others (as in the case of the above narration where Ibn Masʿud's ☙ name is mentioned first) indicates the superiority of that person. Hence, the status of Ibn Masʿud ☙ in the knowledge of the Qurʾan can also be gauged from the above hadith. In this regard, the narration of ʿUmar ☙ has already been mentioned previously, in which the Messenger of Allah ☸ said that whoever intended to recite the Qurʾan as though it were freshly revealed should recite it according to the recitation of ʿAbdullah ibn Masʿud ☙.

OTHER STATEMENTS

Imam Shaʿbi states:

> No Companion of the Messenger ☸ entered Kufa whose knowledge was more beneficial [for the people] or who was a greater jurist than ʿAbdullah ibn Masʿud ☙.

'Allama Dhahabi, describing the status of the great Companion, writes:

> 'Abdullah ibn Mas'ud ﷺ, the learned leader [al-imam al-rabbani], Abu 'Abd al-Rahman 'Abdullah ibn Ummi 'Abd al-Hudhali; Companion and personal servant of the Messenger ﷺ; among the first to embrace Islam; among the veterans of the battle of Badr; among the expert jurists and teachers of the Qur'an; among those who strove to convey [the words of the Messenger ﷺ] very accurately; extremely scrupulous in [his] narrations; and one who would admonish his students upon their negligence in recording the exact words [of the Messenger ﷺ].... [Due to extreme caution] he would narrate very little [himself].... His students would not give preference to any Companion over him.... Surely he was from among the leading Companions, the bearers of sacred knowledge, and the exemplars [a'imma] of guidance (Tadhkirat al-huffaz 1:13–16).

CONCLUSION

The above is some of what has been related concerning the excellence and virtues of 'Abdullah ibn Mas'ud ﷺ. There is no doubt that every Companion is deserving of high praise, especially those who have been complimented by the Messenger ﷺ. As we have learned, 'Abdullah ibn Mas'ud ﷺ was one of the elect Companions, renowned and praised for his learning and deep insight into the religion.

Criticizing any person close to Allah ﷻ means incurring the wrath of Allah (may Allah protect us from it). In a divine [qudsi] hadith, the Messenger ﷺ relates that Allah ﷻ says, "Whoever harbors enmity towards a Friend [wali] of Mine, I declare war against him" (Sahih al-Bukhari). Therefore, it is considered a very serious crime to belittle the position of a Companion in any way, especially one who possessed so many virtues. The Companions are among those whom Allah ﷻ has expressed His pleasure with:

> "Allah is well pleased with them and they pleased with Him. He has prepared for them Gardens under which rivers flow, to dwell therein for ever. That is the supreme success" (al-Qur'an 9:100).

4

The True Position According to Allah ﷻ

SCHOLARS OF ISLAMIC LAW have paid close attention to the question of which opinion on a particular issue in Islamic law would be the true and accurate opinion in the sight of Allah ﷻ. It is believed that the reliable Imams of *ijtihad* [qualified scholarly analysis to derive legal rulings] and jurisprudence (Imam Abu Hanifa, Malik, Shafi'i, Ahmad, etc.) are all dependable and trustworthy, and that their opinions can be adopted by those who follow their schools of thought. It is also asserted that their rulings concerning the various issues of Islamic law are correct and accurate in themselves.

The question we face is: are conflicting views between the Imams simultaneously correct and in agreement with what Allah has decreed as the truth [*haq*], or is there only one view from among them that is the truth according to Allah? If there is only one truly correct position on a given issue in Islamic law, then we must admit that we do not know which position, according to Allah ﷻ, is the truth [*haq*].

The following—an excerpt from Imam Muhammad ibn al-Hasan al-Shaybani's work *Bulugh al-amani*—sheds light on this issue and explains how only one ruling can be the truth [*haq*] in the sight of Allah ﷻ:

Ibn Abi 'l-'Awam narrates from Imam Tahawi and Sulayman ibn Shu'ayb that Shu'ayb al-Kasani said, "Imam Muhammad dictated to us that whenever people are in conflict with one another regarding a particular issue (i.e. when one jurist among them judges a thing to be unlawful [*haram*] and another judges it to be lawful [*halal*])—and the situation is such that both jurists possess the competence to undertake *ijtihad*—even then, the opinion which is the truth according to Allah ﷻ is still one, whether it be the one judging the thing to be unlawful or the one judging it to be lawful. It is not possible that one thing be lawful as well as unlawful at the same time according to Allah ﷻ.

It is the responsibility of the *mujtahid* to attempt his utmost in exercising his jurisprudential capabilities to infer the ruling which he deems to be the truth according to Allah ﷻ. If a jurist attains the truth [i.e. the true ruling according to Allah ﷻ], he has the right to act according to his judgement and has also fulfilled his responsibility. On the other hand, if a jurist does not attain the truth [the true ruling according to Allah ﷻ], he has still fulfilled his responsibility [of endeavoring to uncover the truth] and is therefore also rewarded.

It is not correct for a person to conclude from two conflicting opinions that both can be the truth [*haq*] according to Allah. For instance, one Imam may judge a certain woman to be unlawful [in marriage] for a particular person whereas another Imam may judge her to be lawful for him. In this case, only one of these rulings can be the truth according to Allah ﷻ.

However, since both Imams have fulfilled their responsibility, in making a sincere attempt to arrive at the correct ruling, both will be permitted to act according to their individual judgements, even though, in reality, one of them has certainly erred in his judgement. The reason for this [as mentioned earlier] is that, according to Allah ﷻ, there can only be one true answer for any particular issue in Islamic law."

[Imam Muhammad then concluded:] "This is the opinion of Imam Abu Hanifa and Abu Yusuf and this is our understanding of the issue" (Mufti Muhammad Shafiʿ in his *Kashkol* 101).

PART TWO

1

The Distance to be Kept Between the Feet

ONE QUESTION THAT is probably in the minds of many people is: How should I stand in prayer [*salat*]? Should I stand with my legs wide apart so that my feet touch those of the next person? Should I stand at my own comfort and not touch the feet of the next person? or Should I stand with a gap of four fingers between them as some people do? Questions of this nature have confused the minds of many people, and they would like to discover the precise *sunna* method of standing in prayer.

This chapter attempts to answer these questions and offers the reader a clear view of the correct *sunna* posture. It should be understood at the outset that discussions on this point by the scholars of Islam are very few in comparison to the detailed discussions found on other key issues of prayer. Thus, very limited information is found in the many books of jurisprudence regarding this issue. In fact, the precise views of even the four Imams are quite difficult to determine.

There are a number of hadiths on the issue which emphasize the importance of maintaining orderly rows during the prayer. These narrations are usually accompanied by a warning from the Messenger of Allah ﷺ on the consequence of not straightening the rows for *salat*. One such narration states:

> Straighten your rows, or else Allah will create discord between your hearts (*Sunan Abi Dawud* 1:97).

There are also other narrations which contain similar admonitions.

When a *musalli* [person praying] observes others spreading their feet apart and touching them to the feet of the next person, he cannot help but wonder from where such a method was derived. The upholders of this view present a hadith in which the Companions touched their feet together (i.e. each one joined his feet with those of the person next to him) after receiving admonition from the Messenger of Allah ﷺ to straighten the rows. This hadith, though quoted as being a proof in support of this view, does not in any way make the joining of the feet a *wajib* [necessary] act as the supporters of this opinion so claim. The following sections of this chapter will work to clarify this point by first discussing the different opinions on the issue of positioning the feet in prayer. Thereafter, the above hadith will be independently analyzed in-depth in an attempt to explain its true implications.

To form an orderly row, whether by joining the feet together or not, is undoubtedly a very important requirement for the congregational prayer. It is also the *imam's* responsibility to ensure that this is done correctly before he initiates the prayer. Although, technically speaking, having the rows in perfect order cannot be classified as an integral or *fard* of the prayer, it is definitely an important *sunna* due to the strict instructions that have been related about it from the Messenger of Allah ﷺ.

The Various Opinions

We will begin by stating some of the opinions of the Hanafi school on the issue of feet position in prayer. In all, there seems to be two dominant opinions found in the Hanafi texts. The first of these calls for a gap of four fingers to be left between the feet of a person when he is praying. This opinion is found in Imam Ibn 'Abidin's authoritative commentary on 'Allama Haskafi's *al-Durr al-mukhtar,* where it states:

The gap to be left between a person's feet should be equal to that of four fingers of the hand, because this [amount] is very effective in creating [the posture of] submission and humility [sought in prayer] (*Radd al-muhtar* 1:299).

Leaving a gap equal to four fingers has been described by the jurists [*fuqaha*] as being the superior method, as it sometimes proves quite uncomfortable to stand with the legs spread wide apart for an extended period of time. This discomfort makes concentration difficult and often results in the loss of focus and devotion in the prayer.

The second method according to the Hanafi school can be understood from the following. In *Ma'arif al-sunan,* a commentary of *Sunan al-Tirmidhi* by the late hadith scholar 'Allama Yusuf Binnori, it is stated that there is no mention, among authentic hadith narrations, of a stipulated amount of space to be left between one's own feet during the prayer. For this reason, it could be concluded that the *sunna* method of positioning the feet in prayer is whatever distance a person finds convenient and comfortable while praying (*Ma'arif al-sunan* 2:298).

A hadith is reported in *Sunan al-Nasa'i* which states that

'Abdullah ibn Mas'ud saw a person standing in prayer with his two feet together [i.e. touching each other] and judged it to be against the *sunna*. He advised the person that if he had practised *murawaha* it would have been more preferable (*Sunan al-Nasa'i* 1:142).

The Arabic word *murawaha* usually means to stand on one foot and then the other, alternating between them as one becomes tired. However, another meaning of *murawaha* is to leave a slight gap between the feet, and this seems to be the most probable meaning of this word in reference to the above narration, since the person had been standing with his feet together. If we take this latter meaning of the term *murawaha,* the hadith means that 'Abdullah ibn Mas'ud ﷺ instructed the person to maintain a small gap between his feet, since the *sunna* was not to completely join the feet together (nor to keep them so far apart).

From the above, we learn of the flexibility of the Hanafi school on this issue. It would therefore be permitted for a person to stand with a gap between his feet equal to or greater than the width of four fingers.

In determining the opinion of the Shafiʿis on this issue, a careful study of their literature reveals that their most popular view is that a person should maintain a gap equal to one hand span between his feet (*Nihayat al-muhtaj* 1:347 U). However, it is recommended in *al-Anwar*, another text on Shafiʿi *fiqh*, that the gap should only be four fingers—as is one view of the Hanafis. Furthermore, the great Shafiʿi scholar Imam Nawawi concludes:

> It is undesirable [*makruh*] to join the feet together; it is preferable [*mustahab*] to keep some distance between them. (*Sharh al-Muhadhdhab* 3:266 U).

In total, we have three opinions of the Shafiʿi school: (1) a gap equivalent to one hand span; (2) a gap of four fingers; and (3) as much a gap as the person deems necessary. The first opinion is particular to the Shafiʿi school, whereas the latter two opinions are common to both the Shafiʿi and Hanafi schools.

One has probably noticed by now that not a single opinion mentions that a person's feet must be joined together with the feet of the adjacent person(s). If indeed this was the correct and *sunna* way of standing in prayer, it would have undoubtedly been accepted as such.

THE HADITH ON JOINING THE FEET

There is a hadith in *Sunan Abi Dawud* which describes the Companions joining their feet with each other to form orderly rows. Abu 'l-Qasim al-Jadali reports:

> I heard Nuʿman ibn Bashir ﷺ relate that the Messenger ﷺ faced the people and instructed, "Straighten your rows. By Allah, you should straighten your rows or else Allah will create disagreement between your hearts." Nuʿman ibn Bashir ﷺ then said, "I saw each person join his shoulders

with those of the next person and his knees and ankles with those of the next person" (*Sunan Abi Dawud* 1:104).

This is one of the hadiths put forward as evidence by those who assert that each person's feet should be joined with the next person's during congregational prayer. Some of them are overly particular about this, so much so that if someone standing next to them happens to draw in their feet, these people would adjust their legs even further just to maintain foot contact with their neighbor. They continuously criticize those who do not leave a wide gap between their feet, as though the *sunna* method is only what they claim.

In vain, however, are their attempts to use the above hadith and other similar hadiths to establish that joining the feet in *salat* is necessary [*wajib*]. This is true for a number of simple reasons:

(1) The words which actually describe the joining of the feet are not the words of the Messenger of Allah 鸞, but are rather the words of the narrator. Hence, this portion of the hadith is not a direct statement from the Messenger 鸞 himself [*marfu'*], but rather the narrator's description of the reaction of the Companions to the Messenger's 鸞 warning. In fact, this observation added by the narrator cannot be found in the majority of narrations that emphasize having orderly rows. Hence, it becomes quite clear that the Messenger 鸞 did not command the joining of the feet together, but merely commanded that the lines be straightened. In order to fulfill this command, the Companions employed this method of joining the feet and .

(2) The hadith of Nu'man ibn Bashir 鸞 merely tells us about the behavior of the Companions before the prayer began. In other words, the observed behavior of the Companions was to join their ankles, knees, and shoulders together prior to the prayer's commencement. Nowhere in the hadith does it indicate that this posture was maintained throughout the prayer.

(3) If, for the sake of argument, we were to accept that the joining

of the feet was maintained throughout the prayer, a number of questions arise. One such question is whether the feet should be joined together in all postures of the prayer or only during the standing posture [*qiyam*]. If the answer is that it is required only during the standing posture, then the next questions are: "What is the evidence for that?" and "Why is this arrangement confined to the standing posture only and not required in any other posture?" If the answer is that it is necessary in all postures of prayer, then the question is: "How will people in each row go about joining their feet and shoulders together while in prostration or in the sitting posture?" Clearly it would be quite impossible to achieve this.

Moreover, if the counter-argument is that it is only necessary to have the feet together while in *qiyam* because of its difficulty in the other postures of prayer, then the reply is that it is also very difficult for a row of people to ensure that this *joining* arrangement is maintained between them during the standing posture as well.

(4) Based on the above-mentioned hadith, if it is deemed necessary to join the shoulders and feet together, then why have the knees been excluded from this ruling? In the above narration of *Sunan Abi Dawud*, the Companions joined their knees together as well. It should therefore follow that the joining of the knees also be treated as an obligatory act throughout the prayer. However, one must be warned that standing even for a short while with one's knees joined to the next person's knees can be quite painful. This is even impossible in some cases, when there is a significant size difference between two people standing besides one another.

(5) Another interpretation of the above hadith offered by some scholars is that the narrator Nu'man ibn Bashir only intended to show how the Companions attempted to form extremely straight rows at the instructions of the Messenger of Allah ﷺ, and not that they actually joined their feet, shoulders, and ankles together. It is for this reason that the title of this chapter in *Sahih al-Bukhari*, "Chapter on the

Joining of the Shoulders and Feet Together While Forming the Rows," has been classified by Hafiz Ibn Hajar as an exaggeration. He writes in his commentary, *Fath al-Bari,* that

> [Imam Bukhari's] reason for choosing this specific title is to exaggerate (*mubalagha*) the importance of straightening the rows and filling the gaps in between (*Fath al-Bari* 2:247).

It is deduced from this statement that the above-mentioned narration is not to be taken literally. Imam Shawkani, who is constantly referred to by those who prefer not to follow a school of thought in Islamic jurisprudence, also does not take the hadith's literal interpretation. He writes in his *Nayl al-awtar:*

> [The statement] means: place the parts of the body [shoulders, etc.] in line with each other, so that the shoulder of each person performing prayer is in level with the shoulder of the next person. This way everyone's shoulders, knees, and feet will be in a single straight line (*Nayl al-awtar* 3:65 U).

In clear words, he indicates that the actual reason for joining the shoulders and other body parts, was to straighten the rows and not because the joining itself was an obligatory act.

(6) Anas ﷺ has also stated in a narration of Maʿmar, which Ibn Hajar has recorded in his *Fath al-Bari,* that

> if I were to attempt this [joining the shoulders and feet together] with anybody today, they would scurry away like restive mules (*Fath al-Bari* 2:247).

It is apparent from Anas's ﷺ statement that even the Companions did not continue this practice after the death of the Messenger of Allah ﷺ. If it had been a continuous action of the Messenger ﷺ [*sunna mustamirra*], the Companions would never have abandoned it, let alone speak of it in such a manner.

(7) Once it is established that the primary reason for the Companions joining their feet together was to achieve perfect order in their rows, it can be easily understood that this joining of the feet is not required

any longer, since, in most of the *masjids* and places of worship today, the lines are well marked on the carpets, marble, and floor coverings. By standing together with their heels on the markings, the worshippers will automatically come together in perfectly straight rows. Hence, there is no need to be overly critical and go around ensuring that everyone's feet have been joined together.

Other Points to be Considered

A noteworthy point to mention now is that many of those who assert that the feet be joined together are normally observed widening their feet even during their individual prayers. In fact, on many occasions, they widen them beyond shoulder width. Even if they consider the joining of the feet in congregational prayer to be necessary, it does not mean they must also widen their feet beyond shoulder width. The reason for this is that if every body stood shoulder to shoulder and joined their feet together, the gap between the two feet would only be as wide as the shoulders. It would be quite impossible to spread them any more and still maintain shoulder contact.

Another reason why one should not overspread his feet during individual prayer is that the above-mentioned hadith only describes the Companions joining their feet while in congregation. Hence, this hadith cannot be used as evidence for widening the feet during individual *salat*.

CONCLUSION

In the end, we can conclude, without fear of contradiction, that those who insist on joining the feet together have failed to comprehend the true meaning of the hadith, and, as such, do not have any strong evidence to support their position. It is not possible to follow the Qur'an and hadiths by always employing verbatim translations, which is the methodology of the Literalists [*Zahiriyya*], whose many views majority of scholars have not accepted. The grave consequences of following this type of methodology is quite apparent.

Indeed, it is important to come together during prayer, but this is normally achieved by joining the shoulders together (which has been ordered in the hadiths) and standing with the heels on the lines. It is virtually impossible not to leave any gaps at all as some people insist. Is it too difficult to understand that when someone attempts to fill in the gap between his and the next person's feet, he opens a gap between his own feet?

Therefore, the true *sunna* method would be to either leave a space of approximately four fingers between one's feet or any such gap through which one can achieve a comfortable and humble posture. During the congregational prayer, each person must ensure that he is close enough to the next person as to touch shoulders and that his feet are on the marked lines so that the whole congregation is ordered and comprised of straightened rows.

2

The Position of the Hands in Prayer

UPON ENTERING SOME *masjids*, a person finds a multitude of different people. He observes some standing in prayer with their hands clasped together beneath the navel, some with their hands folded on the chest, and some with their hands just beneath the chest. He also sees a few praying with their hands at their sides.

After observing such a scene, the question that very often arises in the mind of these observers is: "What is the correct method of placing the hands while in prayer?" or "Where did the Messenger of Allah ﷺ place his hands?" The following discussion will seek to answer these questions and determine the *sunna* (and most preferred) method of positioning the hands while standing in prayer.

The first point that needs to be clarified here is that all the positions mentioned in the hadiths are permissible, and the difference of opinion is only concerning which is the most preferable method out of them.

The second point is that there are very few rigorously authenticated [*sahih*] hadiths concerning this issue, and most of the reports which explain the different ways of positioning the hands in *salat* have been classified as either extremely weak or slightly defective. This makes the issue a bit more complicated than others. Nonetheless, it is hoped that by the end of this chapter, the *sunna* and more preferable method of positioning the hands in *salat* will become evident.

FIQH AL-IMAM

THE VARIOUS OPINIONS

The First Difference of Opinion

The first difference of opinion is concerning whether the hands should be clasped together or not. Imam Malik's more popular opinion, as related by Ibn al-Qasim, is that the hands should be left hanging at the sides. A second view of his, related by Ibn al-Mundhir, is that the hands should be brought together and placed on the body.

Imam Abu Hanifa, Imam Shafi'i, and Imam Ahmad, as well as the majority of scholars, are of the opinion that the hands should be clasped together and not left to hang at the side. The great Maliki scholar Ibn 'Abd al-Barr states regarding this:

> There is nothing reported from the Messenger 🕋 which contradicts this [majority opinion], and this is the unanimous view of all the Companions and Followers [tabi'in] (Awjaz al-masalik 2:116).

The Second Difference of Opinion

Now, among those of the latter view, there is a difference of opinion as to exactly where on the body the hands should be positioned after clasping them together. Imam Abu Hanifa and Abu Ishaq al-Marwazi from the Shafi'i school assert that the hands should be positioned below the navel. Imam Shafi'i's view, according to al-Wasit and Kitab al-Umm, is that they should be positioned beneath the chest. This is his most popular opinion. A second opinion of his, as mentioned in al-Hawi, is that the hands should be placed directly on the chest.

There are three opinions related from Imam Ahmad ibn Hanbal, the first of which is similar to that of Imam Abu Hanifa. Ibn Hubayra said this was his more popular opinion. Imam Ahmad's second opinion is similar to that of Imam Shafi'i, and the third opinion is that a person has the choice of either placing his hands beneath his navel or on his chest, since both of these methods are derived from the Sunna.

THE HADITHS ON THIS ISSUE

The scholars state that there are no authentic hadiths that substantiate Imam Malik's opinion of leaving the hands at the sides. Some have mentioned the reason for it to be profound fear, awe, and reverence for Almighty Allah; that once a person is standing before Him, he forgets to bring his hands together and they are left to hang at the sides. Whatever the case maybe, there are reports to be found of some Companions praying with their hands on their sides [*see Musannaf Ibn Abi Shayba* 2:391].

On the other hand, there are numerous narrations which establish that the Messenger 🕮 placed his hands on his body while standing in prayer and did not leave them hanging on his side. These narrations however vary greatly as to where exactly on his body he placed his hands. One very popular narration on this issue is that of Wa'il ibn Hujr 🕮, which is found in numerous hadith collections. The scholars however have labelled this narration as being problematic [*mudtarib*] and inconsistent. In one version of this narration, which is found in *Sahih Ibn Khuzayma,* Wa'il ibn Hujr says,

> I performed prayer with the Messenger of Allah 🕮. He placed his right hand upon the left one on his chest.

The version of *Musnad al-Bazzar* states "near his chest" instead of "upon his chest," and the version of *Musannaf Ibn Abi Shayba* states, "beneath the navel." The first two versions support the view of those who claim it is more preferable to place the hands on the chest or just below it, and the third version supports the Hanafi view. It should be noted, however, that all three versions contain some type of a weakness. Each version will be analyzed in the following sections along with other narrations to determine their status and the reasons for their weakness.

The First Version

1. The version of Wa'il ibn Hujr's 🕮 narration, transmitted by Ibn

57

Khuzayma in his *Sahih,* contains the words "upon his chest" and is probably the weakest of them all. There are a number of reasons for this:

(a) Mu'ammal ibn Isma'il is one of the narrators of this version. He has been called a weak narrator, ever since he erred in his narrations after his books were buried and he was subsequently forced to narrate from memory. Imam Bukhari states, "His narrations are rejected" [*munkar al-hadith*]. 'Allama Dhahabi states, "He makes many errors" [*kathir al-khata'*]. Abu Zur'a states, "His narrations contain many errors." (*Fath al-Mulhim* 2:40)

(b) This narration, although found in many other books through various chains, does not contain the words "on the chest" in any other version. Versions of it are found in *Sunan Abi Dawud, Nasa'i, Ibn Maja,* and in the *Musnad* of Abu Dawud al-Tayalisi. None of them, however, contain the addition "on the chest." 'Allama Nimawi states that this is only found in the version of Mu'ammal ibn Isma'il (and transmitted by Ibn Khuzayma). Hence, it is a weak and unauthenticated version.

(c) Another point is that Mu'ammal ibn Isma'il relates this hadith from Sufyan al-Thawri. Hafiz ibn Hajar al-'Asqalani states that the link between Mu'ammal ibn Isma'il and Sufyan al-Thawri is weak (*Fath al-Bari* 206 U). This is another weakness of this version.

(d) Sufyan al-Thawri himself was of the opinion that the hands should be positioned beneath the navel. So when his narration is found to be in contradiction with his personal opinion, this narration of his will not be accepted according to the principles of hadith study [*usul al-hadith*].

(e) Some have stated that all the narrations of *Sahih Ibn Khuzayma* are authentic. However, this is not true. 'Allama Suyuti states in his *Tadrib al-rawi* that *Sahih Ibn Khuzayma* contains some weak and *munkar* [rejected] reports. Furthermore, Ibn Khuzayma, like Imam

Tirmidhi, routinely comments after every narration stating its level of authenticity. However, following this narration of Wa'il ibn Hujr, he does not make any comments whatsoever regarding its authenticity. This narration therefore cannot be classified as authentic just because it is part of his collection. It is clear that if it had been a rigorously authenticated hadith, he would have surely designated it as such.

(f) Some have said even if this hadith was accepted to be authentic, the placing of the hands on the chest would definitely be considered an isolated [*shadh*] practice—something Allah's Messenger 🕌 did a few times solely to inform his Companions of its permissibility [*bayanan li 'l-jawaz*]. In no way can it be proven from this narration that placing the hands on the chest in *salat* was a permanent practice of the Messenger 🕌.

The Second Version

2. The second version of Wa'il ibn Hujr's narration, found in *Musnad al-Bazzar*, contains the words "near the chest" and is also weak. One of its narrators is Muhammad ibn Hujr regarding whom Imam Bukhari states, "His matter is unsettled." 'Allama Dhahabi states, "Some of his narrations are rejected." (*Majma' al-zawa'id* 2:135) Hence, this version is also weak and must be rejected.

Other Narrations

3. Another narration which mentions the placing of the hands on the chest is the narration of Hulb 🕌 transmitted by Imam Ahmad:

> The Messenger of Allah 🕌 would turn from his right and left side, and would place this [hand] upon his chest (*Musnad Ahmad*).

'Allama Nimawi has established with convincing evidence that there is an error in the wording of this hadith. In place of the words *'ala hadhihi* ["upon the other hand"] the copyist has mistakenly written *'ala sadrihi* ["on his chest"] (*Athar al-sunan* 87). This narration cannot stand as evidence either.

4. Another similar narration found in *Sunan al-Bayhaqi* states:

> 'Ali ☙, [in order to] explain the meaning of the verse, "Therefore turn in prayer to your Lord and Sacrifice" (*al-Qur'an* 108:2), placed his right hand over the center of his left one and positioned them on his chest, as though indicating that the meaning [*tafsir*] of this verse was to position the hands in this manner (*Sunan al-Bayhaqi* 2:30).

However, 'Allama Ibn al-Turkumani al-Mardini, in his book *al-Jawhar al-naqi*, establishes that both the chain [*isnad*] and text [*matn*] in this narration are inconsistent. Imam Bayhaqi has mentioned a similar narration from Ibn 'Abbas ☙ in which there is the narrator Rawh ibn al-Musayyib. About him, Ibn Hibban states:

> He narrates fabrications. It is not permissible to narrate from him.

'Allama Sa'ati writes:

> It is not correct to attribute this exegesis [*tafsir*] to 'Ali or Ibn 'Abbas ☙. The correct meaning of the verse, as Ibn Kathir states, is that it is regarding the Sacrifice [*Qurbani*] (*al-Fath al-Rabbani* 3:174 U).

Of the four narrations that have been analyzed so far, each one has been found to be defective. There are some other narrations similar to these which state that the Messenger ☙ did not position his hands beneath his navel. The explanation of the Hanafis for them is that the Messenger ☙ did, at one time or another, place his hands on his chest or just below it. However, he did this only to demonstrate the permissibility of such a posture [*bayanan li 'l-jawaz*], whereas the normal and routine practice of the Messenger ☙ was to place his hands below his navel. The following narrations will establish this point more clearly.

EVIDENCE OF THE HANAFIS

1. Wa'il ibn Hujr ☙ narrates:

> I saw Allah's Messenger ☙ placing his right hand upon the left one below his navel in prayer (*Musannaf Ibn Abi Shayba, Athar al-Sunan* 90).

This is the third version of Wa'il ibn Hujr's narration, mentioned at the beginning of the chapter, containing the words "below the navel." Some Hanafi scholars have stated that this version cannot be used as conclusive evidence for the Hanafi opinion, because the words "below his navel" are only to be found in some editions of *Musannaf Ibn Abi Shayba,* and not in them all. This is aside from the fact that, as we mentioned, it has an inconsistent text.

However, it is quoted in *Fath al-Mulhim* that 'Allama Qasim ibn Qutlubgah has judged this version to be of sound transmission. 'Allama Muhammad Abu 'l-Tayyib al-Madani writes in his commentary on *Sunan al-Tirmidhi* that this narration has a strong chain, and Shaykh 'Abid Sindhi states, "Its narrators are trustworthy." Also, a number of scholars have verified that the addition, "below the navel," is to be found in many manuscripts of *Musannaf Ibn Abi Shayba*, even if it is not found in the recently published editions [*see Athar al-sunan* 148].

Therefore, despite the problematic nature of Wa'il ibn Hujr's narration, this version of it cannot be rendered totally unacceptable, since there are many other reliable reports that strengthen it.

2. 'Ali ﷺ states:

> To place one palm over the other beneath the navel is from the *sunna* acts of prayer (*Sunan al-Bayhaqi* 312 U, *Musannaf Ibn Abi Shayba* 1:391).

It is a known fact that whenever a Companion utters the words, "It is from the Sunna," regarding any action, it means it is something acquired from the Messenger of Allah ﷺ himself. Hence, 'Ali ﷺ could have only reported this practice as *sunna* after observing Allah's Messenger ﷺ do it.

The problem with this narration is that it contains 'Abd al-Rahman ibn Ishaq in its chain, who has been classified as weak. The Hanafis have not fully relied on this narration as a basis for their opinion, but since there are many other narrations which reinforce it, it could still stand as supplementary evidence.

3. Hajjaj ibn al-Hasan relates:

> Either I heard Abu Mijlaz saying it or I enquired from him, "How should one position his hands [during prayer]?" He replied, "He should place the inner portion of his right hand upon the back of the left one beneath the navel" (*Musannaf Ibn Abi Shayba* 1:390).

The transmission of this hadith is sound [*hasan*], as ʿAllama Ibn al-Turkumani al-Mardini states in his book *al-Jawhar al-naqi*.

4. Ibrahim al-Nakhʿay relates:

> One should place his right hand upon the left one beneath the navel while in prayer (*Musannaf Ibn Abi Shayba* 1:390).

The transmission of this hadith is also sound [*hasan*].

5. Abu Hurayra ﷺ narrates:

> The placing of one hand over the other in prayer should be beneath the navel (*al-Jawhar al-naqi* 2:31 U).

6. Anas ﷺ reports that

> there are three aspects from the characteristics of prophethood [*nubuwwa*]: to open fast early; to delay the predawn meal [*suhur*]; and to position the right hand over the left one beneath the navel while in prayer (*al-Jawhar al-naqi* 2:31 U).

OTHER EVIDENCES FOR THE HANAFI OPINION

The scholars have provided various other reasons as to why the hands are best placed beneath the navel and why this method has been classified as most preferable.

(1) Although most of the hadiths on this issue are weak in one way or another, the narrations presented by the Hanafis have been judged to be more sound than the rest.

(2) The great Hanafi jurist Ibn al-Humam states:

> Due to the inconsistency and contradictions found between the various narrations, it is best to resort to analogy and reasoning. Standing before

the Lord demands a posture which expresses respect and reverence. Since positioning the hands beneath the navel is probably the most respectful way of standing, it will be considered most superior. On the other hand, the reason for women being instructed to position their hands on their chests, is so that greater concealment [and modesty] can be achieved by this (*Fath al-Qadir*).

(3) 'Allama Badr al-Din 'Ayni, the author of the great commentary on *Sahih al-Bukhari, 'Umdat al-Qari,* writes:

> To position the hands beneath the navel holds great virtue. It is a posture which signifies great respect. It displays greater contrast to the postures of the disbelievers.

He also writes:

> This is the same posture in which one stands before the rulers [of this world].

He then writes:

> Placing the hands on the chest creates a similarity with women, hence, that cannot be classified as the *sunna* for men (*'Umdat al-qari* 3:16 U).

CONCLUSION

It could be concluded that although the hadiths presented by the various schools of thought contain some form of weakness or other, the hadiths presented by the Hanafis have received less criticism, and they have many stronger reports to supplement the weaker ones. Therefore, the hadiths presented as evidence for placing the hands on or below the chest cannot be taken to denote the normal practice of Allah's Messenger 🌸. The Hanafis do agree, however, that the Messenger 🌸 sometimes placed his hands upon his chest and below it to express permissibility of such a posture [*bayanan li 'l-jawaz*].

Placing the hands beneath the navel exhibits a greater amount of respect and humility, and just as many postures of prayer for a male differ from that of a female, the method of positioning the hands also differs between them.

3

Reciting Behind the *Imam*

WHETHER OR NOT ONE SHOULD RECITE Surat al-Fatiha behind the *imam* has been a topic of great controversy and dispute since early times. The controversy is not just regarding which is superior and more virtuous, but rather it is a debate concerning the actual permissibility of reciting Surat al-Fatiha when praying behind the *imam*. For this reason, it holds a very important position among the various issues of prayer, and scholars have written lengthy discussions on the subject.

This issue differs from that of *raf' al-yadayn*, which is only about determining whether or not it is more superior to raise the hands at the time of *ruku'*. The issue of *qira'a khalf al-imam* or "reciting behind the *imam*" is far more serious. It is about whether the recitation is *wajib* [necessary] or totally forbidden.

The following study deals with the verses and hadiths on this issue, and the rulings of reciting Fatiha for the *muqtadi* or "one following an *imam*" in the silent [*sirri*] and audible [*jahri*] prayers.

THE VARIOUS OPINIONS

Firstly, there is no difference of opinion concerning whether or not the *imam* or the person praying by himself [*munfarid*] have to recite Surat al-Fatiha. All scholars agree that it is obligatory on both of them to recite Surat al-Fatiha. They also agree that the *muqtadi* is exempted from reciting anything beyond Surat al-Fatiha, whereas the *imam* and the *munfarid* have to recite at least a few short verses or a small chapter in the first two *rak'ats* [units] of the *fard* [obligatory] prayer and in all *rak'ats* of non-*fard* prayers.

The difference is regarding whether or not the *muqtadi* should recite Surat al-Fatiha when praying behind the *imam*.

Imam Malik and Imam Ahmad are of the view that the follower is not required to recite Surat al-Fatiha in the audible prayer, but is required to do so in the silent prayers. Imam Malik has said it is undesirable [*makruh*] for the follower to recite in the audible prayers. (*Fath al-Mulhim* 2:20)

Imam Shafi'i's popular view is that it is necessary for the follower to recite Surat al-Fatiha in both types of prayers—audible as well as silent. This view, although being the popular one, is not necessarily his final opinion. A careful study of his works reveals this opinion to be his former view, as Ibn Qudama states in his book *al-Mughni* (1:601). The words of Imam Shafi'i, as relayed in his book *al-Umm*, inform us that it is not necessary for the *muqtadi* to recite Surat al-Fatiha in the audible prayers; however, it should be recited in the silent prayers. He writes:

> And we say that the follower should *recite* in every prayer performed behind an *imam* in which the *imam* recites in a non-audible tone (*Kitab al-Umm* 7:153 U).

Al-Umm is one of Imam Shafi'i's later works, as affirmed by Hafiz Ibn Kathir in his *al-Bidaya wa 'l-nihaya* (10:252) and 'Allama Suyuti in his *Husn al-muhadhara*. This indicates that what is understood from *al-Umm* is his later opinion, which in most cases is the more correct one.

There is another group of people who claim it is *fard* [obligatory] for the *muqtadi* to recite the Fatiha even in the audible prayers. This is a very isolated and unique position, since even Dawud al-Zahiri and Imam Ibn Taymiya were of the view that the Fatiha should not be recited in the audible prayers.

Imam Abu Hanifa, Abu Yusuf, and Muhammad are unanimous

Reciting Behind the Imam

in their opinions regarding this issue. They state that it is forbidden [*haram*] (though does not nullify the prayer) for the follower to recite any portion of the Qur'an, whether it be the Fatiha or any other verse, in both the silent and audible prayers behind the *imam*. Whatever has been related about Imam Muhammad saying that it is more preferable for the follower to recite in the silent prayers is a weak report. Ibn al-Humam states this opinion to be erroneously attributed to Imam Muhammad. He says,

> The truth is that Imam Muhammad's opinion is the same as that of Imam Abu Hanifa and Imam Abu Yusuf. Imam Muhammad has clearly stated his view to be the same as that of Imam Abu Hanifa and Abu Yusuf in his *Muwatta* and *Kitab al-Athar* (*Fath al-Mulhim* 2:20).

A few points are derived from the above review of opinions concerning the recital of the *muqtadi:*

(1) No Imam considers the reciting of Fatiha to be *fard,* or necessary, for him in the audible prayers.

(2) Some say it is necessary for him only in the silent prayers.

(3) The opinion of the Hanafi school is simple, and that is no recitation should be undertaken by the follower, as his *imam's* recitation is sufficient for him.

Now we will look at the various verses and hadiths on this issue, and determine the closeness of the Hanafi opinion to the Holy Qur'an and Sunna.

THE HOLY QUR'AN ON THIS ISSUE

1. Allah ﷻ says in the Qur'an,

> "So, when the Qur'an is recited, listen to it, and remain silent, that you may receive mercy" [i.e. during the compulsory congregational prayers when the *imam* is reciting] (*al-Qur'an* 7:204).

This verse is sufficient proof that no recitation whatsoever should be

67

undertaken by the follower, and that it is obligatory for him to remain silent and listen attentively while the *imam* is reciting.

It is stated in *Tanzim al-ashtat,* a commentary of *Mishkat al-Masabih,* that this verse issues two commands to the follower: the first, to remain completely silent—which relates to both the silent and audible prayers—and the second, to listen with concentration—which relates only to the audible prayers. This means that the follower should maintain total silence in order to listen attentively to the recitation of his *imam* during the audible prayers; and he should also remain silent in the silent prayers because of the command in the above verse to remain silent, even though he is unable to hear the recitation.

The above-mentioned Qur'anic verse is very general and encompassing in its command. It states that one must remain silent and, if possible, also listen "when the Qur'an is recited," i.e. whether audibly or silently. It does not confine it to any particular state such as "remain silent when you can *hear* the Qur'an being recited," or "...when the Qur'an is being recited *aloud.*" Hence, it becomes clear from this verse that it is necessary for the *muqtadi* to remain silent in the silent and audible prayers while the *imam* is reciting. The *muqtadi* should also listen attentively in the audible prayers.

Some claim that this verse was revealed concerning the Friday sermon [*khutba*] only, and not concerning maintaining silence in prayer. This is an incorrect claim since a number of factors prove otherwise. Hafiz Ibn Taymiya writes in his *Fatawa:*

> It comes to be understood from the pious predecessors [*salaf salih*] that the verse was revealed concerning reciting in prayer, and some have said [it was revealed] concerning the sermon. Imam Ahmad has reported a consensus [among the scholars] that it was revealed concerning prayer (*Majmu' al-fatawa* 23:269).

Ibn Qudama writes in his book *al-Mughni:*

> Imam Ahmad states after a report of Abu Dawud, "The people are unanimous that this verse was revealed concerning the prayer" (1:601).

Ibn Taymiya writes:

> Imam Ahmad has reported a consensus that reciting is not necessary for the *muqtadi* when the *imam* is reciting audibly (*Majmu' al-Fatawa* 23:269).

It is reported in *al-Mughni* that Imam Ahmad explicitly said:

> We have never heard any Muslim scholar state that if a follower observes silence when his *imam* recites aloud, his prayer will not be valid. He further states, "This was [the practice of] the Messenger of Allah ﷺ, the Companions [*Sahaba*], and the Followers [*Tabi'in*]. This is [the opinion of] Malik from Hijaz, Thawri from Iraq, Awza'i from Syria, and Layth from Egypt. None of them have said that a *muqtadi's* prayer will be invalid if he does not recite while his *imam* is reciting" (*al-Mughni* 1:602).

Both Ibn Jarir and Ibn Abi Hatim in their commentaries [*tafasir*], and Imam Bayhaqi in his *Kitab al-qira'a* have related a hadith from the great exegete Mujahid:

> This verse was revealed concerning some Companions of the Messenger ﷺ reciting behind the *imam*.

Although this report is *mursal* (i.e. one in which a Follower reports directly from the Messenger ﷺ without mentioning a Companion in between), it will still stand as strong evidence since it is reported by Mujahid, who is known as one of the greatest exegetes of the Holy Qur'an [*a'lam al-nas bi 'l-tafsir*]. Hence, his *mursal* reports are accepted by the scholars.

Ibn Jarir al-Tabari relates another hadith from Yasir ibn Jabir regarding Ibn Mas'ud ؓ:

> Ibn Mas'ud ؓ was performing prayer when he heard a few people reciting with the *imam*. Upon completing his prayer he remarked, "Has the time not come for you to understand? Has the time not come for you to realize that when the Qur'an is being recited, you must listen to it attentively and remain silent just as Allah has ordered you to?" (*I'la' al-sunan* 4:43, *Tafsir al-Tabari* 11:378)

Hence, all the aforementioned points and statements justify that the verse was indeed revealed concerning prayer in general and not just for the Friday sermon. It is also worth knowing that this is a Makkan verse, whereas the Friday prayer (during which the sermon is delivered) only became obligatory later on in Madina.

2. Allah ﷻ says,

"So recite as much [*"ma"*] of the Qur'an as may be easy [for you]" (*al-Qur'an* 73:20).

This verse commands that some portion of the Qur'an, regardless of its length, should be recited during the prayer. It does not confine the obligation to Surat al-Fatiha but rather indicates that any portion of the Qur'an can be recited to meet the obligation [*fardiyya*]. However, those who hold the view that it is obligatory to recite Surat al-Fatiha in prayer have used this verse with the hadith, "There is no prayer except with Surat al-Fatiha," as proof to substantiate their claim. They state that the article *"ma"* in the above verse is an "unexplained" or *mujmal* term and that the above hadith serves as its explanation. Hence, according to them, the Qur'anic verse means: "So recite Surat al-Fatiha from the Qur'an [during prayer]."

The problem with this explanation is that the article *"ma"* is not an "unexplained" or *mujmal* term, as they propose, but a "general" or *'am* term. According to the principles of jurisprudence [*usul al-fiqh*], the article *"ma"* is normally used in this context, and the verse should read, "Recite whatever is possible for you to recite from the Qur'an." This means that any portion of the Qur'an could be recited to fulfill the obligation laid down by this verse, since its general tone encompasses the whole Qur'an. By confining it to Surat al-Fatiha only, it would abrogate the general nature of the verse.

This does not mean that the Hanafis have disregarded the hadith altogether. Through the hadith, they have rendered the recitation of Surat al-Fatiha to be *wajib* [necessary]. According to Hanafi jurisprudence, there is a difference between *wajib* and *fard*. *Fard* is an obligation that is established through decisive proof [*dalil qat'i*], and *wajib* is an obligation that is established through speculative proof [*dalil zanni*]. Although it is important and necessary to fulfill both types of obligations, there is a difference in the ruling of one who does not fulfill them. For instance, neglecting a *fard* act in the *salat* will render the entire prayer invalid, whereas neglecting a *wajib* will render it deficient but not entirely invalid. A *wajib* act that is neglected can be compensated through the "prostrations of forget-fulness" [*sajdat al-sahw*]; however, neglecting a *fard* act cannot be compensated in this manner. There are many other rulings concern-ing these two types of obligations that can be found in other works of jurisprudence [*fiqh*].

The Hanafis thus conclude that reciting any portion of the Qur'an in prayer is *fard* based on the above-mentioned verse. And based on the above-mentioned hadith, they conclude that the recital of Surat al-Fatiha in prayer is *wajib*. In summary, the *imam* and the person praying alone have to recite Surat al-Fatiha along with some other verses, but the *muqtadi* does not have to recite at all because he has been commanded to remain silent and because his *imam's* recitation is sufficient for him (as will be further discussed under hadith 5).

3. Allah ﷻ says,

"And say your prayer neither aloud nor in a low voice, but follow a way between" (*al-Qur'an* 17:110).

Ibn 'Abbas ﷺ relates the circumstances of revelation for this verse:

This verse was revealed when the Messenger ﷺ was still in the stage of discreetly inviting [*mutawarin*] people to Islam in Makka. He would lead the Companions in prayer and would recite aloud. When the polythe-ists [*mushrikin*] would hear his recitation, they would revile the Holy Qur'an, the One Who revealed it [Allah], and the one who conveyed it [Muhammad ﷺ]. Thus, Allah instructed His Messenger ﷺ, "And say your prayer neither aloud," that the polytheist hear your recitation, "nor in too low a tone," but make it so that the believers can hear you (*al-Ta'liq al-sabih* 1:366, *Sahih Muslim*).

In this verse, Allah 🕮 commanded His Prophet 🕮 to recite loud enough for his Companions behind him to hear, which would only be possible if they remained silent during the prayer. Hence, this proves that the *muqtadi* needs to remain silent, and that the recitation is the responsibility of the *imam* only.

THE HADITHS ON THIS ISSUE

1. Abu Sa'id al-Khudri 🕮 relates:

> The Messenger 🕮 delivered a sermon in which he outlined our Way [Sunna] for us and taught us our prayer. He instructed, "When you prepare for prayer, straighten your rows; then one of you [should become the *imam* to] lead the others in prayer. When he proclaims the *takbir* you also proclaim it; when he recites remain silent; and when he reaches *"ghayr al-maghdubi 'alayhim wala 'l-dallin,"* say *"amin,"* and Allah will answer your prayer (*Sahih Muslim* 1:174).

2. Abu Hurayra 🕮 narrates that the Messenger of Allah 🕮 said:

> The *imam* has been assigned to be followed. When he proclaims the *takbir* you also proclaim it; when he recites remain silent; and when he says *"sami' Allahu liman hamidah,"* say *"Rabbana laka 'l-hamd"* (*Sunan Abi Dawud* 1:96, *Sunan al-Nasa'i* 46).

These two hadiths give a better explanation of verse 1 above. They clearly distinguish between the duty of the *imam* and the follower. Where the Messenger of Allah 🕮 commanded the follower to follow the *imam* in proclaiming the *takbir* and other prayers, he did not command him to recite Surat al-Fatiha with the *imam*, but rather instructed him to remain silent. This proves that if reciting the Fatiha had been necessary for the follower, the Messenger 🕮 would never have ordered the contrary. Therefore, it becomes clear that the *imam's* duty is to recite and the follower's duty is to remain silent and listen to the *imam's* recitation.

It is also understood from hadith 1 that the only time the follower is permitted to say anything is when the *imam* reaches *"wala 'l-dallin,"* when he should say *amin.* The reason why the follower says *amin*—which means "O Allah, accept"—is to strengthen and endorse the *du'a'* [invocation] the *imam* made to Allah in the Fatiha.

Surat al-Fatiha begins with praises to Allah 襟, then follows up with a *du'a'* to Him, in which the servant humbly asks:

> Guide us to the straight path, the path of those on whom You have bestowed Your grace, not [the path] of those who earned Your anger, nor of those who went astray (*al-Qur'an* 1:5–7).

If it had been necessary for every follower to recite Surat al-Fatiha, they would have been ordered to say *amin* at the end of their own recitations; which is not the case since the Messenger 襟 ordered it to be said collectively upon completion of the *imam's* recital of the Fatiha.

Another important point, which is derived from hadith 2, is in the statement, "The *imam* has been assigned to be followed." Here the Messenger 襟 explains that the main reason for the *muqtadi* to remain silent during the prayer is so that he can follow his *imam* by listening to his recitation. It would be very rude for the follower to begin reciting on his own while the *imam* is reciting, as it is virtually impossible to listen attentively to someone else while absorbed in one's own recitation.

3. The next hadith furthers explain why the *muqtadi* has been exempted from reciting and how his obligation stands absolved by the *imam:*

> Jabir 襟 narrates that whoever prays behind an *imam,* his *imam's* recitation is sufficient for him (*al-Jawhar al-naqi* 2:159, *I'la' al-sunan* 4:61, *Musannaf Ibn Abi Shayba* 1:377).

4. The Messenger 襟 said:

> Whoever prays behind the *imam,* his *imam's* recitation is sufficient for him (*'Umdat al-qari* 3:12, *Muwatta Muhammad* 96, *I'la' al-sunan* 4:61).

5. The following hadith of 'Abdullah ibn Shaddad explains this in more detail:

The Messenger of Allah 🕊 led the 'Asr prayer. A person began reciting behind him, so the person next to him gave him a nudge. After finishing his prayer the person asked, "Why did you nudge me?" The other person replied, "The Messenger of Allah 🕊 was in front of you, and I did not approve of you reciting behind him." The Messenger 🕊 heard this and said, "Whoever has an *imam,* the recitation of the *imam* is sufficient for him" (*Muwatta Imam Muhammad* 98, *I'la' al-sunan* 4:70).

6. Someone asked the Messenger 🕊:

> O Messenger of Allah! Is there recitation in every prayer? The Messenger 🕊 said yes. Somebody from amongst the people asked, "[Does that mean] it is necessary?" The Messenger 🕊 replied, "I consider the *imam's* recitation to be sufficient [for the *muqtadi*]" (*Majma' al-zawa'id* 2:110).

The above hadiths have made it clear that "the *imam's* recitation is sufficient for the follower," and that the follower does not have to recite behind the *imam.* If he were to recite, how would he fulfill the obligation of listening and remaining silent? Ibn Taymiya writes in his *Fatawa:*

> The recitation of the *imam* is sufficient for the *muqtadi.* The consensus of the Companions and the Followers proves this. The hadiths from which this [rule] is established are narrated without any Companion being omitted from the transmission [*musnadan*], as well as some with the Companion being omitted from the transmission [*mursalan*]. The legal rulings [*fatawa*] among the Followers were also that the [*imam's*] recitation is sufficient. Above all, it is in total accordance with the Qur'an and Sunna (*Majmu' al-fatawa* 23:271).

7. The Messenger of Allah 🕊 even expressed disapproval at a person who recited behind him, as indicated in the following narration of Abu Hurayra 🕊:

> The Messenger 🕊 turned towards [us] after completing a *salat* in which he had recited aloud and asked, "Did one of you recite with me?" A person replied, "Yes, O Messenger of Allah." The Messenger 🕊 remarked, "I was wondering why I felt as if the words of the Qur'an were being taken from my tongue."

Abu Hurayra relates that when the people heard him say this, they discontinued reciting behind him during the audible prayers (*Sunan al-Tirmidhi* 1:71, *Muwatta Imam Malik* 51, *Sunan al-Nasa'i* 1:146, *Sunan Abi Dawud* 1:146, *Sunan Ibn Maja* 61, *Sunan al-Bayhaqi* 2:157).

8. There is another similar narration from 'Imran ibn Husayn ⬥:

> The Messenger ⬥ was performing the Zuhr prayer when a person behind him began to recite *"Sabbih isma rabbik al-a'la"* [Surat al-A'la]. Upon completing his prayers, the Messenger ⬥ asked who it had been. The person identified himself, so the Messenger ⬥ remarked, "I thought one of you was taking it [the verses] from my tongue" (*Sahih Muslim* 1:172, *I'la' al-sunan* 4:56).

9. There is yet another hadith of this nature in which 'Abdullah ibn Mas'ud ⬥ says,

> The Companions would recite behind the Messenger ⬥. [Once] he said to them, "You have caused me confusion in my recitation of the Qur'an" (*Majma' al-zawa'id* 2:110, *al-Jawhar al-naqi* 1:162).

These hadiths are concrete evidence that the Messenger ⬥ was not too pleased with people reciting behind him. It is also clear that the Companions would not have been reciting very loudly either, as that would constitute gross disrespect on their behalf, which is unthinkable regarding the Companions. Therefore, even though they were reciting in subdued tones, the Messenger of Allah ⬥ admonished them, as it was disturbing his recitation.

The same type of disturbance can occur if the *muqtadi* recites Surat al-Fatiha or some other verses with it while praying behind the *imam*. In either case, it is possible that the *imam* may be led to confusion. This proves that the command of the Qur'an, for the *muqtadi* to remain silent, is indeed concerning both silent and audible prayers.

The Companions and Followers on This Issue

'Allama 'Ayni writes in his commentary on *Sahih al-Bukhari*, *'Umdat al-qari*, that it was the opinion of approximately eighty Companions that the *muqtadi* should not recite behind the *imam*. Some of them very strictly implemented and enforced their opinion. A few of their reports and comments are mentioned here so as to gauge the seriousness of this issue.

1. 'Ata' ibn Yasar enquired from Zayd ibn Thabit ﷺ regarding recitation behind the *imam*. He said,

> There is no recitation behind the *imam* (*Sahih Muslim* 1:215).

2. Malik reports from Nafi' that

> 'Abdullah ibn 'Umar ﷺ was asked whether anything should be recited behind the *imam*. He replied, "Whenever one of you prays behind the *imam*, the recitation of the *imam* is sufficient for him; but when you pray alone, you should recite for yourself." The narrator reports that 'Abdullah ibn 'Umar ﷺ would not recite behind the *imam* (*Muwatta Imam Malik* 51, *I'la' al-sunan* 4:76).

3. 'Ubaydullah ibn Muqsim narrates that

> he enquired from 'Abdullah ibn 'Umar, Zayd ibn Thabit, and Jabir ibn 'Abdillah ﷺ [concerning this issue]. They informed him that there should be no recitation behind the *imam* in any prayer (*Athar al-sunan* 1:116, *I'la' al-sunan* 4:81).

4. In the following report, 'Abdullah ibn Mas'ud ﷺ expresses great disapproval at reciting behind the *imam*. He says,

> Would that the mouth of the person reciting behind the *imam* be filled with dust (*Athar al-sunan* 1:116, *I'la' al-sunan* 4:81).

5. Abu Jamra reports:

> I asked 'Abdullah ibn 'Abbas ﷺ, "Should I recite when the *imam* is in front of me?" He said no (*Athar al-sunan* 1:116, *I'la' al-sunan* 4:81).

6. Ibn 'Abbas ﷺ narrates from the Messenger ﷺ that the recitation of the *imam* is sufficient for the *muqtadi*, whether he recites silently or aloud (*Daraqutni* 1:331, *I'la' al-sunan* 4:82).

7. Musa ibn 'Uqba reports that the Messenger of Allah ﷺ, Abu Bakr,

'Umar, and 'Uthman ﷺ would forbid [people from] reciting behind the *imam* (*'Umdat al-qari* 3:67 U, *I'la' al-sunan* 4:84).

8. Musa ibn Sa'd ibn Zayd ibn Thabit narrates from his grandfather [Zayd bin Thabit ﷺ]:

Whoever recites behind the *imam,* there is no prayer for him (*Muwatta Imam Muhammad* 100, *I'la' al-sunan* 4:87).

9. Ibrahim al-Nakh'ay states:

The first thing the people innovated [in religion] was recitation behind the *imam*—the Companions did not recite behind the *imam* (*al-Jawhar al-naqi* 4:169).

10. This statement is further strengthened by the following one, in which he states:

The first person to recite behind the *imam* was a person accused [of innovation] (*Muwatta Imam Muhammad* 100, *I'la' al-sunan* 4:89).

11. Muhammad ibn Sirin informs us:

I do not consider reciting behind the *imam* to be from the Sunna (*Musannaf Ibn Abi Shayba* 1:377, *I'la' al-sunan* 4:90).

12. 'Abdullah ibn Zayd ibn Aslam reports from his father that

ten Companions of the Messenger ﷺ strongly prohibited reciting behind the *imam*: Abu Bakr al-Siddiq, 'Umar al-Faruq, 'Uthman ibn 'Affan, 'Ali ibn Abi Talib, 'Abd al-Rahman ibn 'Awf, Sa'd ibn Abi Waqqas, 'Abdullah ibn Mas'ud, Zayd ibn Thabit, 'Abdullah ibn 'Umar, and 'Abdullah ibn 'Abbas ﷺ (*Qala'id al-azhar* 2:42 U).

13. 'Ali ibn Abi Talib ﷺ said:

Whoever recites behind the *imam,* his prayer is not valid,

and in another narration he said:

[…] such a person has deviated from the natural path [*fitra*] (*al-Jawhar al-naqi* 2:218, *Musannaf Ibn Abi Shayba* 1:376).

14. Sa'd ﷺ says,

I desire that a burning ember be placed in the mouth of one who recites behind the *imam* (*Musannaf 'Abd al-Razzaq* 2:138, *Musannaf Ibn Abi Shayba* 2:376).

15. A similar statement has been related from 'Umar ﷺ:

Would that there be a stone in the mouth of one who recites behind the *imam* (*Musannaf 'Abd al-Razzaq* 2:128).

It becomes very clear from the above reports that the Hanafis are not isolated in their position, since it was the view of many of the Companions and Followers.

OTHER REASONS FOR NOT RECITING BEHIND THE *IMAM*

(1) The *imam* has been ordered to recite aloud in the audible prayers so that the followers can listen to him. In order for that to happen, they have to remain silent. If the follower is commanded to recite as well, he will not be able to concentrate on his *imam's* recitation. This in turn would mean that the *imam* has been ordered to recite aloud to a congregation which does not need to pay attention to his recitation. It is quite clear that the *Shari'a* would not encourage such a practice.

(2) As mentioned earlier, part of Surat al-Fatiha constitutes a *du'a'* [invocation] for guidance to Allah; and all those who recite this *sura* [chapter] make the *du'a'* for themselves. In the case of the follower, his *du'a'* is made by the *imam* since the *imam's* recitation is sufficient for the entire congregation.

In a typical everyday situation, a group of people who intend to submit a proposal or make a request to someone of authority, would normally not do so on an individual basis; rather, they would appoint someone to represent them. The representative would then act in the interest of the group and would do so without any interference from other group members. Anyone who does not adhere to this arrangement would be frowned upon.

The same is the situation with the *imam* in prayer. He beseeches Allah ﷻ on behalf of the whole congregation, while they stand by in an orderly manner listening to him. Once he completes his *du'a*, they endorse it by proclaiming *amin*, just as the aforementioned group would do so with their signatures. Hence, the hadiths clarify this by stating that the recitation of the *imam* is sufficient for all the members of the congregation.

(3) If a person arrives late for the congregational prayer and finds the *imam* in the bowing posture [*ruku'*], the correct procedure for him to follow would be to first raise his hands and say *"Allahu akbar"* [*takbir*] while standing; and then to join the *imam* in *ruku'*. Although this *musalli* has missed the standing posture [*qiyam*], he is still considered to have acquired that whole *rak'a* with the *imam*, and therefore does not have to make up that *rak'a* later on.

Everyone agrees that if the person did not say the *takbir* while standing, but went directly into the bowing posture instead, his *rak'a* is not valid since he has missed the *takbir* and the standing posture. However, no scholar has stated that his *rak'a* will be invalid because he was not able to recite the Fatiha. This not only proves that Surat al-Fatiha is not *fard* on the *muqtadi*, as the opening *takbir* and standing posture are; but it also proves that his *imam's* recitation is sufficient for him.

(4) When the *imam* makes a mistake in his prayer, the whole congregation is obligated to perform the "prostrations of forgetfulness" [*sujud al-sahw*] with him; and when he recites a "verse of prostration" [*ayat al-sajda*], the whole congregation is also obliged to perform the "prostration of Qur'an recital" [*sajdat al-tilawa*] with him, even if the *imam* recited it silently. Likewise, a single barrier [*sutra*] in front of the *imam* is sufficient for the whole congregation. In light of these commonalities, would it be a stretch of the imagination to take the *imam's* recitation as being sufficient for the entire congregation?

FIQH AL-IMAM

Analyzing the Seemingly Contradictory Hadiths

There are a number of hadiths, authentic as well as weak, which apparently contradict the verses and hadiths that were mentioned earlier in this chapter. These seemingly contradictory hadiths have been used to establish the claim that it is obligatory to recite behind the *imam*. However, in reality, there is no contradiction between these hadiths and those previously mentioned proof texts, as the scholars have reconciled the apparent contradictions between them and have brought their meanings to be in complete harmony with one another. We will now take a look at some of these hadiths.

1. 'Ubada ibn al-Samit ﷺ narrates that the Messenger ﷺ said:

> There is no prayer for the one who does not recite Surat al-Fatiha (*Sahih Muslim*),

and in another narration he says:

> There is no prayer for the one who does not recite Surat al-Fatiha and [some] more [verses] (*Sahih Muslim*).

This hadith has been classified as rigorously authenticated [*sahih*] and is normally presented as evidence for the recitation of Surat al-Fatiha being *fard* on the *muqtadi*. It seems to be in apparent conflict with the Hanafi opinion. However, the scholars have provided many explanations to remove the conflict between it and the previously quoted proof texts of the Hanafis. The following are some explanations which should assist in understanding the true implications of the hadith:

(a) The *imam* and the *muqtadi* are both obligated to recite Surat al-Fatiha according to this hadith, as it seems to entail a general command that also includes the *muqtadi*. The Hanafis do not reject this, but instead state that the obligation upon the follower to recite the Fatiha will be fulfilled through his *imam's* recitation. This is because the Messenger ﷺ has said that the *imam's* recitation is sufficient for the *muqtadi*.

(b) This hadith will be interpreted as concerning the *imam* and the person praying by himself only and will not relate to the follower, since he has been commanded in the Holy Qur'an to remain silent and listen. Hence, the follower is excluded from the obligation of this hadith.

(c) There are rigorously authenticated hadiths (as presented above) that totally prohibit the follower from reciting behind the *imam*. Hence, in purview of those hadiths, he is exempt from the obligation of this hadith, and it becomes clear that this hadith is actually directed at the *imam* and the person praying by himself only.

(d) The first narration only mentions Surat al-Fatiha as being necessary; whereas the second narration also includes the word *"fasa'idan"* which means "and more." What is difficult to understand here is that even though the second narration mentions both the Surat al-Fatiha and "some more verses" as being necessary, only reciting the Fatiha has been considered to be *fard* and not reciting anything beyond it. Hence, whatever explanation is offered for not considering the extra verses as being equally obligatory upon the follower, will also be our explanation for not making even the Fatiha obligatory upon him. The only difference will be that we would have considered the full hadith by declaring the same ruling for both Surat al-Fatiha and the extra verses—that they are both absolved by the *imam's* recitation—and according to the other view, only one half of the hadith would have been considered (i.e. by making only the recital of the Fatiha necessary and not the extra verses).

On the other hand, if the explanation is that the *imam's* recitation of the extra verses is sufficient for the follower, as is sometimes suggested by the proponents of the other view, then that is exactly what the Hanafis state about the Fatiha also.

(e) The obligation of Surat al-Fatiha, as understood from this hadith, is not directed at the *muqtadi* but rather is directed at the *imam* and the person praying alone only. Imam Tirmidhi has narrated the

FIQH AL-IMAM

following statement of Jabir ﷺ with a reliable transmission:

> Whoever performed a *rak'a* in which he did not recite Surat al-Fatiha, it is as though he has not performed it, unless he was [praying] behind the *imam* (*Sunan al-Tirmidhi* 1:71).

This clearly proves that the command in the above hadith is not for the follower. Imam Tirmidhi further mentions the comments of Imam Ahmad concerning the above statement:

> This [Jabir ﷺ] is a Companion of the Messenger ﷺ who has interpreted the statement of the Messenger ﷺ, "There is no prayer for the one who did not recite Surat al-Fatiha," to mean that this is the case only when the person is praying by himself (*I'la' al-sunan* 4:75).

We ask: Who can explain the meaning of a hadith better than a close Companion of the Messenger of Allah ﷺ?

2. 'Ubada ibn al-Samit ﷺ narrates:

> We were performing the Fajr prayer behind the Messenger of Allah ﷺ. He began reciting but experienced difficulty in doing so. Upon finishing he said, "Perhaps you were reciting behind your *imam?*" We replied, "Yes, O Messenger of Allah." So he said, "Do not recite anything besides Surat al-Fatiha, for there is no prayer for the one who does not recite it."

Imam Abu Dawud, Tirmidhi, and Nasa'i have transmitted similar reports to this one in their *Sunans*. A narration from *Sunan Abi Dawud* states:

> The Messenger of Allah ﷺ exclaimed, "I was wondering why the words of the Qur'an were being taken from my tongue. Do not recite any portion of the Qur'an while I am reciting aloud, except Surat al-Fatiha" (*Mishkat al-Masabih* 1:81 from *Sunan Abi Dawud, al-Tirmidhi, al-Nasa'i*).

In another narration from *Sunan al-Tirmidhi*, 'Ubada ibn al-Samit reports:

> The Messenger of Allah ﷺ performed the Fajr prayer but experienced difficulty in reciting, so upon finishing he remarked, "I noticed you reciting behind your *imam!*" We said, "Yes, by Allah." So he instructed, "Do not

recite anything besides the Umm al-Qur'an [Surat al-Fatiha], for there is no prayer for the one who does not recite it."

The apparent wording of the above narration in its various forms indicates that a *muqtadi* is obligated to recite Surat al-Fatiha. The scholars have mentioned a number of reasons why this hadith cannot be taken for its literal meaning. They have either interpreted it in light of the above mentioned hadiths, or they have completely waived it due to its weakness. Some of these interpretations are presented below.

(a) First, present in the chain [*isnad*] of this hadith is a Muhammad ibn Ishaq. Although some have called him a trustworthy narrator, most hadith scholars have criticized him in very harsh terms. Sulayman al-Taymi and Hisham have called him a "flagrant liar" [*kadhdhab*], and Imam Malik has labelled him a "flagrant liar from among the flagrant liars" [*dajjalun min al-dajajila*]. Ibn Zahir, Wahb ibn Khalid, Jarir ibn 'Abd al-Hamid, Daraqutni, and others also have made grave statements about him. Therefore, it will be completely unfair to accept such a transmission as evidence.

(b) Second, its transmission is full of confusion. Makhul sometimes relates the hadith from Muhammad ibn Rabi', sometimes from Nafi' ibn Mahmud, and sometimes from others. With regards to Nafi' ibn Mahmud, hadith experts, such as Ibn 'Abd al-Barr, Tahawi, and Ibn Qudama, state that he is "unknown" [*majhul*]. Since there is a multitude of other rigorously authenticated hadiths regarding this issue, which are not defective in their transmission, there remains no need to employ such hadiths (like the one under discussion), especially when it contradicts the other rigorously authenticated ones.

(c) Third, some hadith experts have classified this hadith as being defective [*ma'lul*] since its transmission has been said to have only reached 'Ubada ibn al-Samit ♦ [*mawquf*] and not the Messenger of Allah ♦ [*marfu'*]. Ibn Taymiya explains in more detail:

This hadith is defective [*mu'allal*], according to the hadith experts [*muhaddithin*], for a number of reasons. Imam Ahmad and others have judged it to be weak. A discussion on its weaknesses has already been detailed at another place [in the book], where it was clarified that the actual authenticated [*sahih*] narration of the Messenger of Allah ﷺ [in this regard] is, "There is no prayer without the Umm al-Qur'an." This hadith has been transmitted by Imam Bukhari and Muslim in their collections [*Sahihayn*], and Zuhri has related it from 'Ubada ؓ through Muhammad ibn Rabi'. As for this hadith, some narrators of Sham [the Levant] have erred in its transmission. The reality of this is that 'Ubada ibn al-Samit ؓ was the *Imam* of Bayt al-Maqdis [Jerusalem] when he related this hadith. They confused his narration, which was meant to end with him [*mawquf*], as having been related directly from the Messenger ﷺ [*marfu'*]." (*Sunan al-Tirmidhi* 1:71)

Hence, this hadith is inadmissible as evidence as it is not a direct report from the Messenger of Allah ﷺ.

(d) Fourth, if we were for a moment to accept the hadith as rigorously authenticated and unblemished, even then, statements like, "Perhaps you were reciting behind your *imam*," indicate that the Messenger ﷺ had not instructed them to recite anything. He would not have asked such a question otherwise.

3. Abu Hurayra ؓ narrates

> that the Messenger ﷺ said: "Whoever performs a prayer in which he does not recite the Umm al-Qur'an, his prayer is incomplete and deficient." A narrator of the hadith enquired from Abu Hurayra ؓ, "I am sometimes behind the *imam* [so what am I to do]?" Abu Hurayra ؓ instructed, "Recite it in your mind" [*fi nafsik*] (*Majmu' al-fatawa* 23:287).

If we look at this narration carefully, we find that it actually consists of two segments: the first is the portion in which Allah's Messenger ﷺ himself emphasizes the importance of Surat al-Fatiha (hence, *marfu'*); and the second is a statement of Abu Hurayra ؓ (hence, *mawquf*) and not of Allah's Messenger ﷺ. It is from the second segment that some attempt to attribute the obligation of reciting Surat al-Fatiha to the *muqtadi*, by taking it to mean, "recite it yourself," and not "recite it in your mind."

Since the first segment of this narration is quite similar to the first hadith analyzed in this section, the explanations mentioned there will also be in effect here. The conclusion is: "The recitation of the *imam* is sufficient for the follower," and hence, the follower will automatically have his obligation of reciting Surat al-Fatiha fulfilled by his *imam*. The second segment of the hadith is explained as follows:

(a) It is a *mawquf* narration, which in this case is a statement of Abu Hurayra ☻, not related directly from the Messenger ☙. Since the second portion (if taken as some interpret it) also contradicts many other rigorously authenticated hadiths that are narrated directly from the Messenger ☙ [*marfu'*], it cannot be used as evidence.

(b) As mentioned earlier, the Hanafis have taken the words, *"iqra'ha fi nafsik,"* in the narration to mean: "recite it in your mind and ponder over it, and do not utter it with your tongue." No doubt, if the *muqtadi* concentrates on his *imam's* recitation, he would be fulfilling this requirement. The Hanafis have not interpreted these words to mean that the *muqtadi* is obligated to recite Surat al-Fatiha.

(c) The words, *"iqra'ha fi nafsik,"* could also be translated as, "Recite it when you are performing prayer individually." The following hadith, which the Messenger ☙ narrated directly from Allah ☙ [*hadith qudsi*], contains a similar expression and supports this translation. Allah ☙ says,

> If the servant remembers Me while he is alone [*fi nafsihi*], I remember him similarly [*fi nafsi*]; and if he remembers Me in a gathering, then I remember him in a gathering more superior to his.

The opposite of being in a gathering with a group of people is being alone. Hence, the meaning of Abu Hurayra's statement will be, "Recite Surat al-Fatiha when you are performing prayer alone," i.e. when not in congregation.

FIQH AL-IMAM

Conclusion

After reaching the end of this discussion, one can quite easily conclude that there is overwhelming evidence in favor of the Hanafi opinion on whether or not one should recite behind the *imam*. The understanding acquired from the verses of the Holy Qur'an and the many hadiths is that the *muqtadi* has two obligations to fulfill: one is to remain silent, and the other to listen carefully. According to the hadiths, the *imam's* recitation is considered sufficient for the follower. The recitation undertaken by the *imam* is considered by the hadiths to be totally sufficient for the *muqtadi*. Since the Qur'an actually prohibits that any word be uttered while the recitation of the Qur'an is taking place, it will be accepted as such; and the *muqtadi* will be required to maintain perfect silence, in both silent and audible prayers.

There should now remain no doubt as to why the follower should remain silent when praying behind the *imam*, even in a silent prayer when he is unable to hear his *imam's* recitation. It has been explained that verse 1 above contains two commands: one of them being the observance of silence, which relates to the silent prayers, and the other of listening attentively, which relates to the audible prayers.

The Hanafis have taken all of these points into consideration and formed an opinion that encompasses all the various aspects of the hadiths. Hence, it could be concluded that their opinion is probably the closest to the Qur'an and Sunna.

4

The Issue of *Amin*—Explained

SAYING *AMIN* (pronounced *aameen*) after completing the recitation of Surat al-Fatiha holds great virtue and is a *sunna* of the Messenger of Allah ﷺ. The Messenger of Allah ﷺ states in one hadith:

> When the *imam* says "*ghayr al-maghdubi 'alayhim wala 'l-dallin*," say *amin*, because the angels say *amin*. And whoever's *amin* coincides with the *amin* of the angels, all his past sins are forgiven (*Sahih al-Bukhari* 1:108).

There is no controversy whatsoever regarding the virtue of saying *amin* at the completion of Surat al-Fatiha. All scholars are unanimous that it is *sunna* to say *amin* at that time. The difference of opinion, however, is regarding whether it should be uttered audibly or silently.

It is established that the Messenger ﷺ said *amin* audibly as well as silently during his lifetime; therefore, it should not be made an issue of great debate. At times, it is taken so seriously that some of those who choose to say it aloud criticize the practice of those who say it silently by labelling them ignorant and even deviant; and some from the latter group criticize the practice of the former group as well.

It must be realized that the difference of opinion is only concerning which method is superior, i.e. is it more virtuous to say *amin* aloud or silently? Ibn al-Qayyim, explaining the nature of this issue, writes:

> This issue is from among the valid differences of opinion in which no criticism should be directed at those who do it [i.e. say *amin* aloud] nor at those who do not [i.e. who say it silently]. This issue is similar to

that of raising or not raising the hands [*raf' al-yadayn*] in prayer (*Zad al-ma'ad* 1:70).

Thus, the following discussion will constitute a combined study of verses of the Holy Qur'an and hadiths of the Messenger 🕮 that are relevant to the issue of *amin,* in order to ascertain the more preferred procedure. As mentioned earlier, it is clearly established that the Messenger 🕮 did say *amin* aloud as well as silently. The Hanafis and many others accept this.

However, the question is: for how long did the Messenger 🕮 say *amin* aloud? Since there seems to be no evidence to establish that *amin* was said aloud on a permanent basis, it is necessary to take a closer look at the various evidences on this issue that have been utilized by the different schools of *fiqh.*

The Various Opinions

The Hanafi opinion is that *amin* should be said inaudibly at all times during the prayer. They uphold that it was said aloud by the Messenger 🕮 a few times, in order to familiarize the Companions with saying *amin* after the Fatiha; after which he would say it silently just like all other invocations and supplications of prayer. Others state that *amin* should be said aloud in all the audible prayers (i.e. Fajr, Maghrib, and 'Isha) and silently in the silent prayers (i.e. Zuhr and 'Asr).

The following points detail how the *imam* and the follower [*muqtadi*] should say *amin:*

(a) All scholars agree that the *imam* should say *amin* silently during the silent prayers. As for the audible prayers, Imam Malik and Imam Abu Hanifa are of the opinion that *amin* should be said silently in them, and another group of scholars says it should be said audibly.

(b) Imam Malik (according to *al-Mudawwanat al-kubra*) and Imam Abu Hanifa are of the opinion that the follower should always say *amin* silently in both the audible and silent prayers. This is also one opinion of Imam Shafi'i. Another group is of the opinion that the followers should say *amin* audibly during the audible prayers and silently during the silent prayers.

As mentioned earlier, the difference of opinion is only concerning which of the two is more virtuous. Technically speaking, saying *amin* aloud or silently is regarded by all the scholars as being a *sunna* act of the prayer and not a *fard*, or integral part of it.

THE QUR'AN ON THIS ISSUE

According to the most accurate definition, *amin* is a verbal noun meaning "accept [our] prayer." Hence, it is a *du'a'* [invocation]. This is clearly indicated in Sura Yunus, where, after mentioning the *du'a'* of Musa 藥, Allah 藥 says,

"Accepted is your prayer (O Musa and Harun)!" (*al-Qur'an* 10:89)

Allah 藥 uses the dual tense in this verse and says *"da'watukuma,"* meaning "the prayer of you both." Since only Musa 藥 is mentioned to have made the *du'a'* and not Harun 藥, the use of this dual tense has been explained as implying that Musa 藥 was making the *du'a'* while Harun 藥 was endorsing it with *amin*. Since *amin* is a *du'a'*, Allah referred to them both as invoking Him and said He had accepted the *du'as* of both.

In the "Chapter on the *Imam* Proclaiming *Amin* Aloud" [*Babu jahr al-imam bi 'l-tamin*], Imam Bukhari quotes the words of 'Ata ibn Abi Rabah, *"Amin is a du'a'"* (*Sahih al-Bukhari* 1:102). Hafiz Ibn Hajar further clarifies this in his commentary, where he states:

> The one saying *amin* is considered a *da'i* [or "invocant"] as mentioned in the words of Allah, "Accepted is your prayer (O Musa and Harun)!" Musa 藥 was making the *du'a'* and Harun 藥 was saying *amin*, as related by Ibn Mardawayh through the narration of Anas 藥 (*Fath al-Bari*).

Thus, once it is established that *amin* is a form of *du'a'*, we must observe the etiquette which Allah 藥 has taught us:

> "Invoke your Lord with humility and in secret. He likes not the aggressors" (*al-Qur'an* 7:55).

Allah ﷻ commands that prayers and *du'as* be made to Him with humility, sincerity, and in silence [*khufya*]. Many examples are provided in the Qur'an of how the various Envoys [*anbiya'*] of Allah (upon them be peace) would invoke Him. Allah ﷻ says, speaking of the calmness of Zakariyya ﷺ when he beseeched his Lord:

"When he called out his Lord (Allah)—a call in secret" (*al-Qur'an* 13:3).

The description of the *du'as* of other Envoys is also mentioned by Allah ﷻ:

"Verily, they used to hasten in performing good deeds; and they used to call on Us with hope and fear; and they used to humble themselves before Us" (*al-Qur'an* 21:90).

At another point, the Qur'an provides a glimpse of the Last Day when the Trumpet will be blown. Allah ﷻ says,

"And all voices will be humbled for the Most Beneficent, and you shall hear nothing but the low sound of their footsteps" (*al-Qur'an* 20:108).

This establishes that since *amin* is a *du'a'*, it should be said silently just like other *du'as*. The various Envoys of Allah preferred to make their invocations silently when they would beseech the All-Hearing [*al-Sami'*] and the Nigh [*al-Qarib*].

In many hadiths, the Messenger ﷺ advised the Companions to invoke Allah ﷻ silently. He informed them that Allah is the Nigh and All-Hearing, and that there was no need for them to invoke Him too loudly. Therefore, since *amin* is also a *du'a'*, it would be more preferable to utter it silently just as other invocations and prayers.

The Hadiths on This Issue

It may have been misconceived from the above analysis that the Hanafis seem to have based their view on mere reasoning and analogy. Therefore, in this section, we will present authentic hadiths to, God-willing, dispel such misunderstandings and to provide concrete proof of the Hanafi opinion being in total accordance with the Sunna.

1. In a narration of Samura ibn Jundub and 'Imran ibn Husayn ﷺ, it is mentioned that

> they had a conversation, [during which] Samura ﷺ related two occasions when the Messenger ﷺ would observe a short silence [*sakta*] [in prayer]—one following the initial *takbir* and the second when completing *wala 'l-dallin*. 'Imran ibn Husayn ﷺ could not acknowledge this, so they wrote to Ubay ibn Ka'b ﷺ. His reply stated that Samura ﷺ has remembered [correctly] (*Sunan Abi Dawud* 1:120).

'Allama Nimawi, commenting on this narration, states:

> The first silence was observed in order to recite the *thana* silently, and the second to say the *amin* silently. It is possible that 'Imran ibn Husayn initially refuted Samura in regards to the second silence, because it was so brief and he did not think it worthy of mention; and therefore acknowledged the first silence because it was longer. It is quite clear that the *amin* was recited during the second silence, because there was no other reason to discontinue the recitation for a brief moment at that instance (*Athar al-sunan* 382).

2. Abu Hurayra ﷺ narrates that the Messenger of Allah ﷺ said:

> When the *imam* recites *"ghayr al-maghdubi 'alayhim wala 'l-dallin,"* say *amin*, because the angels say it and so does the *imam* (*Sunan al-Nasa'i* 1:147).

This hadith proves that the *imam* should say *amin* silently. The reason for this is that the Messenger of Allah ﷺ ordered the Companions to say *amin* and informed them that the angels and the *imam* also say it. If it had been more preferable for the *imam* to say it aloud, the Messenger ﷺ would have had no reason to inform the Companions of the *imam's* saying *amin*, because they would have heard it themselves. Since the Messenger ﷺ informed them that the *imam* also said *amin*, it means that *amin* was normally said in a subdued tone.

3. Shu'ba reports from 'Alqama ibn Wa'il, who narrates from his father, Wa'il, that

> he [Wa'il] performed prayer with the Messenger ﷺ. When the Messenger

⸙ reached *"ghayr al-maghdubi 'alayhim wala 'l-dallin,"* he said *amin* and kept his voice subdued (*Musnad Ahmad, Daraqutni, al-Mustadrak* U, *Nasb al-raya* 1:494).

This hadith has been narrated from Wa'il ibn Hujr ⸙ by Sufyan al-Thawri and Shu'ba. The two reports differ however in that Shu'ba, whose narration is above, relates that the Messenger of Allah ⸙ said *amin* silently; whereas Sufyan relates from Wa'il that the Messenger ⸙ prolonged his voice [*madda biha sawtahu*] while saying *amin*.

Sufyan's report has been used as evidence by those who claim that *amin* was said aloud by the Messenger ⸙. They have criticized Shu'ba's report in a number of ways and, in doing so, have attempted to show Sufyan's report as being the superior narration. On the other hand, the Hanafis have taken Sufyan's report to mean that the initial *"alif"* of *amin* was prolonged and not that the volume of the Messenger's ⸙ voice was raised. The Hanafi scholars have answered all the criticism levelled against Shu'ba's report and have firmly established it to be the more acceptable one regarding this issue [*see Athar al-sunan, Fath al-Mulhim, Darse Tirmidhi*, etc.].

4. Abu Hurayra ⸙ narrates that the Messenger of Allah ⸙ said:

When the *imam* says *wala 'l-dallin*, say *amin* (*Sahih al-Bukhari* 1:108).

Had it been more preferable for the follower to say *amin* aloud, the wording of this hadith could have read, "When the *imam* says *amin*, you say it," as the *imam's amin* would have been the signal to the follower to say *amin*. However, the Messenger ⸙ instructed them to say *amin* after the *imam* recited *"wala 'l-dallin,"* since the *amin* was pronounced silently by the *imam*.

There are in fact some narrations which contain the words, "When the *imam* says *amin*, you say it;" however, this is interpreted as, "When the time comes for the *imam* to say *amin*, you say it." It is not taken literally since the normal practice of the Messenger ⸙ was to say *amin* silently.

THE COMPANIONS AND FOLLOWERS ON THIS ISSUE

1. Abu Wa'il narrates that 'Ali and 'Abdullah ibn Mas'ud Ǵ did not recite *bismi'llah, a'udhu bi'llah,* or *amin* aloud [during the prayer] (*Majma' al-zawa'id* 2:108).

2. Abu Wa'il narrates that 'Umar and 'Ali Ǵ would not recite *bismi'llah* or *amin* aloud (*I'la' al-sunan* 2:215).

3. Imam 'Abd al-Razzaq in his *Musannaf* and Imam Muhammad in his *Kitab al-Athar* have related that the prominent Follower [*tabi'i*] Ibrahim al-Nakh'ay said:

> There are five things the *imam* should say silently: *subhanaka 'llahumma* [*thana*], *ta'awwudh, bismi'llah, amin,* and *Allahumma rabbana laka 'l-hamd* (*Musannaf 'Abd al-Razzaq* 2:87).

OTHER REASONS FOR SAYING *AMIN* SILENTLY

(1) We know it is necessary [*wajib*] to recite the Qur'an aloud in the audible prayers. By saying *amin* aloud, someone could be misled into assuming that it is part of the Qur'an along with the Fatiha; whereas all scholars agree that *amin* is not part of the Qur'an.

(2) Some scholars consider *bismi'llah* to be a verse of Surat al-Fatiha yet do not recite it aloud during the prayer. This proves that invocations, like *amin*—which no scholar considers to be part of the Qur'an—should not be said aloud.

ANALYZING THE SEEMINGLY CONTRADICTORY HADITHS

1. Wa'il ibn Hujr Ǵ says,

> The Messenger Ǵ recited *"ghayri 'l-maghdubi 'alayhim wala 'l-dallin"* and followed it with *amin,* prolonging his voice while saying it [*madda biha sawtahu*] (*Sunan al-Tirmidhi* 1:57, *Abi Dawud* 1:142).

This is Sufyan's report from Wa'il ibn Hujr, which was previously discussed. It was stated above that the Hanafis prefer Shu'ba's report over Sufyan's in this issue.

The word *"madda"* used in this narration literally means "he stretched." Hence, the hadith means that the Messenger 🕊 stretched the initial *alif* of the *amin* and prolonged it, not that he said it aloud. Shu'ba's version of Wa'il ibn Hujr's 🕊 report (hadith 3 above), which supports this interpretation, clearly mentions that the Messenger 🕊 subdued his voice while saying *amin*.

2. Abu Hurayra 🕊 says,

> When the Messenger 🕊 recited *wala 'l-dallin,* he said *amin* after it, which could be heard in the first row (*Sunan Abi Dawud*).

The version of *Sunan Ibn Maja* contains the additional phrase, "The *masjid* echoed with the sound" (*Sunan Ibn Maja* 1:61).

The answer to this hadith is that it is weak and cannot be accepted as evidence, as one of its narrators, Bishr ibn Rafi', has been strongly criticized by a number of hadith experts. Imam Bukhari states, "He is not consistent in his narrations;" Imam Ahmad calls him weak; Imam Nasa'i states, "He is not strong;" and Ibn Hibban states, "He relates spurious narrations." (*Mizan al-i'tidal* U)

The second point to consider here is that if the sound of the *amin* only reached the first row (as the main portion of the narration mentions), then how did the whole *masjid* echo with it (as is added in *Ibn Maja's* version)? Had *amin* echoed throughout the *masjid,* everyone would have heard it. It is not clear how one version states it was heard from the first row only, while the other states it was so loud that the whole *masjid* echoed with its sound. Thus, this hadith is self-contradictory and, as a result, cannot be accepted as evidence in proving that *amin* was said aloud permanently.

A General Explanation and Conclusion

There are other apparently contradicting narrations which state that *amin* was said aloud during the prayer. However, many of these have been judged to be extremely weak and inadmissible as evidence. These narrations have not been discussed here but can be found in larger works such as *Athar al-sunan* and *I'la' al-sunan.*

A general answer for all such narrations is that even the Hanafis accept that the Messenger of Allah 鷺 said *amin* aloud; however, they say it was only said aloud for a short period of time and that there is no evidence to establish it was said aloud on a permanent basis. The few times the Messenger 鷺 said *amin* audibly was to emphasize its importance to his Companions. 'Umar ﷺ did the same with *thana*. He recited it aloud for a few days to teach the Companions, after which he continued to recite it silently. This is further confirmed by a report from Wa'il ibn Hujr ﷺ, transmitted by Hafiz Abu Bishr al-Dulabi in his *Kitab al-asma' wa 'l-kuna,* which states:

> I do not think the Messenger 鷺 said it [*amin*] aloud except to teach us (*Athar al-sunan* 93, *Fath al-Mulhim* 2:50-52, *I'la' al-sunan* 2:186).

Ibn al-Qayyim, concluding on the nature of this issue, writes in *Zad al-ma'ad* under the discussion of *qunut:*

> If the *imam* recites it [*qunut*] aloud a few times to teach the followers, there is no harm in that. 'Umar ﷺ recited *thana* aloud to teach the followers, and Ibn 'Abbas ﷺ recited Surat al-Fatiha during the funeral prayer to teach them it was *sunna.* Likewise, the issue of the *imam* saying *amin* aloud is from the same category (*Zad al-ma'ad* 1:70).

Ibn Jarir al-Tabari states:

> Both types of reports [i.e. those which state the *amin* was said aloud and those which state that it was said silently] have been transmitted from the Messenger 鷺, and both are reliable [*sahih*] (*Fath al-Mulhim* 2:50).

Hence, both types of reports are authentic, but refer to different occasions. The narrations that mention that the Messenger 鷺 said *amin* silently, refer to the normal practice of the Messenger 鷺, and the others refer to the few instances when he said *amin* aloud to teach the Companions.

Had it been the permanent practice of the Messenger 鷺 and the

Companions to say *amin* aloud, it would surely have been narrated from more than just a few Companions. There are five prayers in a day. If *amin* were said aloud in three of them, it would certainly have been widely reported as such.

Besides the narrations of Wa'il ibn Hujr, Abu Hurayra, and a few others (of which most are extremely weak and cannot stand as evidence anyway), few Companions reported that the *amin* was said aloud during the prayer. Even Wa'il himself, who was a resident of Yemen, visited the illuminated city of Madina just a few times, so it is possible that the Messenger 🌼 said *amin* aloud in his presence in order to teach him. Wa'il also mentions something to this effect, as transmitted by Hafiz al-Dulabi:

> I do not think the Messenger 🌼 said it [*amin*] aloud except to teach us (*Darse Tirmidhi* 1:523).

This is not the only report from Wa'il in this regard. Another narration of his, mentioned in *Sunan al-Nasa'i*, states:

> When the Messenger 🌼 recited *"ghayr al-maghdubi 'alayhim wala 'l-dallin,"* he said *amin*. I heard him [say it] since I was behind him (*Sunan al-Nasa'i* 1:147 U).

This indicates that he only heard the Messenger 🌼 say it because he was behind him, and not because it was pronounced loudly.

Hence, even the narrations of Wa'il, which are considered as strong evidence for those who say *amin* aloud, are surrounded by confusion. On the other hand, the evidence of the Hanafi school is from great Companions like 'Abdullah ibn Mas'ud, 'Umar, and 'Ali 🞜, who have plainly reported that one must say *amin* silently.

Therefore, since it is established that *amin* was said silently by the Messenger of Allah 🌼 for the most part of his life, and that many of the Companions and others gave priority to this method, it is the preferred way.

5

Raising the Hands for *Rukuʿ*

SIMILAR TO THE issue of *amin*, the question of whether or not to raise the hands anywhere in the prayer after the opening *takbir*, is not as serious a difference of opinion as has been made out to be. Whether one should raise his hands or not, before and after the bowing [*rukuʿ*], is merely a difference in ascertaining the better of two ways. Sometimes it is taken so seriously that some proponents of raising the hands at these instances, label those who do not raise them as ignorant, deviant, or guilty of reprehensible innovation. These are serious allegations. Likewise, the latter group has also been known to sometimes criticize the former group in a similar way.

It must be remembered that just as *not* raising the hands at any instance beyond the opening *takbir* [*tahrima*] is derived from the hadiths, so is the practice of raising them when bowing. Hence, both methods are permissible according to most scholars. The only difference is that according to some scholars, not raising the hands is more virtuous than raising them, whereas the others assert the contrary view. In the terminology of the jurists [*fuqaha'*], this issue is referred to as the issue of *rafʿ al-yadayn* or "raising of the hands."

The following sections discuss the hadiths and evidences pertaining to this issue. They also seek to demonstrate the strength of the Hanafi position in this issue.

The Various Opinions

Let us first take a look at the different opinions regarding the raising of the hands at various points in the prayer:

(1) Raising the hands while saying the opening *takbir*—all scholars are unanimous that the hands should be raised at this point.

(2) Raising the hands before bowing [*ruku'*] and after returning from it—one group (who will be referred to as "group one" in this chapter) states that it is *sunna* and more virtuous to raise the hands at these instances. Another group, which includes Imam Malik and Imam Abu Hanifa, is of the opinion that it is *sunna* and more preferable not to raise the hands at these instances.

(3) Raising the hands at any other point in the prayer, for instance, when moving into prostration [*sajda*] or returning to the third standing [*qiyam*]—there is no difference of opinion regarding these instances. All the scholars of the *Ahl al-Sunna* are unanimous that it is no longer *sunna* to raise the hands at these instances, since the practice was abrogated.

It should be remembered, however, that since this is not a debate about something being obligatory [*fard*] or unlawful [*haram*], the scholars state that it is permissible for a person following the opinion of group one not to raise his hands, just as it is permissible for a Hanafi or Maliki to raise them. However, it is preferable to follow the preferred practice of one's own school of *fiqh,* since that entails greater reward.

Some History Regarding the Issue

The whole debate concerning the "raising of the hands" revolves around two points. The first is regarding the differences found in the hadiths pertaining to this issue, and the second is regarding the differences found in the practice of the people of the three great cities of Islam during the first century A.H.—Makka, Madina, and Kufa.

Imam Malik based his opinion on the conduct [*ta'amul*] of the people of Madina, who did not observe the practice of raising the hands. Hence, he was of the opinion that one should not raise the hands anywhere after the opening *takbir*. It states in *al-Mudawwana*:

> Imam Malik said, "I do not consider the raising of the hands to be part of any *takbir* of the prayer, neither of any descending or ascending motion, except at the beginning of prayer." Ibn al-Qasim states, "Raising the hands [at any other point] was considered a weak practice according to Imam Malik" (*al-Mudawwanat al-kubra* 1:71).

This is Imam Malik sitting in the capital of Islam of the time, the city of Madina, where the Messenger of Allah 🕌 and the rightly guided Caliphs [*Khulafa' rashidun*] had resided, stating that *raf' al-yadayn* was a weak practice.

The opinions of Imam Shafi'i, on the other hand, were usually based on the fiqh of Makka. Hence, he preferred the raising of the hands, as it was the practice of most of the inhabitants of Makka in accordance with the teachings of 'Abdullah ibn al-Zubayr ⚬.

Other than these two cities, the most significant center of Islamic learning was Kufa. 'Umar ⚬ had sent 'Abdullah ibn Mas'ud ⚬ to Kufa as its teacher, in addition to approximately fifteen hundred other Companions who had previously taken up residence there. 'Ali ⚬ had transferred the center of the Islamic caliphate to Kufa as well, where he also took up residence. Hence, the people of Kufa, based on the teachings of Ibn Mas'ud and 'Ali ⚬, did not practice the raising of the hands. The great hadith master 'Allama 'Iraqi reports in his book *Sharh al-Taqrib* that Muhammad ibn Nasr al-Marwazi said regarding the inhabitants of Kufa:

> We are not aware of any city, in which all its inhabitants had completely abandoned the practice of raising the hands at all instances of ascending or descending in prayer, besides the people of Kufa. None from among them would raise their hands except at the initial *takbir* (*Ithaf al-sadat al-muttaqin bi sharh Ihya' 'ulum al-din* 3:54).

Hence, only one city from among the three great centers of Islam gave preference to raising the hands. The practice in the other cities was the contrary. This is very strong evidence in favor of the Hanafi opinion, because many of the people of Kufa must have travelled to Makka but still chose not to adopt the practice of the people of Makka in raising the hands.

Imam Tirmidhi, in his *Sunan,* composed two chapters concerning this issue: one containing the hadiths of raising the hands, and the other containing the hadiths of not raising them. At the end of the first chapter, he remarks concerning the raising of the hands, "This is the opinion of a few [*ba'd*] Companions." At the end of the second chapter, on *not* raising the hands, he remarks, "This is the opinion of more than one Companion." The expression used—*ghayru wahidin,* "more than one"—indicates a greater number than the term *ba'd* "few." These remarks of Imam Tirmidhi indicate that the practice of not raising the hands was a very widespread one.

The Differences Found in the Narrations

The hadiths regarding *raf' al-yadayn* are of three types:

(1) There are those which clearly mention that the Messenger of Allah ﷺ raised his hands at the time of *ruku'.*

(2) There are those which mention that Messenger of Allah ﷺ never raised his hands except when uttering the opening *takbir.*

(3) There are those which describe the complete prayer of the Messenger of Allah ﷺ, but do not mention whether or not he raised his hands after the opening *takbir.*

The hadiths of the first category stand as evidence for group one, whose opinion is of raising the hands; whereas the second category of hadiths stand as evidence for those whose opinion is not to raise the hands. Although the hadiths of the first category seem to out-number those of the second, this does not mean anything, because the hadiths of the third category could also be used in conjunction with the second as evidence for not raising the hands. The reason for this is that not mentioning something only evidences that it was not a popular practice. It is also very difficult to accept that while demonstrating the prayer of the Messenger 🌸, a narrator could have failed to mention something as significant as raising the hands, had it been an important aspect of the prayer. Hence, along with the hadiths of the third category, which are supplementary evidence for those of the second category, the hadiths in support of not raising the hands would actually outnumber those in support of it.

To elaborate further, it must be understood that the Messenger's 🌸 not raising his hands is a "nonexistent" action, and people do not mention nonexistent actions in their conversations. For instance, if an individual returning home from the *masjid*, happened to fall down and hurt himself, the report would state, "He fell down," since his falling down became an existent action (something that actually took place). On the other hand, if this same person arrived home without any accident, nobody would remark, "He did not fall," since this is a nonexistent action. It is just another one of several hundred other such incidents that did not occur.

The case of these hadiths is similar because, since the Messenger of Allah 🌸 did not raise his hands at all, the narrators did not report it. If it had been a regular practice of the Messenger 🌸 that he failed to do sometimes, the narrator would certainly have mentioned it.

This can be likened to the example of a person who has a fixed time for eating. If, for some reason, he failed to eat at that time, someone could remark that he did not eat, since eating at that time should have been an existent action for him but did not occur. Nobody would comment on his not eating at any other time, since eating at other times is normally a nonexistent action for this person, and nonexistent actions are normally not mentioned.

Now, the hadiths of the third category do not mention anything about the raising of the hands being a habitual action of Allah's

Messenger ﷺ. As a result, these hadiths can also be used as evidence, along with those of the second category, for the Hanafi point of view. This would significantly increase the number of hadiths in favor of the Hanafi opinion, causing them to outnumber the hadiths of the first category.

Another Complication

Another complicating aspect of this issue is that there are other hadiths which inform of the Messenger ﷺ raising his hands at various other instances within the prayer. More specifically, there are seven instances in the *salat* where the Messenger ﷺ is reported to have raised his hands at one time or another: (1) at the initial *takbir;* (2) before and after bowing [*ruku'*]; (3) before descending into prostration [*sajda*]; (4) between the two prostrations [*sujud*]; (5) when beginning the second *rak'a;* (6) when beginning the third *rak'a;* (7) in fact, some narrations mention that he raised his hands at the change of every new posture in the prayer.

The opinion of group one is that one should raise his hands at the first and second instances mentioned above, while the opinion of Imam Abu Hanifa and Imam Malik is that one should raise his hands at the first instance only. The question that arises here is: "Why has group one adopted the first two instances only and not the others?" Whatever their reason is for adopting only two instances and abandoning the rest will be the reason for Imam Abu Hanifa and Imam Malik adopting the first instance only and abandoning the others.

Undoubtedly, all of the Imams have their reasons for not classifying the raising of the hands as being *sunna* in all seven instances, in spite of the hadiths which mention that the Messenger ﷺ frequently raised his hands during *salat*. By the end of this chapter, it should become clear why such a practice was discarded, and why the raising of the hands was restricted to the opening *takbir* only.

THE HADITHS ON RAISING THE HANDS

Group one normally presents the narrations of Ibn 'Umar ❁ and Malik ibn al-Huwayrith ❁ as their primary sources of evidence, since both of these Companions have reported the raising of the hands at the time of bowing. However, both of these Companions have also reported the raising of the hands regarding all seven instances mentioned above. Group one has only accepted those narrations of the two Companions which mention that the Messenger of Allah ﷺ raised his hands at the opening *takbir* and when bowing, and have disregarded the other narrations.

The Hanafi scholars did not base their opinion on these narrations but on those reports whose narrators are consistent. Their primary source are the narrations of 'Abdullah ibn Mas'ud ❁, who states that the hands were raised at the initial *takbir* only, and not repeated at any other time in the prayer. All reports from him explain the same practice.

Weakness of 'Abdullah ibn 'Umar's ❁ Narrations

Now we come to the issue of the narrations of 'Abdullah ibn 'Umar, which are normally quoted by those who claim that the Messenger ﷺ frequently raised his hands in *salat*. It is well known that Imam Malik received many narrations from 'Abdullah ibn 'Umar ❁. In fact, his famous chain of transmission, which runs through Nafi' to 'Abdullah ibn 'Umar ❁, is known as "the golden chain" [*silsilat al-dhahab*]. However, in this issue, Imam Malik did not base his opinion on these narrations, but rather adopted the narrations of Ibn Mas'ud ❁ instead, and gave preference to the practice [*ta'amul*] of the people of Madina, which was to raise the hands at the initial *takbir* only.

Second, Ibn Abi Shayba and Imam Tahawi have related another hadith of Ibn 'Umar ❁ through Mujahid, in which there is also no mention of raising the hands. If this was a constant practice of the Messenger ﷺ, then why is it not mentioned in this narration?

Furthermore, although there are many hadiths of Ibn 'Umar ﷺ regarding the raising of the hands, there are many inconsistencies found in them. Such confusion in the reports of a narrator will not allow his narrations to be adopted in the presence of other reports that are more precise and consistent. For example, in one of his narrations, which is mentioned in Imam Tahawi's *Mushkil al-athar,* it states that the hands were raised at every movement of the prayer, whereas in his other narrations, this is not mentioned.

THE HADITHS ON NOT RAISING THE HANDS

We will now present the narrations of various Companions, including those of Ibn 'Umar ﷺ, which state that the Messenger ﷺ raised his hands for the opening *takbir* only.

The Hadiths of 'Abdullah ibn Mas'ud ﷺ

1. 'Alqama reports that

> 'Abdullah ibn Mas'ud ﷺ said: "Should I not demonstrate the prayer of the Messenger of Allah ﷺ for you?" He performed the prayer, and did not raise his hands except at the initial *takbir* (*Sunan al-Tirmidhi* 1:59, *Sunan al-Nasa'i* 1:161, *Sunan Abi Dawud* 1:116).

Imam Tirmidhi classifies this hadith as sound [*hasan*]. 'Allama ibn Hazm classifies it as rigorously authenticated [*sahih*] (*al-Muhalla* 4:88), and 'Allama Ahmad Muhammad Shakir, rejecting the criticism of some scholars, writes in his commentary of *Sunan al-Tirmidhi:*

> This hadith has been authenticated by Ibn Hazm and other hadith masters [*huffaz*], and whatever has been stated about it containing defects is incorrect.

It is mentioned in the *al-Jawhar al-naqi* that its narrators are those of *Sahih Muslim* (*I'la' al-sunan* 3:45).

2. 'Alqama reports that

> 'Abdullah ibn Mas'ud ﷺ asked: "Should I not inform you of Allah's

Messenger's 鑿 prayer?" He stood up and raised his hands at the outset and did not do so again (*Sunan al-Nasa'i* 1:158, *I'la' al-sunan* 3:48).

3. 'Alqama narrates from 'Abdullah ibn Mas'ud 鑿:

The Messenger of Allah 鑿 would raise his hands at the opening *takbir*, then would not raise them again (*Sharh Ma'ani 'l-athar* 224).

4. 'Abdullah ibn Mas'ud 鑿 relates:

I prayed with the Messenger of Allah 鑿, Abu Bakr, and 'Umar 鑿. They did not raise their hands except at the beginning of prayer (*Nasb al-raya* 1:526, *Majma' al-zawa'id* 2:101).

Judging from the above hadiths, it can be concluded quite easily that the Messenger 鑿 did not raise his hands regularly during the course of prayer. Ibn Mas'ud, 'Ali 鑿, and other Companions would never have narrated such reports had they observed the Messenger of Allah 鑿 and the Caliphs [*Khulafa'*] regularly raising their hands? It has also been observed that all the narrations of Ibn Mas'ud 鑿 are consistent in that they relate the hands being raised only at the beginning of prayer and not at any other instance.

The Hadiths of 'Abdullah ibn 'Umar 鑿

The following narrations of Ibn 'Umar 鑿 speak of the hands being raised at the opening *takbir* only.

5. Salim reports that his father (Ibn 'Umar 鑿) said:

I observed that when the Messenger of Allah 鑿 would begin his prayer, he would raise his hands while levelling them: some say at shoulder level. Thereafter, he would not raise them again before the bowing or after it. Some have added that he would not raise them between the two prostrations [*sujud*] either" (*Sahih Ibn 'Awana* 2:90 U).

In this narration, Ibn 'Umar 鑿 actually confirms that the Messenger of Allah 鑿 did not raise his hands at the time o f *ruku'*. Imam Humaydi, the *shaykh* [teacher] of Imam Bukhari, has also reported this very hadith through his own chain, which is one of the most reliable chains (*Musnad al-Humaydi* 2:277). It is an agreed upon fact that all of the hadiths of *Sahih Ibn 'Awana*, where this hadith is found, are rigorously authenticated [*sahih*].

6. Salim reports from his father that the Messenger of Allah ﷺ would raise his hands to shoulder level when beginning the prayer (*al-Mudawwanat al-kubra* 2:71 U). Imam Malik rejected *raf' al-yadayn* at the time of bowing due to this hadith.

7. 'Abdullah ibn 'Abbas and Ibn 'Umar ﷺ report that the Messenger of Allah ﷺ said:

> The hands are to be raised at seven instances: at the beginning of prayer, when setting sight on the House of Allah, at Safa, Marwa, 'Arafat, Muzdalifa, and when saluting the [black] stone (*Nasb al-raya* 1:521).

In this hadith, there is no mention of the hands being raised at the time of bowing [*ruku'*].

The Hadiths of Jabir ibn Samura ﷺ

8. Jabir ibn Samura ﷺ narrates:

> The Messenger of Allah ﷺ approached us and remarked, "Why is it that I see you raising your hands as though they are the tails of restive horses? Remain calm in prayer" (*Sahih Muslim* 1:181, *Sunan al-Nasa'i* 1:176, *Sunan Abi Dawud* 1:150).

In this hadith, the Messenger ﷺ prohibits the raising of the hands while performing prayer. This could only mean at the time of bowing, prostration, and the like. It cannot be considered prohibited to raise them when proclaiming the opening *takbir*, since the raising of the hands at that time is not considered to be inside the prayer and, as such, does not interfere with the calmness recommended in the *salat*.

Some scholars however assert that this hadith is regarding the prohibition of raising the hands while making *salam* at the end of *salat*. This is a misconception that has probably risen from another similar hadith regarding *salam*, which states:

Whenever we prayed with the Messenger of Allah 🕌, we would say, "*al-salamu ʿalaykum wa rahmatullah, al-salamu ʿalaykum wa rahmatullah,*" and we would gesture with our hands towards our sides. The Messenger 🕌 asked, "What are you gesturing towards with your hands, as though they are the tails of restive horses? It is sufficient for you to leave your hands on your laps and make *salam* to your brother on your right and left" (*Sahih Muslim* 1:181).

This misconception may have occurred because of a statement in both narrations mentioning raising the hands "as though they were the tails of restive horses." This may have lead some scholars to conclude that both narrations are concerning one and the same incident [i.e. the raising of the hands while saying *salam*]. However, if both narrations are analyzed and the circumstances of each investigated, it is evident, *insha Allah*, that both are concerning two different and separate incidents. Some of these differences are highlighted below:

(a) In the first hadith (Jabir ibn Samura's 🕊 narration), it states that the Companions were engrossed in their own prayers when the Messenger 🕌 addressed them. The second hadith mentions that they were performing prayer behind Allah's Messenger 🕌, after which he addressed them.

(b) The first hadith states that the Messenger 🕌 prohibited them from "raising their hands during prayer," and in the second hadith he prohibited them from "gesturing to the right and left with their hands when making *salam.*"

(c) In the first hadith, the Messenger of Allah 🕌 also instructed them to exercise calmness in prayer after prohibiting them from raising their hands, whereas in the second one he only instructed them on how to properly perform the *salam*.

(d) In the first hadith, the Messenger 🕌 uses the words "in prayer" whereas *salam* is made at the end of prayer. This means the hadith is concerning observing calmness throughout the prayer, and not just at the time of making *salam*.

FIQH AL-IMAM

(e) If the first hadith were taken for a moment to be referring to calmness during *salam*, it would then mean that remaining calm in the prayer itself, when bowing for example, would be even more important. If raising of the hands during *salam* is prohibited, it would more conclusively be prohibited throughout the prayer.

The Hadiths of 'Abdullah ibn 'Abbas ﷺ

9. 'Abdullah ibn 'Abbas ﷺ reports that the Messenger of Allah ﷺ said:

> The hands should not be raised except at seven instances: at the beginning of prayer, when entering the Masjid al-Haram ["the Sanctified Masjid"] and setting sight on the House of Allah, when standing on Safa, Marwa, and when standing [*yaqifu*] with the pilgrims in 'Arafat, and at Muzdalifa (*Nasb al-raya* 1:290 U, *Mu'jam al-Tabarani* 1:389 U).

10. 'Abdullah ibn 'Abbas ﷺ also narrates:

> The hands should not be raised except at seven instances: when beginning the prayer, when setting sight on the House of Allah, at Safa, Marwa, 'Arafat, Muzdalifa, and when pelting the *jamarat* [stone pillars representing the Satan at Mina] (*Musannaf Ibn Abi Shayba* 1:237).

The Hadiths of Bara' ibn 'Azib ﷺ

11. Ibn Abi Layla reports that he heard Bara' ﷺ narrate to a group of people, among whom was Ka'b ibn 'Ujra ﷺ:

> I observed the Messenger of Allah ﷺ raise his hands at the initial *takbir* when beginning the prayer (*Daraqutni* 1:293).

It is mentioned in the *Musannaf* of Ibn Abi Shayba that Ibn Abi Layla was also known not to raise his hands [except at the initial *takbir*] (1:237).

12. Bara' ibn 'Azib ﷺ narrates that

> when the Messenger of Allah ﷺ would begin the prayer, he would raise his hands up to his ears, then not do so again.

One version of this narration adds: "only once" (i.e. he would raise them only once), and another adds: "then he would not raise them again until completing the prayer" (*Musannaf Ibn Abi Shayba* 1:236, *Sunan Abi Dawud* 1:109 U).

This further clarifies that the Messenger of Allah ﷺ only raised his hands at the beginning of the *salat*. Like these narrations, there are countless others which inform us that the hands were not regularly raised beyond the first *takbir*. For those seeking further clarification, additional narrations and commentary can be found in the following books: *Nasb al-raya* of 'Allama Zayla'i, 2:389–416, *Awjaz al-masalik* of Shaykh Zakariyya Khandelwi 1:202–210, and *I'la' al-sunan* of Shaykh Zafar 'Uthmani 3:43–72.

The Companions and Followers on This Issue

1. Aswad reports:

   I performed prayer with 'Umar ◈, and he raised his hands only when beginning the prayer" (*Musannaf Ibn Abi Shayba* 1:237).

2. 'Abd al-Malik states:

   I observed that Sha'bi, Ibrahim al-Nakh'ay, and Abu Ishaq did not raise their hands except at the beginning of the prayer" (*Musannaf Ibn Abi Shayba* 1:237).

3. 'Asim ibn Kulayb reports from his father, who was a companion of 'Ali ibn Abi Talib ◈, that

   'Ali ◈ would raise his hands only at the initial *takbir* when beginning his prayer; thereafter, he would not raise them again at any other place in the prayer (*Muwatta Imam Muhammad* 94, *Musannaf Ibn Abi Shayba* 1:236).

4. Ibrahim al-Nakh'ay reports that

   'Abdullah ibn Mas'ud ◈ would raise his hands at the beginning of the prayer, then would not raise them again (*Musannaf Ibn Abi Shayba* 1:236).

5. Mujahid reports:

> I did not see 'Umar ❀ raise his hands except at the beginning of prayer (*Musannaf Ibn Abi Shayba* 1:236).

The narrators of this hadith are those from whom Imam Bukhari has related in his *Kitab al-tafsir* [see *Sahih al-Bukhari* 2:725].

6. Imam Malik reports that

> Na'im ibn 'Abdillah al-Mujmir and Abu Ja'far al-Qari informed him that Abu Hurayra ❀ would lead them in prayer. He would say the *takbir* every time he moved from one posture to another, and would raise his hands when saying the *takbir* at the beginning of the prayer (*Muwatta Imam Muhammad* 90).

7. Abu Ishaq reports that

> the companions of 'Abdullah ibn Mas'ud and 'Ali ❀ would not raise their hands except at the beginning of prayer. Waki' confirms that they [the companions] would not raise them thereafter (*Musannaf Ibn Abi Shayba* 1:236).

8. Isma'il reports that

> Qays would raise his hands when entering into prayer, after which he would not raise them [again] (*Musannaf Ibn Abi Shayba* 1:236).

The narrator Qays has the honor of transmitting from all ten of the Companions who were given glad tidings of Paradise by the Messenger of Allah ❀ in one sitting ['ashara mubashshara].

9. It is reported from Aswad and 'Alqama that

> they would raise their hands when beginning the prayer, after which they would not raise them again (*Musannaf Ibn Abi Shayba* 1:237).

10. Sufyan ibn Muslim al-Juhani reports that

> Ibn Abi Layla would raise his hands at the beginning [of prayer] when saying the *takbir*.

11. It is reported from Khaythama and Ibrahim al-Nakh'ay that they

would only raise their hands at the beginning of prayer (*Musannaf Ibn Abi Shayba* 1:236).

12. It is reported regarding Shaʿbi that he would raise his hands at the initial *takbir* [only], then would not do so again (*Musannaf Ibn Abi Shayba* 1:236).

13. Abu Bakr ibn ʿAyash reports:

> I have never seen a jurist do such a thing, i.e. raising the hands at any point other than at the initial *takbir* (*Sharh Maʿani ʾl-athar* 1:228).

Here are the likes of Abu Bakr, ʿUmar, ʿAli, Ibn Masʿud, Ibn ʿUmar, Abu Hurayra, and many other Companions ﷺ, followed by Shaʿbi, Ibrahim al-Nakhʿay, Abu Ishaq, Qays, Aswad, ʿAlqama, and Ibn Abi Layla, all from the Followers—they were reported to have not raised their hands except at the initial *takbir*. It is quite clear that they would not have omitted the "raising of the hands" at the time of bowing, had it been the regular practice of the Messenger of Allah ﷺ.

OTHER REASONS FOR NOT RAISING THE HANDS

(1) Not raising the hands beyond the opening *takbir* is most in conformance with the Holy Qurʾan. Allah ﷺ says,

> "Successful indeed are the believers, those who humble themselves [*khashiʿun*] in their prayers" (*al-Qurʾan* 23:2).

The word *khushuʿ* means humility and humbleness. Similarly, in another verse Allah ﷺ says,

> "Stand before Allah in a devout frame of mind [*qanitin*]" (*al-Qurʾan* 2:238).

From these verses, it is understood that both humility and calmness are required in *salat*. The Messenger ﷺ prohibited the raising of the hands during prayer (as in hadith 8, p. 106) because it interfered with the maintenance of humility and calmness in it. Not raising the hands so frequently will help achieve the peace, tranquillity, and devotion encouraged by Allah ﷻ in the Qur'an.

Furthermore, according to the principles of hadith [*usul al-hadith*], when some hadiths are in apparent conflict with others—as in this case—those most in conformance with the Qur'an will be regarded as more superior.

(2) Raising the hands at the opening *takbir* is a *sunna* by consensus, and raising them before and after bowing is where the difference of opinion lies. Raising the hands beyond these two instances is unanimously viewed as not being *sunna*. Now let us determine whether the *takbir* at the time of descending into *ruku'* and the *tasmi'* [*sami'allahu liman hamidah*] when returning from it, are similar to the opening *takbir* or to the *takbirs* at other instances in the prayer.

They are not similar to the opening *takbir* because the opening *takbir* is an integral [*rukn*] of *salat,* whereas the *takbir* and the *tasmi'* for *ruku'* are *sunna*. The *takbirs* at all other instances in the prayer, however, are also *sunna* and the hands are not raised when saying them. Since the *takbir* and *tasmi'* when bowing resemble these other *takbirs* in their being *sunna,* it should follow that the hands should not be raised at the time of bowing either, as they are not raised for these other *takbirs*.

(3) Since there are two types of hadiths found—those which state the hands were raised when bowing and those which state on the contrary—it is important to find out which practice abrogated the other. Whenever an abrogation [*naskh*] occurred regarding any particular action of prayer, it was always regarding an action that was initially commanded and practised. Nonexistent practices were not abrogated. For instance, in the earlier period of Islam, it was permissible to talk and move around during prayer. Both of these actions were later prohibited and no longer remain valid. This is what abrogation is; when a practice is cancelled after having been existent.

We cannot say that something which was never practised to begin with, became abrogated by an injunction commanding its performance. That would just be considered a new command. Similarly, it should be understood here that raising the hands at the time of bowing, while being initially allowed, was later abrogated, just as the Hanafis have said.

(4) The narrations on this issue are of two types. There are those which outline the method of the Messenger's ﷺ prayer and whether he raised his hands or not. Many differences are found in these narrations. Some state that the Messenger ﷺ raised his hands at every *takbir*, whereas others state that he raised them for the initial *takbir* only and so forth.

The second type of narrations are those in which the Messenger ﷺ issues direct commands about raising the hands in prayer. Unlike the first category, there is no confusion or inconsistency found in these narrations. They all mention that the Messenger ﷺ prohibited the raising of the hands in prayer. For instance, hadith 8 above (p. 106) clearly prohibits the raising of the hands while engrossed in prayer. According to the principles of hadith [*usul al-hadith*], the narrations which contradict each other will be rejected, and those which are consistent will be accepted. Hence, since the hadiths of the second category are very consistent in their prohibition of raising the hands, they will be preferred over the first category, which are inconsistent.

(5) The narrators of the hadiths who, like 'Abdullah ibn 'Umar ﷺ, mention the Messenger ﷺ raising his hands at the time of bowing, have themselves been reported to have not raised their hands. However, the primary narrator of the hadiths which mention the Messenger ﷺ as having not raised his hands, is 'Abdullah ibn Mas'ud ﷺ. He has not been reported to have adopted any method besides what is mentioned in his narrations. This means that Ibn Mas'ud's hadiths hold a stronger position in this issue, since, according to the principles of hadith [*usul al-hadith*], the narrations of a narrator whose personal practice contradicts his narrations are usually not accepted.

(6) Those who narrated that the hands were not raised, were higher ranking jurists [*fuqaha'*] than those who narrated that it was a constant practice. For instance, it is well known that 'Abdullah ibn Mas'ud ﷺ was a greater jurist than 'Abdullah ibn 'Umar ﷺ; and Ibn Mas'ud's students, 'Alqama and Aswad, were greater jurists than Nafi', who reported from Ibn 'Umar ﷺ. Hence, according to the principles of hadith [*usul al-hadith*], the narrations of Ibn Mas'ud ﷺ, 'Alqama, and Aswad on this issue are preferred over the narrations of Ibn 'Umar and his students, due to their status in jurisprudence [*fiqh*].

(7) Since Ibn Mas'ud ﷺ was older than Ibn 'Umar ﷺ, he had more opportunity to stand in the first row closer to the Messenger ﷺ, giving him a closer view of the Messenger's prayer. Ibn 'Umar ﷺ, due to his young age, would not stand in the front rows. Hence, Ibn Mas'ud's ﷺ narrations will be regarded as stronger than Ibn 'Umar's in this issue.

Besides this, Ibn Mas'ud ﷺ enjoyed a very close relationship with the Messenger ﷺ. 'Allama Dhahabi, describing the status of Ibn Mas'ud ﷺ, writes:

> 'Abdullah ibn Mas'ud ﷺ, the learned leader [*al-imam al-rabbani*], Abu 'Abd al-Rahman 'Abdullah ibn Ummi 'Abd al-Hudhali; Companion and personal servant of the Messenger ﷺ; among the first to embrace Islam; among the veterans of the battle of Badr; among the expert jurists and teachers of the Qur'an; among those who strove to convey [the words of the Messenger ﷺ] very accurately; extremely scrupulous in [his] narrations; and one who would admonish his students upon their negligence in recording the exact words [of the Messenger ﷺ].... [Due to extreme caution] he would narrate very little [himself].... His students would not give preference to any Companion over him.... Surely he was from among the leading Companions, the bearers of sacred knowledge, and the exemplars [*a'imma*] of guidance (*Tadhkirat al-huffaz*).

Imam Tahawi relates a very interesting incident:

> Mughira ibn Muqsim reports, "I mentioned to Ibrahim al-Nakh'ay the hadith of Wa'il ibn Hujr ﷺ regarding the Messenger of Allah ﷺ raising

his hands before and after bowing." Ibrahim said, "If Wa'il has seen the Messenger 畿 raising his hands once, then Ibn Mas'ud 釜 has seen him fifty times not raising them" (*Sharh Ma'ani 'l-athar*).

'Urwa ibn Murra stated:

> When I entered the *masjid* [mosque] of Hadhramaut, I heard 'Alqama ibn Wa'il narrate from his father that the Messenger 畿 would raise his hands before and after the bowing posture. I mentioned this to Ibrahim al-Nakh'ay, who responded angrily, "Is Wa'il ibn Hujr the only one to have seen the Messenger 畿? Did not Ibn Mas'ud 釜 and his companions also see him?" (*Muwatta Imam Muhammad* 92).

(8) One other reason for not raising the hands at the time of bowing is that we find all of the various invocations of prayer accompanied by a specific body motion. For instance, there is *takbir* before bowing and *tasmi'* when returning from it, and likewise, when descending into the prostration there is a *takbir.* Since there was no accompanying body motion for the beginning and ending of prayer, raising the hands was allocated for the opening *takbir,* and the turning of the head for *taslim* [*salams*]. Now, if the hands are also to be raised at the time of bowing, then the *takbir* and *tasmi'* at that time will be accompanied by two actions (i.e. bowing down and raising the hands) and in turn contradict the standard of having only one motion for every invocation.

CONCLUSION

The hadiths, which mention that the hands were raised at the time of bowing, do not constitute sufficient evidence to establish that the raising of the hands remained a permanent practice of the Messenger 畿. Therefore, raising the hands before and after bowing cannot be called a *sunna mustamirra,* or "a permanent or continuous practice of the Messenger 畿," due to the many authentic narrations which state that the hands were never raised after the opening *takbir.* The practice of the rightly guided Caliphs [*Khulafa' rashidun*] and many of the prominent Companions was also to not raise them, and hadith 8 (p. 106) actually prohibits raising them. All of these points indicate that raising the hands when bowing is a *sunna matruka,* or "an earlier practice of Allah's Messenger 🌸 which he later abandoned;" hence, it would be *sunna* and more preferable not to raise the hands before and after bowing.

To expound further, the Hanafis do acknowledge that the Messenger 🌸 raised his hands at the various instances in the *salat* that are outlined in the hadiths; however, they recognize this as a temporary practice. It was only at the time of the opening *takbir* that he raised them regularly. Not a single narration is found from those presented by group one which establishes that the hands were raised by the Messenger 🌸 on a permanent basis before and after bowing.

One narration of Ibn 'Umar 🌸, which is sometimes mentioned, ends with the words, "Thus, this remained the practice of Allah's Messenger 🌸 in prayer until he met with Allah 🌸." This narration however is either extremely weak or fabricated due to it containing 'Isma ibn Muhammad in its chain of narrators. This narrator has been described as follows: (a) Yahya ibn Ma'in calls him a "flagrant liar [*kadhdhab*] who fabricates hadiths;" (b) 'Uqayli states, "He narrates nonsense from reliable narrators" (*Mizan al-i'tidal* 3:68); (c) Ibn 'Adi states, "None of his narrations are free from defect" (*Mizan al-i'tidal* 2:582).

It also contains another narrator, 'Abd al-Rahman ibn Quraysh, who has also been criticized and called a fabricator (*Mizan al-i'tidal* 2:582).

Hence, all the hadiths which have been brought forth as evidence by group one, only mention that the Messenger 🌸 raised his hands at the time of bowing, just as some hadiths also explain that he raised them at various other instances as well. None of these hadiths, however, state that these additional raises were a constant and lifelong practice of the Messenger 🌸.

6

Sitting in Prayer: *Tawarruk* or *Iftirash?*

ONE OTHER ISSUE that has become quite popular today is that of determining the exact way one should sit in the *qa'da* or "sitting posture" of prayer. The abundant treasures of hadiths outline two different methods the Messenger of Allah 🕊 used for his sitting posture. Some hadiths indicate that the Messenger 🕊 sat in the *tawarruk* position, and other hadiths indicate that he sat in the *iftirash* position. Hence, we could gauge from this that the Messenger of Allah 🕊 at one time or another during his blessed life sat in both of these positions.

The *tawarruk* position is when a person sits with the left posterior on the ground; his right foot placed vertically with toes pointing towards the *qibla;* and the left foot on its side emerging from under the right foot.

Slightly different is the *iftirash* position, which is to place the left foot on its side and to sit on it; and to keep the right foot vertical, while resting on the bottom of the toes, turning them toward the *qibla.*

THE VARIOUS OPINIONS

According to the Hanafis, the more superior and preferred method is that a person use the *iftirash* position in all sittings of the prayer. However, though it is not the preferred method, it would be permissible, in light of rigorously authenticated [*sahih*] hadiths, to sit in the *tawarruk* position as well.

Another group of scholars states that it is more preferable for a person to use the *tawarruk* position in all the sittings of the prayer. A third group states it is more preferable to use the *iftirash* position in the first sitting and *tawarruk* in the "final" one. This means that while performing a two *rak'a* salat with one sitting at the end, a person will use the *tawarruk* position in that sitting, since it is the "final" one. The view of the fourth group is slightly different from this, in that a person will use the *iftirash* position in the "first" sitting of every prayer and *tawarruk* in the second. This means that a person performing a two *rak'a* prayer with only one sitting, will sit in the *iftirash* position for that sitting, since it is the "first" one; and if the *salat* is a three or four *rak'a* one, then he will sit in the *iftirash* position for the first sitting and *tawarruk* in the second sitting.

The difference of opinion on this issue, however, is not a very serious one, as it is about determining which of the two valid and permissible actions is more preferable. The following section will outline the reasons why the Hanafi school has given preference to the *iftirash* position, and it will also seek to clarify precisely when and why the Messenger ﷺ used *tawarruk*.

The Hadiths on *Iftirash*

The Hanafis state that the Messenger ﷺ, for the greater part of his life, sat in the *iftirash* position for all sittings of his prayer, and Imam Tirmidhi has stated it to be the practice of the majority of scholars. As for the few times the Messenger ﷺ did do *tawarruk*—as some narrations state—it was either due to his weakness and not being able to sit in *iftirash* in the latter part of his life, or it was merely to inform the Companions of its permissibility [*bayanan li 'l-jawaz*]. The following hadiths mention the Messenger's ﷺ use of *iftirash* while sitting in the *salat*.

1. 'A'isha ﷺ said,

   The Messenger of Allah ﷺ would spread his left foot and keep the right one standing (*Sahih Muslim* 1:195).

2. 'Abdullah ibn 'Umar ﷺ states in his narration:

   It is a *sunna* of prayer that you keep your right foot standing and fold the left one (*Sahih al-Bukhari* 1:114).

The following hadiths will further clarify the posture illustrated in the above two narrations.

3. Ibn 'Umar ﷺ narrates that

   among the *sunnats* of prayer is that you keep the right foot standing with the toes pointed towards the *qibla,* and [that you] sit on the left foot (*Sunan al-Nasa'i* 1:173).

4. Wa'il ibn Hujr ﷺ said,

   I came to Madina to observe the Messenger of Allah's ﷺ prayer. When he sat for *tashahhud,* he spread his left foot and kept the right one standing (*Sunan al-Tirmidhi* 1:65).

Imam Tirmidhi reports this to be a rigorously authenticated [*sahih*] hadith, and then states that this was the practice of the majority of the learned scholars and is the view of Sufyan al-Thawri, Ibn al-Mubarak, and the people of Kufa.

All of these hadiths speak of the *iftirash* position being generally used by the Messenger ﷺ, and do not imply that he sat in any other position. This means it was a common practice for him to sit in the *iftirash* position. One objection raised here by the second group (mentioned above) is that these hadiths only refer to the sitting posture of the first sitting and not the second. Hence, according to them, a person should only sit in *iftirash* in the first sitting and use *tawarruk* in the second sitting. This objection however is not a valid one, because of Wa'il ibn Hujr's ﷺ above statement:

   I came to Madina [especially] to observe the Messenger's prayer.

This means that his main purpose of visiting the Messenger of Allah ﷺ was to observe how he prayed. So, for Wa'il ibn Hujr ؓ to specifically mention *iftirash* as the only sitting posture used by the Messenger ﷺ, and not mention any other sitting method, informs us that this Companion only observed the Messenger ﷺ using *iftirash* in all the sittings of the prayer.

5. Abu Humayd al-Sa'idi said,

> [...] then, when he [the Messenger ﷺ] sat for *tashahhud*, he spread his left foot and raised the right one on its toes, and recited the *tashahhud* (*Sharh Ma'ani 'l-athar* 1:260).

Abu Humayd has related this hadith in a totally general context as well, and does not mention whether or not this posture is restricted to the first sitting only.

6. One narration of Abu Wa'il states:

> When he [the Messenger ﷺ] sat for *tashahhud*, he spread his left foot and sat on it, then began to supplicate raising his index finger (*Sharh Ma'ani 'l-athar* 1:259).

This hadith describes the Messenger ﷺ to be sitting in *iftirash* while making the supplication after *tashahhud*. Therefore, since it is quite obvious that the supplication [*du'a'*] is usually made in the final sitting of the prayer, it has also been concluded from this hadith that the Messenger ﷺ used *iftirash* in the final sitting.

7. Ibrahim narrates that

> when the Messenger ﷺ would sit during his prayer, he would spread his left foot, until the above surface of the foot had become dark [through sitting constantly in this position] (*Sunan Abi Dawud*).

8. Samura ؓ said,

> The Messenger ﷺ forbade sitting on the ground with the knees drawn up [*iq'a'*] and *tawarruk* (*Sunan al-Bayhaqi, al-Mustadrak*).

From all of the above hadiths, we can infer that the Messenger of Allah ﷺ mostly sat in the *iftirash* position, which clearly indicates that it is *sunna* and therefore the preferred posture for sitting.

Some scholars have stated one other reason for the preference of *iftirash* over *tawarruk*. They say *iftirash* is slightly more difficult than *tawarruk,* and the more difficult a form of worship is the more reward it entails. 'A'isha ◌ relates that the Messenger of Allah ﷺ said,

> The reward is in proportion to the hardship [you undertake] (*Sahih al-Bukhari, Muslim*).

It was mentioned at the beginning of this chapter that according to some narrations, the Messenger ﷺ also sat in *tawarruk.* The following section deals with the hadiths on *tawarruk* and provides insight into the reasons why the Messenger ﷺ sometimes sat in this position, even though his usual practice was of *iftirash.* The Hanafi scholars have offered many explanations as to why he sometimes sat in *tawarruk.*

The Hadiths on *Tawarruk*

1. It is narrated from Yahya ibn Sa'id that

> Qasim ibn Muhammad demonstrated for them the method of sitting [in prayer]. He raised the right foot and spread the left one, then sat with his left posterior [on the ground] and did not sit on his foot. He then said, "Abdullah, son of 'Abdullah ibn 'Umar ◌, demonstrated it this way for me and informed me that his father, Ibn 'Umar ◌, would [also] sit in this fashion" (*Sharh Ma'ani 'l-athar* 257).

This hadith is used as evidence by those who claim that the Messenger ﷺ generally sat in the *tawarruk* position, and by it they also attempt to prove the superiority of this position. However, we will discover that their claim is weak for a number of reasons:

(a) Ibn 'Umar ◌ sat in *tawarruk* (as in the above hadith) only because he was experiencing some weakness in his legs and was unable to sit in *iftirash*. It is reported that he would sometimes sit in the *tarabbu'*, or cross-legged, posture as well, but would forbid others from doing so. The following narration of 'Abdullah ibn 'Umar ⬥ explains this in more detail:

> Abdullah, son of 'Abdullah ibn 'Umar ⬥, would observe his father sitting cross-legged in prayer. He states, "I also [once] sat in that position while I was still young, but my father forbade me saying, 'It is a *sunna* of prayer that you raise your right foot and spread the left one.' I remarked to him, 'You sit in that position [i.e. cross-legged],' so he replied, 'My legs do not support me'" (*Sharh Ma'ani 'l-athar* 257-258, *Sahih al-Bukhari*).

This hadith clearly establishes that according to Ibn 'Umar ⬥, the *sunna* and preferred way of sitting is in the *iftirash* position. It was only due to weakness in his legs that Ibn 'Umar ⬥ could not sit that way and eventually resorted to sitting in *tawarruk* and, at times, in *tarabbu'* [cross-legged]. We can conclude from this that both the *tarabbu'* and *tawarruk* positions are secondary and alternative positions that are used only when there is difficulty with sitting in *iftirash*.

(b) One other reason why this hadith is unable to stand as evidence against the narrations presented by the Hanafis, is because it is a mere description of somebody's action [*hadith fi'li*]. The Hanafis, on the other hand, have narrations containing verbal commands [*ahadith qawliyya*] for *iftirash* [*see* hadith 2 and 3 above]; and a verbal command, according to one of the principles of hadith [*usul al-hadith*], takes precedence over a narration which describes only an action.

2. Abu Humayd al-Sa'idi ⬥ said,

> When the Messenger ⬥ reached the final sitting [*rak'a*], in which the prayer was to be completed, he spread his left foot and sat [leaning] on one side, in *tawarruk* (*Sunan al-Tirmidhi* 1:67).

This is another hadith used by those who claim that *tawarruk* should be used in the final sitting. The Hanafis have explained the implications of this hadith as follows:

(a) This was the posture adopted by the Messenger 🕋 in his final days when it became too difficult for him to sit in *iftirash*. The Messenger 🕋 himself mentioned in some narrations that he "had become heavy" due to advanced age.

(b) Abu Humayd al-Sa'idi, the narrator of the hadith, has also narrated on another occasion that the Messenger of Allah 🕋 sat in *iftirash* only [*see* hadith 5 above]. Hence, both of his narrations could be reconciled by stating that his first narration describes the Messenger's 🕋 regular posture, while this one highlights the Messenger's 🕋 practice in his final years.

(c) Another reason why the Messenger 🕋 occasionally sat in the *tawarruk* posture could have been to display the permissibility of it [*bayanan li 'l-jawaz*], i.e. that it was not unlawful to sit that way. This means that the Messenger 🕋 used the *tawarruk* posture on a few occasions to teach the Companions that it was a permissible and alternate way of sitting if the need arose.

From the above points, we gather that the *tawarruk* posture was used by the Messenger of Allah 🕋 mostly in his final years, due to weakness in his legs which prevented him from sitting in the *iftirash* position. If any hadith describes the Messenger 🕋 as having used *tawarruk* prior to that, then it was simply to indicate the permissibility of it and not to indicate its preference over *iftirash* or of it being his permanent practice.

CONCLUSION

Both types of hadiths are to be found in the books of hadith, i.e. those of *iftirash* and those of *tawarruk*. The Hanafis after studying them carefully have concluded that the Messenger 🕋 sat in both of these positions at one time or another. They are both permissible and a person has the choice of sitting in either of the two positions during his prayer. However, since the Messenger 🕋 used the *iftirash* position for most of his life, and it was his continuous practice (as the hadiths of Ibn 'Umar ﷺ confirm), it would be more virtuous and rewarding to do the same and sit in the *iftirash* position. In the event of inability, the recourse would be to sit in *tawarruk*.

The narrations that mention *tawarruk* do not describe it as being a permanent practice of the Messenger ﷺ but rather only mention it as being a practice of his which he did to display its permissibility [*bayanan li 'l-jawaz*]; or that he resorted to it in the latter part of his life due to his weakness and inability to sit in *iftirash*. In this way, the Hanafis have managed to reconcile between the various narrations and provided suitable interpretations for them all.

7

The *Sunna* Prayer of Fajr

THE MESSENGER OF ALLAH 🕌 laid great emphasis on the *sunna* prayer of Fajr, saying, "It is more superior than the world and everything within it" (*Sahih Muslim* 1:251). Likewise, there are a number of narrations from which the importance of this *sunna* prayer can be understood. This means that a person should ensure that it is performed prior to the *fard* prayer, since no *sunna* prayer is permissible until after sunrise, once the *fard* prayer of Fajr is performed.

So what is one to do if he arrives late to the *masjid* for Fajr, and finds the congregational prayer about to begin or already in progress? On the one hand, he remembers the emphasis regarding the *sunna* prayer of Fajr, yet on the other, he knows the hadith of the Messenger 🕌 stating that once the call to commence [*iqama*] has been made, only the *fard* prayer should be performed. The Messenger of Allah 🕌 said:

> Once the call to commence [*iqama*] is made for the prayer, there is no prayer except the *fard* prayer [*maktuba*] (*Sahih Muslim* 1:247).

The worshipper [*musalli*] is unsure of what to do in this situation. Should he hurry and perform the *sunna* prayer, then catch up with the *imam* for the *fard* prayer, or should he abandon the *sunna* prayer altogether and join in the congregation? There is a difference of opinion among the scholars on this issue.

THE VARIOUS OPINIONS

One opinion is that it is necessary for this person to immediately join the congregation for the *fard* prayer, and that it is no longer permissible for him to perform the *sunna* prayer during the congregational *fard* prayer, just as is the ruling for other prayers.

Imam Abu Hanifa and Imam Malik are of the opinion that the person should attempt to perform his *sunna* prayer, as long as he thinks he can complete it quickly and join in the *fard* prayer before it ends, i.e. even if he catches only the last sitting. This means that he must be confident of not missing the congregation completely, otherwise he should leave performing the *sunna* and join the congregation; because, technically speaking, the congregational *fard* prayer is more important.

One point to remember, however, is that once the congregational *fard* prayer begins, the *sunna* prayer should not be performed where the main congregation is in progress. It should be performed outside the main prayer-hall (*masjid*) area.

Another view of some Hanafi scholars is that a person should only attempt to perform the *sunna* prayer if he feels confident of acquiring at least one *rak'a* behind the *imam*. This means that he must be certain of catching up with the *imam* before he stands up from the bowing [*ruku'*] of the second *rak'a* of the *fard*.

This difference of opinion is only concerning the two-*rak'ats sunna* of Fajr, and there is no controversy regarding the *sunna* in other prayers. All the scholars are unanimous that once the congregation for those prayers commences, no other *sunna* prayer is permissible, because although the *sunna* prayers in them are important, they are not as emphasized as the *sunna* of Fajr. Also, if a person happens to miss the *sunna* prayer of Zuhr for instance, he can make it up after the *fard*, since it is not a prohibited time for it.

IMPORTANCE OF THE *SUNNA* PRAYER OF FAJR

1. 'A'isha ☙ said,

   The Messenger of Allah ☙ was not as regular in any supererogatory [*nafl*] prayer as he was in the two *rak'ats* before Fajr (*Sahih Muslim* 1:251).

2. 'A'isha ☙ said,

   I did not observe the Messenger of Allah ☙ hasten towards any supererogatory [*nafl*] prayer as fast as he would to perform the two *rak'ats* before Fajr (*Sahih Muslim* 1:251).

3. 'A'isha ☙ reports that the Messenger of Allah ☙ said,

   The two [*sunna*] *rak'ats* of Fajr are more superior than the world and everything within it (*Sahih Muslim* 1:251).

4. 'A'isha ☙ reports that the Messenger of Allah ☙ said regarding the two [*sunna*] *rak'ats* at the break of dawn:

   They are more beloved to me than the entire world (*Sahih Muslim* 1:251).

5. Abu Hurayra ☙ narrates that the Messenger of Allah ☙ said,

   Do not abandon the *sunna rak'ats* of Fajr, even if horses trample over you (*Sunan Abi Dawud* 1:186, *Athar al-sunan* 1:224).

All the above hadiths explain the significance of and emphasis placed on the *sunna* prayer of Fajr. Since the *sunna rak'ats* of other prayers are not as greatly emphasized as the *sunna* of Fajr, they are treated differently.

THE COMPANIONS AND FOLLOWERS ON THIS ISSUE

There are also many other rigorously authenticated hadiths which confirm that the Companions of the Messenger ☙ would attempt to complete their *sunna* prayer prior to joining the congregational *fard* prayer of Fajr if it had already commenced.

FIQH AL-IMAM

1. Imam Tahawi reports from Nafi':

   I wakened Ibn 'Umar ✿ for the Fajr prayer, while the prayer had already commenced. He arose and performed the two *rak'ats* [*sunna* first] (*Sharh Ma'ani 'l-athar* 1:375).

2. Abu Ishaq says,

   'Abdullah ibn Abi Musa related to me from his father regarding the time Sa'id ibn al-'As called them. He had called Abu Musa, Hudhayfa, and 'Abdullah ibn Mas'ud ✿ before the Fajr prayer. When they departed from him, the congregation had already begun, so 'Abdullah ibn Mas'ud ✿ positioned himself behind a pillar in the *masjid* and performed two *rak'ats* *sunna* first, then joined the congregation (*Sharh Ma'ani 'l-athar* 1:374).

3. Abu 'Uthman al-Ansari reports:

   'Abdullah ibn 'Abbas ✿ arrived while the *imam* was leading the Fajr prayer. Since Ibn 'Abbas ✿ had not yet performed the two *rak'ats* [*sunna*], he performed them behind the *imam* [i.e. separately], then joined in the congregation (*Sharh Ma'ani 'l-athar* 1:375).

4. Imam Tahawi has transmitted a report about Abu 'l-Darda' ✿:

   He would enter the *masjid* while everybody would be in rows performing the Fajr prayer. He would first perform his two *rak'ats* in a corner of the *masjid*, then join everyone in the [*fard*] prayer (*Sharh Ma'ani 'l-athar* 1:375).

5. Abu 'Uthman al-Nahdi says,

   We would arrive at [times to the *masjid* where] 'Umar ibn al-Khattab ✿ [was the *imam*], not having performed the two *rak'ats* [*sunna*] of Fajr. 'Umar ✿ would have already started the prayer, so we would first perform our two *rak'ats* at the rear of the *masjid*, then join in the congregation (*Sharh Ma'ani 'l-athar* 1:376).

6. 'Abdullah ibn Abi Musa ✿ narrates:

   'Abdullah ibn Mas'ud ✿ arrived while the *imam* was leading the Fajr prayer. He performed the two *rak'ats* [*sunna*] behind a pillar, as he had not yet performed them (*Musannaf 'Abd al-Razzaq* 1:444).

7. Haritha ibn Mudrib narrates:

'Abdullah ibn Mas'ud and Abu Musa ☙ left Sa'id ibn al-'As [after visiting him]. The congregation [for Fajr] had just begun, so 'Abdullah ibn Mas'ud ☙ performed two *rak'ats* [*sunna*], then joined in the prayer with everyone else. As for Abu Musa, he joined in the row [immediately] (*Musannaf Ibn Abi Shayba* 2:251).

8. Abu 'l-Darda' ☙ would say regarding the *sunna* of Fajr,

Yes, by Allah! If I ever enter [the *masjid*] and find everyone in prayer, I proceed to a pillar of the *masjid* and perform two *rak'ats* quickly; then I join the congregation and perform my Fajr with them (*Musannaf 'Abd al-Razzaq* 1:443).

9. Abu 'l-Darda' ☙, according to another report, states:

I [sometimes] approach the people while they are standing in rows performing Fajr. I perform two *rak'ats* [*sunna*] then I join them (*Musannaf Ibn Abi Shayba* 2:251).

10. It is reported regarding Ibn 'Umar ☙:

He would sometimes join in the congregation [immediately] and at other times he would first perform his two *rak'ats* at one side of the *masjid* (*Musannaf Ibn Abi Shayba* 2:251).

11. Sha'bi narrates regarding Masruq:

He entered the *masjid* to find the people engaged in the Fajr prayer. Since he had not yet performed the two *rak'ats* [*sunna*], he performed them at one side, then joined the congregation in prayer (*Musannaf Ibn Abi Shayba* 2:251, *Musannaf 'Abd al-Razzaq* 2:444).

12. It is reported that Hasan al-Basri had instructed:

When you enter the *masjid* and find the *imam* in prayer and you have not yet performed the two *rak'ats* of Fajr, perform them [first]; then join the *imam* [in the *fard* prayer] (*Musannaf 'Abd al-Razzaq* 2:445, *Sharh Ma'ani 'l-athar* 1:376).

These are just some of the many hadiths which highlight the practice of the Companions and Followers. A great jurist [*faqih*] like 'Abdullah

ibn Mas'ud ♦, as well as many other prominent Companions, such as
Abu 'l-Darda' and Ibn 'Umar ♦, would first perform the two-*rak'ats*
sunna of Fajr and then proceed to join the main congregation. Hasan
al-Basri, a prominent Follower [*tabi'i*] who requires no introduction,
orders in clear words that the *sunna* prayer be performed before joining the congregation.

OTHER REASONS FOR THE HANAFI OPINION

(1) The emphasis regarding the *sunna* of Fajr is far greater than that
of any other *sunna* prayer. It has been ordered that the *sunna* of Fajr
be performed even if there is a danger of horses trampling over the
person. Due to this emphasis, there should remain no doubt as to
why the Hanafis excluded the *sunna* prayer of Fajr from the command
of the hadith that informs us of only *fard* prayers being permissible
once the congregation begins.

(2) It is *sunna* to make a lengthy recitation of the Qur'an during the
fard of Fajr. Hence, it is possible that one could quickly perform his
two *rak'ats sunna* first and then join in with the *imam* during the
first *rak'a*, the second *rak'a*, or just before the *imam* makes the *salam.*
This is normally difficult in other prayers where a relatively shorter
recitation is made and the number of *rak'ats* recommended before
them is four.

(3) In the above hadith, the command regarding the impermissibility of any non–*fard* prayer at the time of congregation cannot be
taken as a general command encompassing all prayers. If it was an
absolutely general command, then it would also be prohibited for
someone to perform the *sunna* prayer in his house once he was aware
that the congregation had commenced in the *masjid*. However, many
scholars have permitted that the *sunna* prayer be performed at home,
even though the congregation may have already begun in the *masjid*.
Consequently, this leaves no room to criticize the Hanafi school for
excluding the *sunna* of Fajr from the prohibition. Many other scholars

have also not taken the command to be an absolutely general one.

(4) The word *"maktuba"* has been used in the hadith to describe the *fard* prayer. The general meaning of this word includes the missed [*qada'*] prayers also, which indicates that it would be permissible to perform the missed prayers even after the congregation has begun. However, some scholars do not allow this. From this, it is understood that the hadith (*see* beginning of chapter) is not taken literally, just as its command is not taken in a general sense.

After mentioning these points, it could be concluded that the Hanafi school has reconciled both types of hadiths by saying that the person should only perform the *sunna* prayer first if he feels he can acquire the congregational-*fard* prayer before it ends. Otherwise, he should enter immediately into the congregation with the *imam*. In this way, the person benefits by attaining the reward of the *sunna* prayer of Fajr and also the reward of performing the *fard salat* in congregation.

ONE MORE POINT TO REMEMBER

At times, some narrations are quoted which explicitly exempt the Fajr *sunna* from the command of the hadith (which mentions the impermissibility of prayer once the congregational *fard* prayer has commenced). However, those narrations are usually weak, and have neither been used as a basis for the Hanafi position nor as evidence to prove the Hanafi opinion against other opinions.

Likewise, there are some narrations which specifically indicate that the *sunna rak'ats* of Fajr are included in the prohibition of the hadith. The narrations mention details of a Companion confirming with the Messenger 廬: "Are the *sunna rak'ats* of Fajr also invalid if they are performed after the congregation has begun?" The Messenger 廬 of Allah answers him in the affirmative saying, "Yes! They are also invalid." These narrations, being even weaker than the others, will not stand as evidence to strengthen the other group's opinion.

8

How Many *Rak'ats* in *Witr*?

WITR HAS BEEN noted to be one of the most complex issues of prayer. There are approximately seventeen aspects concerning the *witr* prayer around which there lie differences of opinion. However, in this chapter we will focus mainly on the following three issues: (1) How many *rak'ats* is the *witr* prayer? (2) How many *salams* in the *witr* prayer? (3) Is performing one *rak'a* sufficient for *witr*?

There are numerous hadiths which report the number of *rak'ats* to be performed in *witr*. However, due to many inconsistencies found in them, it becomes very difficult to formulate an opinion that is in complete agreement with the *literal* meaning of each narration. It is therefore necessary to interpret some of these narrations in order to harmonize their meaning with other similar narrations.

In this chapter, various narrations on the *witr* prayer will be analyzed in depth in an attempt to establish those procedures of performing *witr* that are most in conformance with the *sunna*.

1. HOW MANY *RAK'ATS* IS THE *WITR* PRAYER?

The first discussion is concerning the number of *rak'ats* that should be performed for *witr*.

THE VARIOUS OPINIONS

According to Imam Shafiʻi, *witr* could be performed in units of one, three, five, seven, nine, or even eleven *rakʻats*. He states in his book *Kitab al-Umm* that one *rakʻa* can be performed as *witr*. However, ʻAllama Qastalani relates in his commentary of *Sahih al-Bukhari, Irshad al-sari,* that Qadi Abu ʼl-Tayyib was of the opinion that it is undesirable [*makruh*] to perform just one *rakʻa* for *witr.* (*Irshad al-sari* 2:259)

Qadi Abu ʼl-Tayyib is regarded as one of the greatest scholars of Shafiʻi *fiqh* and was also one of its main teachers in Iraq during his time. He studied under Imam Daraqutni, and among his students were the likes of Khatib al-Baghdadi and Abu Ishaq al-Shirazi.

Following this, there is a difference of opinion among the Shafiʻis as to how the *rakʻats* of *witr* should be performed. One opinion is that during Ramadan, three *rakʻats* should be performed with one set of *salams*, and in other months with two sets—one in the second *rakʻa* and the other in the third. Another opinion states that one set of *salams* should be made if the *witr* is being performed in congregation, and two sets if it is being performed individually.

The opinions of Imam Malik and Ahmad are similar to that of Imam Shafiʻi with just a few minor differences. The commentator of *Sifr al-saʻada* relates an opinion of Imam Ahmad which states that a single *rakʻa* of *witr* is undesirable [*makruh*]. According to the Imam, a person must perform some *rakʻats* before performing the *witr*. A similar opinion has been reported from Imam Malik as well. He relates a hadith in his *Muwatta* on the authority of Saʻd ibn Abi Waqqas in which the Companion is described as performing a single *rakʻa* for *witr*. Following this narration, Imam Malik states:

> Our practice is not based on this, since *witr* [in our opinion] is at least three *rakʻats* (*Muwatta Imam Malik* 77).

The above review of opinions can be concluded as follows. According to Imam Shafiʻi, *witr* can be performed in any number of odd *rak'ats,* ranging from one to eleven. Imam Ahmad's main and more popular view is that the *witr* be performed as one *rak'a* and the *rak'ats* performed prior to it be considered as *qiyam al-layl* or *tahajjud* [night-vigil prayer] (*al-Mughni*). Imam Malik also does not recommend performing a single *rak'a* for *witr.* He recommends that at least three *rak'ats* be performed. Imam Abu Hanifa's opinion is simply that *witr* should be performed as three continuous *rak'ats* with two sittings—one in the second *rak'a* and the other in the third—with *salams* to be performed in the final sitting only.

THE HADITHS ON THIS ISSUE

Before looking at the apparently conflicting hadiths, we will first look at those hadiths which clearly state that *witr* consists of three *rak'ats.*

1. It is reported from Abu Salama that

   he asked 'A'isha ﷺ regarding the prayer of the Messenger of Allah ﷺ during Ramadan. She explained, "The Messenger of Allah ﷺ would not perform more than eleven *rak'ats,* neither in Ramadan nor out of it. He would perform four *rak'ats,* and do not ask of their beauty and length; followed by another four, and do not ask of their beauty and length; after which he would perform three [*witr*]." 'A'isha ﷺ continued, "I asked, 'O Messenger of Allah! Do you sleep before you perform *witr.*' He replied, 'O 'A'isha! My eyes sleep, but my heart does not'" (*Sahih al-Bukhari* 1:154, *Sahih Muslim* 1:254, *Sunan al-Nasa'i* 1:248, *Sunan Abi Dawud* 196).

In this narration, Umm al-mu'minin [Mother of the Believers] 'A'isha ﷺ mentions that the *witr* prayer performed by Allah's Messenger ﷺ consisted of three *rak'ats.*

2. Sa'd ibn Hisham ﷺ relates that

   'A'isha ﷺ informed him that the Messenger of Allah ﷺ did not make *salams* in the second *rak'a* of *witr* (*Sunan al-Nasa'i* 1:248, *Muwatta Imam Muhammad* 151).

3. This narration has also been mentioned by Imam Hakim with a slight variation:

> The Messenger of Allah ﷺ would not make *salams* in the first two *rak'ats* of *witr* (*al-Mustadrak* 1:304).

Imam Hakim then states, "[This narration is] authentic according to the conditions of Imam Bukhari and Muslim." 'Allama Dhahabi agreed with him.

4. The following is another variation of the above narration related by Imam Hakim:

> The Messenger of Allah ﷺ would perform three *rak'ats* of *witr* making *salams* only at the end [in the final *rak'a*]. This was the practice of the Leader of the Faithful 'Umar ibn al-Khattab ◈ and it is from him that the people of Madina acquired this practice (*al-Mustadrak* 1:304).

5. Sa'd ibn Hisham ◈ narrates:

> The Messenger of Allah ﷺ, after completing the 'Isha prayer, would enter his home and perform two *rak'ats*, followed by another two more lengthier than the first. Thereafter, he would perform the *witr* prayer without any interval in between [i.e. without *salams* in the second *rak'a*]. He would then perform two *rak'ats* sitting down with the bowing and prostration also sitting down (*Musnad Ahmad* 6:156 U).

6. 'Abdullah ibn Qays narrates:

> I asked 'A'isha ◈, "How many *rak'ats* of *witr* did the Messenger of Allah ﷺ perform?" She replied, "Four with three, six with three, or eight with three. He would not perform more than thirteen *rak'ats* for *witr* or less than seven" (*Sunan Abi Dawud* 1:200).

In this hadith, the whole *tahajjud* prayer has been described as *witr*, whereas in reality only three *rak'ats* were *witr*, and the remaining four, six, or eight *rak'ats* were *tahajjud*. This is the reason why Umm al-mu'minin 'A'isha ◈ distinguished between the three *rak'ats* of *witr* and the various other *rak'ats* in the above narrations.

7. 'Abd al-'Aziz ibn Jurayj narrates:

I asked 'A'isha ☺ regarding the chapters the Messenger of Allah ☺ would recite in *witr*. She replied, "He would recite *'Sabbih isma rabbik al-a'la'* [Surat al-A'la] in the first *rak'a*, *'Qul ya'ayyuha 'l-kafirun'* [Surat al-Kafirun] in the second, and *'Qul huwallahu ahad'* [Surat al-Ikhlas] along with the *'Mu'awwadhatayn'* [Surat al-Falaq and al-Nas] in the third" (*Sunan Abi Dawud* 1:208, *Sunan al-Tirmidhi* 1:106, *Sunan Ibn Maja* 1:82).

Imam Tirmidhi has declared this hadith to be sound [*hasan*].

8. Imam Hakim has related a very similar narration from 'A'isha ☺ through 'Amra bint 'Abd al-Rahman and has stated it as being in accordance with the strict conditions of both Imam Bukhari and Muslim. 'Allama Dhahabi has also verified this by stating that the hadith has been transmitted through a reliable chain of narrators (*al-Mustadrak* 1:305).

9. Muhammad ibn 'Ali reports from his father, who narrates on the authority of his father, 'Abdullah ibn 'Abbas ☺, that

the Messenger of Allah ☺ rose at night, cleaned his teeth with a *siwak* [toothstick], and performed two *rak'ats* of prayer, then went back to sleep. He again rose, used the *siwak* and made *wudu,* and thereafter performed another two *rak'ats* of prayer, [on and on] until he had completed six *rak'ats* [in this manner]. He then performed three *rak'ats witr* followed by two *rak'ats* [*nafl*] (*Sahih Muslim* 1:261, *Sunan al-Nasa'i* 1:249).

10. 'Abdullah ibn 'Abbas ☺ has also reported the following narration regarding the Messenger's ☺ *witr* prayer:

During the night before dawn, the Messenger of Allah ☺ would perform eight *rak'ats* [*tahajjud*] and three *rak'ats witr*, followed by two *rak'ats* [*nafl*] (*Sunan al-Nasa'i* 1:249).

11. 'Abdullah ibn 'Abbas ☺ narrates:

The Messenger of Allah ☺ would perform three *rak'ats witr*. He would recite *"Sabbih isma rabbik al-a'la"* [Surat al-A'la] in the first *rak'a*, *"Qul ya'ayyuha 'l-kafirun"* [Surat al-Kafirun] in the second, and *"Qul huwallahu ahad"* [Surat al-Ikhlas] in the third (*Sunan al-Tirmidhi* 1:106, *Sunan al-Nasa'i* 1:249, *Sunan Ibn Maja* 82).

137

Numerous other Companions in their narrations have also mentioned the Messenger's 🌸 recitation of these three *surats* [chapters] during *witr* in the above mentioned order:

(1) 'Abd al-Rahman ibn Abza 🌸 (*Musannaf Ibn Abi Shayba* 2:298).

(2) Ubay ibn Ka'b 🌸 (*Musannaf Ibn Abi Shayba* 2:300).

(3) 'Ali ibn Abi Talib 🌸 (*Sunan al-Tirmidhi* 1:106).

(4) 'Abdullah ibn Abi Awfa 🌸 (*Majma' al-zawa'id* 1:241 U).

(5) 'Abdullah ibn Mas'ud 🌸 (*Majma' al-zawa'id* 1:241 U).

(6) Nu'man ibn Bashir 🌸 (*Majma' al-zawa'id* 1:241 U).

(7) Abu Hurayra 🌸 (*Majma' al-zawa'id* 1:241 U).

(8) 'Abdullah ibn 'Umar 🌸 (*Majma' al-zawa'id* 1:241 U).

(9) 'Imran ibn Husayn 🌸 (*Musannaf Ibn Abi Shayba* 2:298)

(10) Abu Khaythama through his father Mu'awiya ibn Khadij 🌸 (*Majma' al-zawa'id* 1:241 U).

The narrations of these Companions further support the opinion that *witr* consists of three *rak'ats*.

12. Thabit al-Bunani reports that Anas ibn Malik 🌸 addressed him saying:

> O Thabit! Take this from me, for you will not hear it from anyone more trustworthy than myself, since I heard it from the Messenger of Allah 🌸, who acquired it from Jibril, and Jibril acquired it from Allah 🌸. The Messenger of Allah 🌸 performed the 'Isha prayer while I was in his company, followed by six *rak'ats* [*nafl*], during which he made *salams* at every second *rak'a*. Thereafter, he performed three *rak'ats witr* with *salams* at the very end (*Kanz al-'ummal* 4:196 U).

The great historian and hadith master Ibn Asakir has narrated this hadith through a reliable chain.

From the above narrations, a number of points are derived: (1) it is established that *witr* is three *rak'ats*; and (2) that the three *rak'ats* are to be performed together and concluded with *salams* at the end of the third *rak'a*.

THE COMPANIONS AND FOLLOWERS ON THIS ISSUE

1. Miswar ibn Makhrama reports:

   We finished burying Abu Bakr ﷺ, when 'Umar ﷺ remembered that he had not yet performed *witr*. He stood up and we formed rows behind him. He lead us in three *rak'ats* and made *salams* only at the end [in the third *rak'a*] (*Musannaf Ibn Abi Shayba* 2:293 U, *Musannaf 'Abd al-Razzaq* 3:20 U).

2. Ibrahim al-Nakh'ay reports that 'Umar ibn al-Khattab ﷺ said,

   I would not neglect the three *rak'ats* of *witr,* even if I were to receive red camels in exchange (*Muwatta Imam Muhammad* 150).

   In those times red camels were considered valuable assets.

3. Hasan al-Basri was informed that

   'Abdullah ibn 'Umar ﷺ would make *salams* in the second *rak'a* of *witr*. Hasan al-Basri informed that 'Umar ﷺ was a greater jurist than [his son], and his practice was to say the *takbir* and stand up from the second *rak'a* [for the third without making *salams*] (*al-Mustadrak* 1:304).

4. Makhul reports:

   'Umar ibn al-Khattab ﷺ would perform three *rak'ats* of *witr* without *salams* in between (*Musannaf Ibn Abi Shayba* 2:295).

5. 'Abdullah ibn Mas'ud ﷺ says,

   The *rak'ats* of *witr* are three similar to the daytime *witr* prayer (i.e. Maghrib) [(*Muwatta Imam Muhammad* 150, *Majma' al-zawa'id* 2:242 U)].

6. Ibrahim al-Nakh'ay reports that 'Abdullah ibn Mas'ud ﷺ said,

   One *rak'a* does not suffice for *witr*. (*Muwatta Imam Muhammad* 150).

7. It is reported from Anas 🌼 that

   witr is three *rak'ats* (*Musannaf Ibn Abi Shayba* 2:293).

8. Abu Mansur reports:

   I asked Ibn 'Abbas 🌼 regarding the number of *rak'ats* in *witr*. He replied, "Three *rak'ats*" (*Sharh Ma'ani 'l-athar*).

9. 'Ata' reports that 'Abdullah ibn 'Abbas 🌼 said:

   Witr is similar to the Maghrib prayer (*Muwatta Imam Muhammad* 150).

10. Hasan al-Basri reports:

    Ubay ibn Ka'b 🌼 would perform three *rak'ats* for *witr* and would make *salams* only at the end of the third *rak'a* (*Musannaf 'Abd al-Razzaq* 2:294).

11. Abu Ghalib reports that

    Abu Umama 🌼 would perform three *rak'ats* for *witr* (*Musannaf Ibn Abi Shayba* 2:294).

12. 'Alqama, the student of 'Abdullah ibn Mas'ud 🌼, reports that

    witr is three *rak'ats* (*Musannaf Ibn Abi Shayba* 2:294).

13. It is reported that Ibrahim al-Nakh'ay would say:

    There is no *witr* consisting of less than three *rak'ats* (*Musannaf Ibn Abi Shayba* 2:294).

14. Abu 'l-Zanad reports:

    'Umar ibn 'Abd al-'Aziz designated the *rak'ats* of *witr* to be three based on the ruling of the jurists, with *salams* to be made only at the end (*Sharh Ma'ani 'l-athar*).

15. It is reported that Hasan al-Basri said:

    The Muslims have reached a consensus concerning *witr* being three *rak'ats* with *salams* only at the end (*Musannaf Ibn Abi Shayba* 2:294).

The reason for quoting the statements of so many Companions and Followers [*tabi'in*] is that their opinions and practices hold a high status in Islamic law. Whenever a conflict is found between the hadiths concerning a certain issue, the scholars turn to the actions and statements of the Companions to remedy that conflict. The Companions undoubtedly possessed great insight into the reality of these issues, due to them being blessed with the close company of the Messenger 鐵. The scholars therefore hold their opinion in high regard and normally adopt those hadiths which conform to their practice. Likewise the opinions of the Followers are also regarded since they succeeded the Companions and were the bearers of their knowledge.

The more prominent Companions like Sayyidina 'Umar, 'Ali, 'Abdullah ibn Mas'ud, 'Abdullah ibn 'Umar, Anas ibn Malik, 'Abdullah ibn 'Abbas, 'A'isha, Ubay ibn Ka'b, and Abu Umama 鐵 all stated in clear terms that *witr* consists of three *rak'ats*. Those who came after them, like Ibrahim al-Nakh'ay, 'Alqama, Abu Ishaq, Qasim ibn Muhammad, and others, held the same opinion. Even the renowned *fuqaha' sab'a*, "the seven great jurists" of the earlier period [*see* p. 143], concluded that *witr* was three *rak'ats*. This was such a widely accepted opinion that Hasan al-Basri reported consensus [*ijma'*] on it.

2. How Many *Salams* in the *Witr* Prayer?

The Hanafi opinion in this matter is that, like every other prayer, only one set of *salams* should be made in *witr*. According to this opinion, one must not make two sets of *salams* and cause the third *rak'a* to be performed separately.

The opinion of other scholars is that the *musalli* [person praying] should first perform two *rak'ats* and then, after terminating them with *salams,* perform the third *rak'a* separately with another set of *salams*.

There are a number of reasons which establish the superiority of the Hanafi position in this issue.

(1) None of the narrations mentioned above declare that two sets of *salams* should be made within the three *rak'a* prayer. On the contrary, many of them have stated that the three *rak'ats* are to be performed

continuously without any break in between. It is quite evident that if there had been an interval in between the second and third *rak'ats*, the narrators would have certainly mentioned it.

(2) The narrations of 'A'isha ♦ portray *witr* to be like any other set of three *rak'ats*, as they do not mention the Messenger ♦ making an extra set of *salams* in the second *rak'a*. It should be noted that 'A'isha ♦ is considered the most knowledgeable person regarding the Messenger's ♦ *witr* prayer. This is due to her close observance of the Messenger's ♦ *witr* prayer while at home, where he was habitually performing it. Hence, without further debate, her explanation that *witr* consists of three *rak'ats* should be accepted.

(3) Some narrations, which have been reported from 'Abdullah ibn 'Umar ♦, state that *witr* was performed as a single *rak'a*. Many scholars claim that Ibn 'Umar ♦ never actually saw the Messenger ♦ performing the *witr* prayer, and that his narrations cannot be preferred over those of 'A'isha and Ibn 'Abbas ♦, both of whom were known to have seen Allah's Messenger ♦ performing the prayer.

(4) One narration states:

> The Messenger of Allah ♦ prohibited the "incomplete prayer" [*butayra*, lit. an animal which has had its tail cut off]—where a person performs a single *rak'a* as *witr*.

Although this narration is said to contain some weaknesses, its prohibition of performing *witr* as one *rak'a* holds; due to it being authentically transmitted through a number of reliable chains [*asnad*]. In his *Lisan al-Mizan*, Hafiz Ibn Hajar has related this narration through a strong chain under the biography of 'Uthman ibn Muhammad, one of its narrators. With the exception of 'Uqayli—known for his extreme strictness in the criticism of narrators (even though his criticism here is only of a mild nature)—most scholars of hadith have judged 'Uthman ibn Muhammad to be reliable. Hakim al-Naysaburi has related a narration from him in his *Mustadrak* and called it authentic, which 'Allama Dhahabi has verified. Hence, the status of the hadith can be no lower than *hasan* [sound], and the prohibition mentioned in it of performing one *rak'a* separately will stand as a strong command [*see Fath al-Mulhim* 2:309].

(5) Many of the elect Companions, like 'Umar ibn al-Khattab, 'Ali ibn Abi Talib, Ibn Mas'ud, Ibn 'Abbas, Hudhayfa ibn al-Yaman, Anas ibn Malik, Ubay ibn Ka'b ؓ all performed *witr* with only one set of *salams* at the end of the *salat*. Some of their narrations have been mentioned above and others can be found in the numerous collections of hadiths; the chapters (on *witr*) of which are especially replete with the narrations of 'A'isha ؓ on *witr*. Therefore, the *sunna* method of performing *witr* would be to perform them as a continuous set of three *rak'ats* as practised by these great Companions.

(6) In some hadiths, the Maghrib prayer, which contains only one set of *salams* at the end, has been called "the *witr* prayer of the day." Therefore, "the *witr* prayer of the night" should also be offered like the Maghrib *salat*—with only one set of *salams* in the last *rak'a*.

There is a report which mentions that the Messenger of Allah ﷺ prohibited that the *witr* be performed like the Maghrib prayer. What this actually means is that one should not perform the *witr* alone, like Maghrib, without performing any dual set of *rak'ats* [*shuf'a*] before it. The report does not mean that one must make *salams* in between and separate the last *rak'a* from the first two.

(7) The "seven great jurists" [*fuqaha' sab'a*] all agreed that the *witr* was to be performed as three *rak'ats* with *salams* only at the end. These seven jurists would be consulted by the people on various issues, and whatever the majority of them agreed on would be accepted as the legal ruling [*fatwa*]. In his book, Imam Tahawi has related their unanimous opinion that *witr* should be performed as three *rak'ats* with *salams* made only in the last *rak'a*. The seven jurists were: Sa'id ibn al-Musayyib, 'Urwa ibn al-Zubayr, Qasim ibn Muhammad, Abu Bakr ibn 'Abd al-Rahman, Kharija ibn Zayd, 'Ubaydullah ibn

'Abdillah, and Sulayman ibn Yasar (may Allah be pleased with them all) [(*Awjaz al-masalik* 1:434)].

(8) Hasan al-Basri reported a consensus [*ijma'*] on the opinion that *witr* was three continuous *rak'ats* without any intervals in between; which means that it was a widely accepted view.

These points make it easy to conclude that the *witr* is indeed three *rak'ats* with a single set of *salams* to be performed in the third, and final, *rak'a*. This was the widely held opinion among the Companions and Followers (may Allah be pleased with them).

Some Confusing Narrations

1. Sa'd ibn Hisham asked 'A'isha ༺ to describe for him the *witr* prayer of the Messenger ﷺ. She replied:

> We would prepare his *siwak* [toothstick] and water for his ablution [*wudu'*]. Allah would have him wake up during the night whenever He willed, and the Messenger ﷺ would clean his teeth with the *siwak* and complete his ablution. He would then perform nine *rak'ats* and would sit on the eighth *rak'a* only, in which he would remember Allah, praise Him, and invoke [*du'a'*] Him. Thereafter, he would stand up without making *salams* and perform the ninth *rak'a*, then he would sit down, and [again] he would remember Allah, praise Him, and invoke Him. He would then make the *salams* [loud enough] for us to hear. After *salams*, he would perform another two *rak'ats* sitting down. So, my son, these were eleven *rak'ats*. When the Messenger ﷺ became of age and heavier, he would perform [only] seven *rak'ats*, and his practice in the [final] two *rak'ats* would be the same as his earlier practice [of performing them seated]. So these were [in total] seven *rak'ats* (*Sahih Muslim* 1:256).

The apparent wording of this narration suggests that the Messenger's ﷺ *witr* prayer was a total of nine *rak'ats*, in which he would sit only at the end of the eighth *rak'a* and complete the prayer with *salams* in the ninth. The hadith then states that this was his earlier practice, for later on he reduced the number of *rak'ats* to seven, sitting briefly in the sixth and ending with *salams* in the seventh.

In *Sunan al-Nasa'i, Muwatta Imam Malik,* and a number of other hadith collections, the same narration has been transmitted through the same chain with the following addition, "The Messenger of Allah 🕮 would not make *salams* in the second *rak'a* of *witr.*" In the version of *al-Mustadrak,* it states, "The Messenger of Allah 🕮 would perform three *rak'ats witr* with *salams* only at the end." In *Musnad Ahmad,* it states:

> After the Messenger of Allah 🕮 had performed the 'Isha prayer, he would enter his home and perform two *rak'ats,* followed by another two lengthier than the first. He would then perform *witr* without any interval in between, after which he would perform a final two *rak'ats* seated.

The following points come to light after studying the various transmissions of this narration:

(a) At most, the Messenger of Allah 🕮 would perform a total of eleven *rak'ats* at night. Included in this were the *witr* and the two *rak'ats* that succeeded it.

(b) Three *rak'ats* out of the eleven were *witr.*

(c) He would sit in the second *rak'a* of *witr* without making any *salams.*

(d) After *witr,* he would perform two *rak'ats* seated.

(e) He would sit at the end of every second *rak'a.*

From these points we learn that the various narrations concerning *witr* are indeed describing the same procedure of performing *witr.* The reason why they appear to be conflicting is due to the different words used in most of them.

The version in *Sahih Muslim* only states the total number of *rak'ats* performed, without offering much detail as to how they were performed in connection with the *tahajjud* prayer. The reason for this is that 'A'isha 🕮 was specifically asked about the *witr* prayer and not about *tahajjud.* Hence, she did not feel it was necessary to provide any details about the *rak'ats* of *tahajjud* performed before the *witr.* So, providing details on the *witr*, she said, "The Messenger of Allah ﷺ would sit without making *salams* on the eighth *rak'a*." This eighth *rak'a* was in reality the second *rak'a* of *witr*, which was being performed after the six *rak'ats* of *tahajjud;* then, on the ninth *rak'a* (the third *rak'a* of *witr*), he would make *salams* and thus complete his *witr* prayer.

It was common knowledge at that time that the Messenger ﷺ always performed his *tahajjud* prayer in sets of two; so 'A'isha ﷺ did not provide any detail about them and thus mentioned the total number of *rak'ats* together. Lastly, she ended by saying that the Messenger ﷺ would perform yet another two *rak'ats* seated after performing the ninth *rak'a*, bringing the total number of *rak'ats* to eleven.

This is most likely the soundest interpretation for this hadith, as it encompasses all the variations of Sa'd ibn Hisham's narration, and at the same time reconciles the apparent conflicts between them. In summary, the Messenger ﷺ would perform the *tahajjud* prayer in sets of two, as stated in the above-mentioned narration in *Musnad Ahmad* (and probably all other narrations on *tahajjud*); and thereafter perform the three continuous *rak'ats* of *witr*, with *salams* made only at the end. After the final *salams*, he would then perform two more *rak'ats* sitting down.

2. 'A'isha ﷺ narrates:

> The Messenger's ﷺ prayer at night would be thirteen *rak'ats*, five of which would be *witr;* and he would sit only at the end.

The apparent wording of this hadith describes the *witr* prayer of the Messenger ﷺ as being a continuous set of five *rak'ats*. However, just as in the previous narration, the apparent meaning in this narration is not to be taken as the implied meaning. The reason for this is that 'A'isha ﷺ only specified the total number of *rak'ats* performed by the Messenger of Allah ﷺ at night and included in it the two *rak'ats* of *nafl* performed sitting down after the three *rak'ats* of *witr*. This is what she refers to when she says, "Five of which would be *witr*" (i.e. including the two *rak'ats* of *nafl*).

When she says, "he would sit only at the end," it means he would not sit for any lengthy period of time during the prayer to make extra supplication [*du'a'*] and remembrance [*dhikr*] except at the very end. He sat only briefly in every other *rak'a* to recite the *tashahhud*. Furthermore, she did not even mention that he made *salams* in the third *rak'a* of *witr*, as it was common knowledge that *salams* had to be made in the third *rak'a*. What 'A'isha ⁎ was referring to when she said, "he would sit only at the end," was the final sitting of the Messenger's ⁎ two *rak'ats nafl salat* that followed his *witr* (i.e. the Messenger ⁎ would only sit for an extended period of time in the final sitting of his last set of two *rak'ats nafl salat*).

Some Hanafi scholars have explained this narration in a slightly different way. They state that it is known that the Messenger ⁎ would perform the *rak'ats* of *tahajjud* standing up or sitting down, and the *witr* prayer he would always perform standing up, while the two *rak'ats* following the *witr* he would mostly perform sitting down. Hence, if the hadith is approached with these points in mind, the apparent meaning of the hadith cannot be taken.

What really happened, they explain, is that the Messenger ⁎, according to his normal routine, performed the *witr* along with the *tahajjud* prayer standing up and then sat down to perform the two *nafl rak'ats*. 'A'isha ⁎ described his prayer by saying, "he would sit only at the end"—that the Messenger ⁎, after having performed the first eleven or so *rak'ats* (*tahajjud* and *witr*) standing, sat down and performed the last two *rak'ats* of *nafl*. She states that he sat down to perform the last two *rak'ats* of *nafl* after having performed all the other prayers standing up. [*See Darse Tirmidhi* 2:210–220, *Fath al-Mulhim* 2:219]

This makes the above narration of 'A'isha ⁎ very clear and dispels the notion that the Messenger ⁎ performed a lengthy prayer comprised of many *rak'ats*, with only one sitting at the end and no sitting postures in between the various *rak'ats* he performed. The following narration of Ibn 'Abbas ⁎ further corroborates this explanation:

The Messenger of Allah ﷺ performed eight *rak'ats* and seven *rak'ats* in Madina, i.e. Zuhr and 'Asr [together] and Maghrib and 'Isha [together] (*Sahih Muslim* 1:246).

No scholar has taken this statement to imply that each of the four *rak'ats* of Zuhr and 'Asr, and the three of Maghrib and four of 'Isha were combined together in such a way that there was no interval between them.

The reason why scholars have disregarded such an interpretation is because it suggests a new method of prayer that is inconsistent with the normal method of prayer used regularly by the Messenger ﷺ and his Companions ﷺ. In the same way, those narrations which apparently suggest a method for *witr* contrary to the normal practice of prayer being a minimum of two *rak'ats*, will have to be interpreted accordingly and not taken literally.

3. Is One *Rak'a* Sufficient for *Witr*?

'Abdullah ibn 'Umar ﷺ narrates:

> Someone asked the Messenger ﷺ about prayer at night. The Messenger ﷺ said, "The prayer at night should be performed in sets of two. Then, when one anticipates the break of dawn, he should perform one more *rak'a* which will convert what he has performed into *witr* for him" (*Sahih al-Bukhari* 1:135, *Sahih Muslim* 1:257).

In another version of this narration it states, "*Witr* is a single *rak'a* [performed] towards the end of the night." The version in *Sunan Ibn Maja* states, "The prayer of the night is [performed] in sets of two, and the *witr* is a *rak'a* [performed] before dawn."

Some scholars have deduced from these narrations that the *witr* is a single *rak'a* to be performed on its own separately. This deduction however does not bring out the real meaning of this hadith as all the characteristics of prayer have not been taken into consideration. The following points should be considered:

(a) May Allah ﷻ bless the great Shafi'i scholar Hafiz Ibn Hajar al-'Asqalani, who states in his *Fath al-Bari:*

> It could be contended that this [*hadith*] is not absolutely clear with regards to the intervals [between the second and third *rak'ats* of *witr*]. It is possible that the Messenger ﷺ intended by his statement, "he should perform one more *rak'a*," that this *rak'a* should be performed together [*mudafatan*] with the two *rak'ats* before it (*Fath al-Bari* 2:385 U).

Hence, the real meaning of this hadith is that a person should perform the *tahajjud* prayer in sets of two throughout the night, and upon reaching the end of his vigil [*qiyam al-layl*], he should add an extra *rak'a* to the final set of two and make it three *rak'ats*. This way, the *rak'ats* of his *tahajjud* and *witr* prayer will add up to an odd number and thereby be in accordance with the Messenger's ﷺ statement:

> Then, when one anticipates the break of dawn, he should perform one more *rak'a*, which will convert what he has performed into *witr* for him (*Sahih al-Bukhari* 1:135, *Sahih Muslim* 1:257).

(b) The Messenger ﷺ said regarding the sacred pilgrimage [*haj*]:

> The Pilgrimage is 'Arafa (*Sunan al-Tirmidhi, Ibn Maja, al-Daraqutni*).

This narration is also not to be taken literally, as it would mean that a person's pilgrimage is completed by him merely proceeding to the plain of 'Arafat, standing there for some time, and then returning home without even entering into pilgrim sanctity [*ihram*]. This is obviously not a valid interpretation since it has neglected many integral aspects of the worship. In actuality, the hadith is only expressing the importance of standing [*wuquf*] in 'Arafat, as it is one of the integrals of the pilgrimage; and not that it is the only integral act to be performed for *haj*.

Similarly, by stating that the *witr* is one *rak'a* performed before the end of the night, the Messenger ﷺ is only defining the distinctive factor between *witr* and two *rak'ats* of *tahajjud*; that adding an extra *rak'a* to the last two *rak'ats* of *tahajjud* would render all three *rak'ats* into *witr*, thus allowing the person to fulfill his requirement of *witr*.

(c) The personal practice of Ibn 'Umar ﷺ, although appearing otherwise from the above hadith, was to perform three *rak'ats* of *witr* together; as is indicated in the following narration of Imam Malik:

> Ibn 'Umar ﷺ would state that the Maghrib prayer is the *witr* of the day (*Muwatta Imam Malik* 77).

If the Maghrib prayer (which everyone agrees is three continuous *rak'ats*) has been stated as being the *witr* of the day, then it follows that the *witr* prayer itself should be performed as three continuous *rak'ats* as well.

In light of the above, it is very difficult to establish that *witr* could be performed as just one *rak'a*. Hafiz Ibn Hajar relates in his *Fath al-Bari* that Ibn al-Salah said:

> We cannot infer from the narrations of *witr*, despite their being so many, that the Messenger ﷺ only performed a single *rak'a* for *witr* (*Fath al-Bari* 2:15).

Hence, any narration which states that the *witr* prayer was anything but three *rak'ats* cannot be taken literally. Instead, it has to be analyzed and suitably interpreted so as to draw out its true meaning and harmonize it with the other narrations that mention the *witr* as being three *rak'ats*.

A FINAL QUESTION

After reading the hadiths of this chapter, one might ask why these narrations differ from one another in describing the *witr* prayer? The answer to this is very simple. There are two types of narrators. Firstly, there are those who refer to the whole combination of night prayer [*tahajjud*] and *witr* as being *witr*, and do not mention any distinction between the two. They state only the total number of *rak'ats* the Messenger ﷺ performed at night, since it was common knowledge anyway that the final three *rak'ats* of the *tahajjud* prayer would be set aside for *witr*. Hence, they include the whole night-vigil [*tahajjud*] prayer when mentioning the *witr* prayer. Examples of this can be found above in the section titled "Some Confusing Narrations."

As opposed to this, the second type of narrators do not refer to all of the *rak'ats* as being *witr*, but rather describe the *tahajjud* and *witr* prayers separately in terms of the number of *rak'ats* performed for each. Hence, they do not leave any room for speculation. The majority of the second type of narrations state very clearly that the *witr* consists of three *rak'ats*. Examples of this can be found above in the section titled "The Hadiths on This Issue." Imam Tirmidhi, quoting the words of Ishaq ibn Ibrahim Rahway [or Rahuya], concludes:

> The narrations that state that the Messenger 🌸 performed thirteen *rak'ats* *witr* actually mean (as Ishaq says) that he performed thirteen *rak'ats* including the three *rak'ats* of *witr*, and [it follows from this] that the whole night prayer was referred to as *witr* (*Sunan al-Tirmidhi* 1:105).

Imam Abu Muhammad al-Manbaji, a Hanafi jurist and hadith scholar, writes:

> One way of reconciling between the [conflicting] narrations is to say that [initially] the Messenger 🌸 used to perform one *rak'a* as *witr* and even instructed others in this; but his final position was to perform [the *witr* as] three *rak'ats* (*al-Lubab fi 'l-jam'i bayn al-sunnati wa 'l-kitab* 1:173).

CONCLUSION

In conclusion, the *witr* should be performed as a three *rak'a* prayer, since that is how, according to the majority of narrations, the Messenger of Allah 🌸 performed his *witr* prayer. These three *rak'ats* should be performed together without separating the third *rak'a* from the first two. Performing one *rak'a* *witr* has been classified as being an incomplete prayer by the Messenger 🌸. Evidence of this is the fact that there is no other example of a prayer consisting of just one *rak'a* in Islamic jurisprudence. Hence, the *witr* prayer should be performed continuously just like the Maghrib prayer and not on its own as a single *rak'a*.

Furthermore, it has been made clear that the practice of the Messenger ﷺ was to perform *witr* at night after the *tahajjud* prayer. He would perform the *tahajjud* prayer in sets of two *rak'ats* until the time of Fajr drew close, at which time he would add an extra *rak'a* to the final set, thus converting both the last two *rak'ats* set and the additional *rak'a* into *witr*. Surely, this explanation is what the Messenger ﷺ intended when he said,

> Then, when one anticipates the break of dawn, he should perform one more *rak'a*, which will convert what he has performed into *witr* for him (*Sahih al-Bukhari* 1:135, *Sahih Muslim* 1:257).

And Allah ﷻ knows best.

9

Prayer After 'Asr

UPON STUDYING the books of hadith, a person will eventually come across some narrations in which the Messenger of Allah ﷺ prohibits a person from performing *salat* after the 'Asr prayer. In some narrations, however, the Messenger ﷺ himself is stated to have performed two *rak'at*s at that very time. This indicates a conflict between the two types of narrations.

In this chapter, we will discuss and attempt to resolve this apparent contradiction in order to answer the pertinent question: "What is the meaning of the Messenger ﷺ prohibiting any form of prayer after 'Asr if he himself performed them on occasion?" This chapter will also discuss whether or not it would be permissible for any one other than the Messenger ﷺ to perform *salat* at that time. The following will work to clarify the religious [*shar'i*] ruling regarding these *rak'at*s after 'Asr, and also bring to light whether the above prohibition is indeed general or rather bound by particular circumstances.

THE VARIOUS OPINIONS

Imam Abu Hanifa is of the opinion that it is not permissible for a *musalli* to perform the *tahiyyat al-masjid* [two *rak'at*s upon entering the *masjid*] or any other supererogatory [*nafl*] prayer after he has performed the 'Asr prayer. However, according to the Imam, making up missed [*qada'*] prayers is permissible. Another group's view is that it is impermissible to perform supererogatory prayer [*nawafil*] after 'Asr, but permissible to make up missed prayers or other nonobligatory prayers which are performed for a particular reason, such as the funeral prayer, *tahiyyat al-masjid*, or *tahiyyat al-wudu'* [two *rak'ats* after ablution].

The above difference of opinion informs us that the time after the 'Asr prayer is one in which each group agrees that some form of prayer or another is undesirable. The reason for this is that there are many hadiths which prohibit prayer after 'Asr; and it is due to these prohibitive hadiths that the Hanafis have disallowed all forms of nonobligatory *salat* to be performed in this time. However, there are other hadiths that speak of the Messenger 🕌 performing two *rak'ats* after 'Asr. These hadiths seem to be in conflict with those that prohibit it; therefore, we will first analyze these hadiths to gain a deeper understanding of this apparent conflict.

Analyzing the Seemingly Contradictory Hadiths

The conflicting narrations are of two kinds—those that portray the Messenger 🕌 performing two *rak'ats* after 'Asr only once (implying that he never did so again); and those which indicate that the Messenger 🕌 performed these two *rak'ats* on a regular basis. Both types of narrations are addressed in this section.

1. 'A'isha 🌸 narrates:

> The Messenger of Allah 🕌 [once] missed the two *rak'ats* before the 'Asr prayer; so after finishing 'Asr, he made them up, then never performed them again [at that time] (*Mu'jam al-Tabarani, Majma' al-zawa'id* 2:223).

2. A similar narration of Umm Salama 🌸 has been transmitted by Imam Ahmad in his *Musnad* (*Ma'arif al-sunan* 2:135, *Musnad Ahmad* 229:2 U).

3. Ibn 'Abbas 🌸 relates:

The Messenger of Allah ﷺ performed two *rak'ats* after 'Asr, as some items [of charity] had arrived [to be distributed] and had occupied him from performing the two *rak'ats* [*sunna*] after Zuhr. So he made them up after 'Asr, then he did not do so again (*Sunan al-Tirmidhi* 1:45).

From the above three narrations, we learn that the two *rak'ats* after the 'Asr prayer were performed only once by Allah's Messenger ﷺ. All three narrations state clearly that the Messenger ﷺ was making up the two *rak'ats* of *sunna* prayer which he had missed after Zuhr. These hadiths also indicate that the prayer after 'Asr was in no way a special prayer that the Messenger of Allah ﷺ regularly performed at that time. This, however, is contradicted by the following hadiths, which mention that the Messenger ﷺ performed two *rak'ats* after 'Asr quite regularly.

4. 'A'isha ◉ narrates:

The Messenger ﷺ would never visit me during the day after the 'Asr prayer, except that he would perform two *rak'ats* (*Sahih al-Bukhari* 1:83).

5. It is related from Abu Salama that

he asked 'A'isha ◉ regarding the two *rak'ats* the Messenger ﷺ would perform after 'Asr. She told him that he would perform them before ['Asr], until he happened to once miss them or forgot to perform them due to being occupied with something; so he performed them after 'Asr. He then continued to perform them, [because] whenever he would perform any [new] prayer [once], he would continue to perform it regularly thereafter (*Sahih Muslim* 1:277).

6. 'A'isha ◉ narrates that

the Messenger ﷺ never neglected the two *rak'ats* after 'Asr while he was in her company (*Sahih Muslim* 1:277).

These hadiths demonstrate that the Messenger of Allah ﷺ performed the two *rak'ats* on a regular basis. They state that whenever he would perform any new prayer (once), he would take it upon himself to continue them regularly. In this case, it was the two *rak'ats* of Zuhr he was making up and not a new prayer; but since he was performing them out of their usual time, he thereafter continued to perform them regularly after 'Asr. In either case, these hadiths seem to be in conflict with the former set of hadiths, which state that he performed the two *rak'a* prayer after 'Asr only once. The following has been mentioned concerning this apparent conflict.

Hafiz ibn Hajar reports that the second set of three hadiths (4,5, and 6) are of a higher degree of authenticity than the first three. This means that, according to Ibn Hajar, the hadiths which state that the Messenger 靐 performed the two *rak'ats* regularly have a higher degree of authenticity than those which mention that he performed them only once.

To expound on this point, it is quite true that the narration of Ibn 'Abbas (hadith 3) has only been designated as sound [*hasan*] by Imam Tirmidhi, whereas all the hadiths mentioned after it are either from *Sahih al-Bukhari* or *Muslim* and are rigorously authenticated [*sahih*]. Thus, Ibn 'Abbas's narration cannot stand in comparison. Secondly, hadith 1, which is transmitted from 'A'isha 靐, is said to have in its transmission the narrator Qattat, who has been called "a flagrant liar" [*kadhdhab*]. Hence, it is too weak to stand up against the other rigorously authenticated [*sahih*] narrations of 'A'isha 靐.

The hadith of Umm Salama (no. 2), however, is not defective and, as such, cannot be overlooked. The narration states that the Messenger 靐 performed two *rak'ats* after 'Asr only once, and it negates him performing them at any other time. This means that we have a single rigorously authenticated [*sahih*] hadith conflicting with three others of the same authenticity. We have 'A'isha's 靐 narrations, transmitted by Imam Bukhari and Muslim, which are affirmative [*muthbit*] in establishing that these two *rak'ats* were regularly performed by the Messenger 靐; and we also have the rigorously authenticated hadith of Umm Salama 靐 that states to the contrary. Hence, we are still left with two conflicting texts, both of which are authentic: one a negative [*manfi*] text (i.e. in support of the prohibition) and the other an affirmative [*muthbit*] one (i.e. not in support of the prohibition).

Hafiz Ibn Hajar al-'Asqalani attempts to correlate the two types of narrations by putting into effect a rule from the principles of hadith [*usul al-hadith*], which states that an affirmative [*muthbit*] text shall take precedence over a negative [*manfi*] one (i.e. an affirmative narration holds more strength than a negative one). He concludes that since 'A'isha's narrations are the affirmative ones, they will take precedence over Umm Salama's negative narration. He further states that 'A'isha's affirming that the Messenger regularly performed two *rak'ats* after 'Asr was according to her personal knowledge of his actions, and Umm Salama's negation of it was according to her own observation of the Messenger's *salat*.

Hafiz Ibn Hajar's explanation could have been conclusive, as it appears to have resolved the conflict between the two types of narrations; however, the great jurist and hadith scholar, 'Allama Taqi 'Uthmani, states in his *Darse Tirmidhi* (1:427) that a hadith in *Sahih Muslim* contradicts the basis of Hafiz Ibn Hajar's explanation—that both 'A'isha and Umm Salama were narrating from their own personal observations. The hadith in *Sahih Muslim* reveals that 'A'isha's knowledge regarding the Messenger's performance of this prayer was in actuality acquired from Umm Salama.

7. The following hadith explains this in further detail:

Kurayb narrates that he was sent by 'Abdullah ibn 'Abbas, 'Abd al-Rahman ibn Azhar, and Miswar ibn Makhrama to 'A'isha, the wife of the Messenger of Allah. They instructed him to convey their *salams* [greeting of peace] to her and enquire from her about the [performance of] two *rak'ats* after 'Asr. They told him to say that they had been informed of her performing the prayer, whereas it had reached them that the Messenger had prohibited it. Ibn 'Abbas said, "Umar and myself would deter people from performing them."

Kurayb says, "I visited her and conveyed their message. She told me to ask Umm Salama. I came out and informed them of what she had told me; so they sent me to Umm Salama with the same questions. Umm Salama said, 'I heard the Messenger of Allah prohibit them, and then I saw him perform them [himself]. The [first] time he performed them, he had completed 'Asr then entered the house to find some Ansari women from the Banu Haram tribe with me. So, as he began to perform the prayer, I sent a young girl and instructed her to stand by his side and say, 'O Messenger of Allah, Umm Salama says that she has heard you prohibit the performance of these two *rak'ats,* and now she sees you performing them.' She also told her that if he gestures with his hand then move back. The girl went to him and he gestured with his hand so she moved back. When he completed the prayer he said, 'O daughter of Ibn Umayya [Umm Salama], you asked me regarding the two *rak'ats* after 'Asr. A group of people from the 'Abd al-Qays tribe had come to me… and occupied me from performing the two *rak'ats* after Zuhr, so these were the [two *rak'ats*]'" (*Sahih Muslim* 1:277).

This hadith without doubt implies that Umm Salama ♦ was the source of 'A'isha's ♦ knowledge regarding the Messenger ♦ performing the two *rak'ats* after 'Asr. This is because the Messenger ♦ performed them while he was in Umm Salama's company, and 'A'isha was aware of that. The following narration clarifies this even further:

8. It is narrated from 'Abd al-Rahman ibn Abi Sufyan that

Mu'awiya ♦ sent a person to 'A'isha ♦, asking her about the two *rak'ats* after 'Asr. She replied that the Messenger ♦ had not performed them in her company, but Umm Salama had told her that he had performed them while with her. Therefore, Mu'awiya ♦ sent someone to [enquire from] Umm Salama. She said, "He [once] performed them by me, and as I had never seen him perform them before, I enquired from him, 'O Messenger of Allah, what were the two *rak'ats* I saw you perform after 'Asr? You have never performed them before.' He replied, 'They are the two *rak'ats* I [usually] perform after Zuhr, but some camels, collected as charity [*sadaqa*], had been brought to me [for distribution], so I forgot to perform them until I had completed 'Asr [i.e. after which time I completed them]. When I did remember, I did not think it was appropriate to make them up in the *masjid* with people looking, so I performed them while with you'" (*Sharh Ma'ani 'l-athar* 1:302).

This hadith, in conjunction with the previous one, clearly establishes that the Messenger of Allah ♦ did not initially perform the prayer in 'A'isha's ♦ company, but in the company of Umm Salama ♦.

'Allama 'Uthmani writes that even after extensive research, he could still not find a conclusive explanation to dispel the apparent conflict between these narrations. Nonetheless, he states that after giving some more thought to the issue, it appeared that the incident of the Messenger ﷺ performing the two *rak'ats* after 'Asr initially took place in the company of Umm Salama ؓ. This is confirmed by 'A'isha ؓ in the two narrations (hadith 7 and 8) mentioned above.

Thereafter, since the Messenger's ﷺ habit was of continuing any practice he had begun, he began to perform two *rak'ats* after the 'Asr prayer in 'A'isha's ؓ company on a daily basis, but Umm Salama ؓ remained unaware of this. This is probably why she insisted that he never performed them again after that one instance, and 'A'isha claimed that he always performed them in her company. 'Allama 'Uthmani concludes that this appears to be the best possible explanation to reconcile the hadiths and dispel the contradiction (*Darse Tirmidhi* 1:428).

Up to this point, the discussion has been regarding the differences found in the hadiths regarding how many times the Messenger of Allah ﷺ performed the two *rak'ats* after 'Asr. We now come to another important question: What is the ruling for the *Umma* concerning these two *rak'ats* after 'Asr. The scholars hold different views in this regard.

One group claims it is *sunna* to perform the two *rak'ats* after 'Asr, even though the Messenger ﷺ had forbidden all nonobligatory prayers at that time. They cite the narrations of 'A'isha ؓ, which have been mentioned above, as evidence to support their claim. This group asserts that since the Messenger ﷺ performed them, it is permissible for others to do so as well. However, the Hanafi scholars and many others, state that these two *rak'ats* cannot be considered a general *sunna* on the basis of these hadiths alone. In fact, it is prohibitively disliked [*makruh tahrimi*] to perform any nonobligatory prayer at that time. There are numerous other narrations and reasons that clearly prohibit prayer after 'Asr.

An Exclusive Practice of Allah's Messenger ﷺ

The main reason the Messenger ﷺ performed the two *rak'ats* after 'Asr, as the hadiths state, was to make up for the two missed *sunna rak'ats* of Zuhr (*see* hadith 7). The reason for this is that it was an exclusive practice of the Messenger ﷺ to make up any missed *sunna* prayers. This, however, is not the case for the rest of the *Umma*.

Hence, the Messenger of Allah ﷺ performed the two missed *rak'ats* of Zuhr *sunna* after 'Asr, and thereafter continued to perform two extra *rak'ats* every day after 'Asr; which was due to his exclusive habit to continue any new prayer even if he had performed it just once. The following narrations explicitly provide the same explanation.

9. 'A'isha ◈, after narrating the incident in which the Messenger ﷺ performed the two *rak'ats* after 'Asr, states:

> Whenever he would perform a [new] prayer once, he would continue it [thereafter on a regular basis] (*Sahih Muslim* 1:277).

This hadith illustrates the exclusive habit of the Messenger ﷺ. The following hadiths will make the matter even more clear.

10. 'A'isha ◈ narrates:

> The Messenger ﷺ would perform prayer after 'Asr but would prohibit [others from] it; and he would fast continuously [*yuwasilu*, i.e. without eating in between for long periods] but would prohibit [others from] it (*Sunan Abi Dawud* 1:182).

This hadith clearly indicates that just as the Messenger ﷺ would observe continuous fasts himself and prohibit the Companions from doing so, he would also prohibit others from performing the two *rak'ats* after 'Asr but would observe them himself. This narration has been related by Imam Abu Dawud who does not make any comments after mentioning it; which means that the narration is a strong one. It is well-known among hadith scholars that whenever Imam Abu Dawud is silent after a hadith (i.e. does not comment on its grade), it means that the hadith is strong.

11. Umm Salama ♣, after observing the Messenger of Allah ﷺ performing the two *rak'ats,* enquired from him:

> O Messenger of Allah, can we make them up [as well] if they are missed? He said no (*Sharh Ma'ani 'l-athar* 1:306).

'Allama Haythami states that this hadith has been related by Imam Ahmad in his *Musnad* and Ibn Hibban in his *Sahih.* He further states that the narrators in Imam Ahmad's chain are mentioned within the chains of *Sahih al-Bukhari* (*Majma' al-zawa'id* 2:223).

From the above hadith, we learn that Umm Salama ♣ was prohibited from making up the *sunna* prayers after 'Asr if she happened to miss them. This indicates that making them up was an exclusive practice of Allah's Messenger ﷺ. It is related by 'Allama 'Ayni that al-Khattabi said: "This prayer [the two *rak'ats* after 'Asr] is also from among the unique practices [*khasa'is*] of the Messenger ﷺ." Ibn al-'Uqayli has stated the same.

All of the above reports lead to the same conclusion that the performance of the two *rak'ats* after 'Asr was indeed an exclusive practice of the Messenger ﷺ and, as such, was not legislated as being *sunna.* This is confirmed by the fact that many narrations actually prohibit any form of supererogatory prayer at that time.

The Hadiths Prohibiting Prayer After 'Asr

1. Abu Sa'id al-Khudri ♣ narrates that the Messenger ﷺ said,

> There is no [supererogatory] prayer following Fajr until the sun rises, nor after 'Asr until the sun sets (*Sahih al-Bukhari* 1:82-83).

2. 'Amr ibn 'Abasa narrates that the Messenger ﷺ said,

> Perform the Fajr prayer; thereafter, abstain from any prayer while the sun is rising until it has fully risen. And perform the 'Asr prayer; thereafter abstain from any prayer until the sun sets (*Sahih Muslim* U).

3. Ibn 'Abbas ♣ narrates that the Messenger ﷺ prohibited prayer after 'Asr (*Sunan al-Nasa'i* 96).

4. It is narrated about 'Ali ibn Abi Talib ❀ that

> he performed two *rak'ats* after 'Asr on the way to Makka. 'Umar ❀ called for him and expressed his anger saying, "By Allah, you are aware that the Messenger ❀ has prohibited us from performing them." (*Sharh Ma'ani 'l-athar* 1:303)

5. 'Ali ❀ narrates that

> the Messenger ❀ would perform two *rak'ats* after every prayer except after Fajr and 'Asr (*Sharh Ma'ani 'l-athar* 1:303).

6. 'A'isha ❀ narrates that

> the Messenger ❀ would never perform any prayer without following it up with two *rak'ats*, except Fajr and 'Asr, in which case he would perform two *rak'ats* before them (*Sharh Ma'ani 'l-athar* 1:303 U).

7. Mu'awiya ibn Abi Sufyan ❀ delivered a sermon saying:

> O people! You perform such a prayer which we have never seen the Messenger ❀ perform, despite having remained in his company. He has prohibited the two *rak'ats* after 'Asr (*Sharh Ma'ani 'l-athar* 1:304).

8. Sa'ib ibn Yazid ❀ narrates that

> he saw 'Umar ❀ beating Munkadir for performing prayer after 'Asr (*Sharh Ma'ani 'l-athar* 1:304).

9. 'Abdullah ❀ narrates:

> 'Umar disliked the performance of prayer after 'Asr, and I dislike what 'Umar dislikes (*Sharh Ma'ani 'l-athar* 1:304).

10. Jabala ibn Suhaym narrates:

> I heard Ibn 'Umar ❀ relate that he would observe [his father] 'Umar ❀ beat a person if he found him performing prayer after 'Asr, until the person would terminate his prayer (*Sharh Ma'ani 'l-athar* 1:304).

11. Tawus narrates that

> he asked 'Abdullah ibn 'Abbas ❀ regarding the two *rak'ats* after 'Asr. He forbade him and recited: "It is not fitting for a believer, male or female,

when a matter has been decided upon by Allah and His Messenger, to have any option about their decision" (*al-Qur'an* 33:36). [(*Sharh Ma'ani 'l-athar* 1:304)]

CONCLUSION

The outcome of this discussion can be summed up as follows. There is some conflict in the narrations which mention the Messenger 鸞 performing prayer after 'Asr. Some rigorously authenticated hadiths indicate that he did so only once, and other rigorously authenticated hadiths reveal that he performed them quite regularly. To remove the conflict between the narrations and explain the reality of the situation, the Hanafis have established that this was a unique practice of the Messenger 鸞.

The Messenger 鸞 had only performed them initially to make up for the two *sunna rak'ats* of Zuhr, which he had missed due to being with some guests. He thereafter began to regularly perform two *rak'ats* after 'Asr, as it was his unique habit to continue any form of prayer he would initiate. Numerous hadiths have been presented to substantiate this explanation.

Moreover, also highlighted above are a large number of narrations that explicitly prohibit the performance of prayer after 'Asr. In light of this weighty evidence, Hanafis scholars have concluded that the strongest and most correct view regarding supererogatory prayers after 'Asr, is that it is prohibited. As for those hadiths which are brought forth to prove the general permissibility of prayer after 'Asr, they cannot be accepted here as proof of permissibility since they only illustrate an action exclusive to Allah's Messenger 鸞.

10

Prayer During the Friday Sermon

THE MESSENGER OF ALLAH ﷺ has instructed that whenever a person enters the *masjid*, he should perform two *rak'ats* of prayer before sitting down. This prayer is called *tahiyyat al-masjid* [greeting of the *masjid*], and it is a *sunna* prayer.

However, these two *rak'ats* are not to be performed at times in which prayers are undesirable [*makruh*]. Islamic law has designated the following times as undesirable: (1) after the Fajr prayer until sunrise; (2) after the 'Asr prayer until sunset; (3) from the beginning of sunrise until the sun is a spear's length above the horizon [i.e. when a distance equal to the sun's diameter appears between the sun and the horizon]; (4) from the time the sun is at its highest point in the sky until it moves on [*istiwa'*]; and (5) from when the sun turns yellow before sunset until after it has set.

Hence, it is recommended to perform the *tahiyyat al-masjid* upon entering the *masjid* at any time other than these disliked times. There is however one other exception to this general rule. Since the Messenger of Allah ﷺ forbade any form of prayer or conversation during the Friday sermon [*khutba*], it is not allowed that a person perform the *tahiyyat al-masjid* upon entering the *masjid* while the sermon is in progress. This is the opinion of the Hanafis and many others.

Some scholars state that a person entering the *masjid* at such a time should still perform a set of two *rak'ats* prior to sitting down and listening to the *imam's* sermon. They go as far as designating it a desirable act even at that time.

The following is a discussion regarding this very issue. It seeks to determine the exact procedure a person should follow when he enters the *masjid* during the Friday sermon. The evidence used by the Hanafi school to establish the impermissibility of performing *salat* while the sermon is in progress will be presented first; after which we will analyze the few seemingly contradictory narrations that are used to prove the permissibility of prayer in this time.

The Qur'an on This Issue

Allah ﷻ says,

> "So when the Qur'an is recited, listen to it and remain silent, that you may receive mercy" (*al-Qur'an* 7:204).

As we discussed earlier in chapter 3, "Reciting Behind the *Imam,*" this verse was revealed concerning *salat* (and, according to some opinions, concerning the sermon too). Now, since the sermon has been likened to prayer and since the verses of the Qur'an are recited in it, the command of this verse shall apply to the sermon as well; which means that a person would have to observe silence during the sermon and listen attentively to what is being said. This also means that the person should not occupy himself in prayer during the sermon.

It is related from 'Umar ﷜ that the two sermons on Friday are equal to two *rak'ats* of prayer. This is probably why the *rak'ats* of Friday prayer are only two, whereas the *rak'ats* of Zuhr are four. He states:

> The sermon is equivalent to two *rak'ats;* therefore, whoever misses the sermon should perform four *rak'ats* [of Zuhr] instead (*Musannaf Ibn Abi Shayba* 2:128, *Musannaf 'Abd al-Razzaq*).

It should be remembered that this was his personal view, and the ruling of the majority of scholars is that a person should still join the two *rak'ats* Friday congregation with the *imam* even if he happened to miss the sermon.

Prayer During the Sermon

Since the sermon is similar to the prayer, it could be concluded from this that one should also remain silent and listen carefully while the sermon is in progress, just as one would while in prayer. The wisdom behind disallowing all forms of prayer, remembrance [*dhikr*], supplication [*du'a'*], and even enjoining the right and forbidding the wrong [*amr bi 'l-ma'ruf* and *nahy 'an al-munkar*]—which is permissible on all other occasions—is due to the fact that if a person engages in *tahiyyat al-masjid* or any other activity while the sermon is in progress, he will not be able to listen attentively to the *imam's* sermon.

THE HADITHS ON THIS ISSUE

1. Abu Hurayra ﷺ narrates that the Messenger of Allah ﷺ said:

   Whoever says, "Remain silent," while the *imam* is delivering the sermon, he has nullified [his reward] (*Sunan al-Tirmidhi* 1:114).

2. Abu Hurayra ﷺ narrates from the Messenger of Allah ﷺ:

   When you say, "Remain silent," to your companion on Friday while the *imam* is delivering the sermon, you have nullified [your reward] (*Sahih Muslim* 1:281, *Sharh Ma'ani 'l-athar*).

Since merely reminding another person to keep quiet during the Friday sermon has been prohibited by these hadiths, it follows that *tahiyyat al-masjid,* which is a supererogatory [*nafl*] action, must also be disallowed while the Friday sermon is being delivered. The following hadith further clarifies this deduction:

3. 'Abdullah ibn 'Umar ﷺ narrates that

   he heard the Messenger of Allah ﷺ say, "When one of you enters the *masjid* to find the *imam* on the pulpit [delivering the sermon], then no prayer or conversation [is permitted] until the *imam* finishes" (*Majma' al-zawa'id* 2:184).

This hadith in itself may have been classified by some as being defective due to the narrator in its chain, Ayyub ibn al-Nahik. There is mixed criticism about him. Some scholars of hadith have called him trustworthy, while others have called him weak. However, despite this, there are many other aspects which bolster its acceptability. Ibn Abi Shayba has related some other narrations of Ibn 'Umar ﷺ (the narrator of this hadith) which would indicate that Ibn 'Umar's personal opinion and practice was in conformance with his narration. This adds strength to his narration.

One of the principles of hadith [*usul al-hadith*] is that any narration supported by the constant practice of the Companions and Followers will acquire enough strength to be used as evidence. This means that the message of the above hadith, despite the criticism leveled at its chain, can be accepted. The fact that there are many other rigorously authenticated [*sahih*] hadiths that relay the same message as the above hadith makes it even more legitimate to use as proof.

We will see in the following paragraphs that this opinion was not an isolated one but was rather the opinion of numerous Companions and Followers.

4. It is related from Salman al-Farsi ﷺ that the Messenger ﷺ said:

> A person who performs the ritual bath [*ghusl*] on Friday, attains as much purity as he can, applies oil or some scent found in the house; then departs for the *masjid* and does not force two people apart [to sit between them]; and performs as much prayer as Allah has willed for him, and then maintains silence while the *imam* speaks, will have all his sins from the present Friday to the next forgiven (*Sahih al-Bukhari* 1:122, *Sharh Maʿani 'l-athar* 1:369).

5. A similar narration of Abu Hurayra ﷺ in *Sahih Muslim* has the following variation:

> [...] and performs what has been ordained for him, then observes silence until the *imam* finishes his sermon... (*Sahih Muslim* 1:283).

6. Another narration of Abu Hurayra and Abu Saʿid al-Khudri ﷺ contains the following variation:

> [...] and performs what Allah ﷻ has ordained for him, then observes silence when the *imam* appears... (*Sunan Abi Dawud* 50 U).

7. Nubaysha al-Hudhali narrates from the Messenger of Allah ﷺ:

> When a Muslim performs *ghusl* [ritual bath] on Friday, approaches the *masjid* without inconveniencing anybody; and if he finds that the *imam* has not yet appeared, he engrosses himself in prayer for as long as possible; and if he finds the *imam* present, he sits silently and listens attentively until the *imam* completes the Friday prayer... (*Musnad Ahmad*).

Imam Haythami states regarding the above hadith that "Imam Ahmad has narrated this hadith and its narrators are those of Sahih al-Bukhari except for the *shaykh* [teacher] of Ahmad, who is trustworthy" (*Majma' al-zawa'id* 2:171).

None of the above hadiths mention that it is virtuous or even permissible to perform prayer once the *imam* has appeared for the sermon. The reason why this has been prohibited was previously stated; it is due to the *musalli's* inability to attentively listen to the *imam's* sermon and to the verses of the Qur'an he is reciting.

THE COMPANIONS AND FOLLOWERS ON THIS ISSUE

1. It is related from 'Abdullah ibn 'Abbas and Ibn 'Umar ﷺ that

   they disliked any prayer or conversation on Friday once the *imam* had appeared [to deliver the sermon] (*Musannaf Ibn Abi Shayba* 2:124).

2. It is narrated from Ibn 'Umar ﷺ that

   he would remain in prayer on Friday, and when the *imam* would appear he would stop praying (*Musannaf Ibn Abi Shayba* 2:124).

3. 'Uqba ibn 'Amir has been reported as saying that

   prayer while the *imam* is on the pulpit [*minbar*] is a disobedience [*ma'siya*] (*Sharh Ma'ani 'l-athar* 1:370).

4. It is narrated from Ibn Shihab al-Zuhri that

   a person [who enters the *masjid* on Friday while the *imam* is delivering the sermon] should sit down and not engage himself in any prayer (*Sharh Ma'ani 'l-athar* 1:369).

5. It is narrated from Khalid al-Hadhdha' that

> Abu Qilaba arrived while the *imam* was delivering the sermon. He sat down and did not perform any prayer (*Sharh Ma'ani 'l-athar* 1:369).

6. Abu Malik al-Qurazi narrates that

> the "sitting" of the *imam* on the pulpit [*minbar*] signals an end to all prayer, and his "sermon" [signals an end] to all talking (*Sharh Ma'ani 'l-athar* 1:370).

7. Ibrahim al-Nakh'ay says,

> 'Alqama was asked, "Do you speak while the *imam* is delivering the sermon or after he has arrived [to deliver it]?" He said no (*Sharh Ma'ani 'l-athar* 1:370).

8. It is related from Mujahid that

> he disliked to pray while the *imam* was delivering the sermon (*Sharh Ma'ani 'l-athar* 1:370).

Another important point is that the angels have also been reported to wrap up their registers as soon as the sermon begins. The following hadiths reveal that as the *imam* begins his sermon, the angels put away their records in order to listen to the sermon.

9. There is a narration of Abu Hurayra ◈ in *Sahih al-Bukhari,* as well as in other collections, regarding the angels recording the names and times of the worshippers arriving for the sermon on Friday. Towards the end of this hadith, the Messenger of Allah ◈ says,

> Thereafter, when the *imam* appears, the angels wrap up their records and begin to listen to the admonition [*dhikr*] (*Sahih Muslim* 1:283, *Sahih al-Bukhari* 1:127, *Sunan al-Nasa'i* 205).

10. A narration from Abu Umama ◈ states:

> When the *imam* appears, the records [of the angels] are put away (*Majma' al-zawa'id* 2:177).

11. A narration from Abu Sa'id al-Khudri ◈ states:

When the muezzin calls for prayer [*adhan*] and the *imam* sits on the pulpit, the records [of the angels] are wrapped up, and they enter the *masjid* listening attentively to the admonition [*dhikr*] (*Majma' al-zawa'id* 2:177).

12. In his commentary on *Sahih Muslim,* Imam Nawawi has stated that the same (i.e. that no prayer during the sermon) was the practice of 'Umar, 'Uthman, and 'Ali ﷺ (*Sharh Sahih Muslim* 1:288).

13. 'Allama Shawkani states that the great hadith master Zayn al-Din 'Iraqi has related the same practice from Muhammad ibn Sirin, Qadi Shurayh, Ibrahim al-Nakh'ay, Qatada, and Zuhri.

14. Ibn Abi Shayba has also reported this opinion from Sa'id ibn al-Musayyib, Mujahid, 'Ata', and 'Urwa ibn al-Zubayr.

These narrations highlight and further establish the position of the Hanafis on the issue of prayer during the Friday sermon. Their opinion is that it is impermissible to perform *salat* while the sermon is in progress.

ANALYZING THE SEEMINGLY CONTRADICTORY HADITHS

1. Jabir ﷺ narrates:

Sulayk al-Ghatafani arrived on Friday and sat down while the Messenger ﷺ was delivering the sermon. The Messenger ﷺ ordered him to stand and perform two *rak'ats* and to make them short (*Sahih Muslim* 1:287).

This hadith is used by those who claim that it is permissible to perform two *rak'ats* during the sermon. This however is very difficult to accept due to the following reasons:

(a) This hadith cannot stand as evidence for prayer being permissible at the time of the sermon, because it speaks of a lone and isolated incident. It was only once that the Messenger ﷺ ordered somebody to rise and perform two *rak'ats* during the sermon. In fact, there are a number of narrations which state that the Messenger ﷺ ordered people to sit down during the sermon.

There is one hadith about a desert Arab [*a'rabi*] who had come to Allah's Messenger ﷺ to complain about drought, then had appeared a week later to complain about heavy floods. This person arrived during the Friday sermon, but the Messenger ﷺ did not command him to perform two *rak'ats*. Anas ﷺ narrates:

> A person entered [the *masjid*] on a Friday from the door opposite the pulpit upon which the Messenger ﷺ was delivering the sermon. He faced the Messenger ﷺ and said, "O Messenger of Allah, properties have been destroyed and the pathways blocked. Pray to Allah that he send us rain." The narrator says that the Messenger ﷺ raised his hands and prayed, "O Allah, grant us rain." It began to rain, and, by Allah, we did not see the sun for a week. Thereafter, the person arrived through the same door the following Friday while the Messenger ﷺ was delivering the sermon. He faced the Messenger ﷺ and said, "O Messenger of Allah, property have been destroyed and the pathways blocked. Pray to Allah to stop the rain" (*Sahih al-Bukhari* 1:137).

Another narration tells us that the Messenger ﷺ once observed a person during the sermon who was hurrying over people's shoulders. The Messenger ﷺ told him:

> Sit, for you have inconvenienced [the people] (*Sunan al-Nasa'i* 207, *Abi Dawud*).

It is quite clear that the Messenger ﷺ did not order him to perform any prayer, but told him to sit down quickly. In another narration of Jabir ﷺ, it states:

> [On one occasion] the Messenger ﷺ positioned himself on the pulpit and said, "Be seated." Ibn Mas'ud ﷺ [who had just entered] sat down instantly by the door of the *masjid*. When the Messenger ﷺ saw him he said, "Come forth, O 'Abdullah ibn Mas'ud" (*Sunan Abi Dawud* 156).

Again, the Messenger ﷺ did not order him to perform prayer, but instead told him to come forth and sit. A hadith in *Sahih Muslim* states:

> 'Umar ﷺ was once delivering the sermon when 'Uthman ﷺ arrived. 'Umar

⚜ admonished him for not having performing the ritual bath [*ghusl*], but did not order him to perform any prayer (*Sahih Muslim* 1:280).

None of these incidents indicate a command for prayer while the sermon is in progress. In fact, they instruct that one should sit down while the *imam* is delivering the sermon, which proves that the one occasion on which the Messenger ⚜ ordered Sulayk al-Ghatafani ⚜ to stand and pray was due to another reason. The hadith of Sulayk ⚜ therefore cannot be used to prove the desirability of prayer during the Friday sermon. The full account of Sulayk al-Ghatafani's incident is as follows:

> Once, while the Messenger ⚜ was sitting on the pulpit waiting to begin the sermon, a Companion named Sulayk ibn Hudba al-Ghatafani ⚜ who had on very torn and worn clothing entered the *masjid*. The Messenger ⚜, after seeing his poverty-stricken state, ordered him to stand and pray. He did this so the other Companions could also observe his condition. The Messenger ⚜ remained silent until he had finished his prayer; then, after seeing that the other Companions had taken a look at him, he encouraged them to contribute to him, which they did with open hearts.

One can clearly see that this was a very special circumstance, in which the Messenger ⚜ ordered Sulayk ⚜ to stand up and pray so that his condition would become known to the Companions. Consequently, this command cannot be classified as generally applicable as it was issued only once to this particular Companion.

(b) The above explanation should be sufficient to understand the true nature of the incident. Another explanation mentioned by some scholars is that the Messenger ⚜ gave the order to pray before commencing the sermon and then waited silently until the Companion had completed his prayer. The Messenger ⚜ did not recite or say anything while Sulayk ⚜ prayed, as is understood from a hadith in *Sahih Muslim*:

> Sulayk al-Ghatafani ⚜ entered the *masjid* on Friday while the Messenger ⚜ was sitting on the pulpit [and had not yet stood for the sermon]" (*Sahih Muslim* 1:287).

It is a proven fact that the Messenger of Allah 🌸 would deliver his sermons standing. Hence, for him to be sitting down (as the narration states) means that he had not yet begun the sermon; so Sulayk's prayer was not performed during the Messenger's 🌸 sermon but before it. This point is further substantiated by Imam Nasa'i's inclusion of this narration under a chapter entitled, "Chapter on Prayer Before the Sermon." This clearly indicates that according to Imam Nasa'i, this incident took place before the sermon had begun.

(c) There are some narrations, however, which indicate that the Messenger 🌸 had already begun the sermon when Sulayk 🌸 entered. The meaning of these narrations is that he was just about to begin the sermon when Sulayk 🌸 walked in.

(d) There are also other narrations which mention that Allah's Messenger 🌸 interrupted his sermon and remained silent until Sulayk finished his prayer. The narration in *Musannaf Ibn Abi Shayba* contains the following words:

> The Messenger 🌸, when ordering the Companion to perform two *rak'ats*, discontinued his sermon until he had finished the two *rak'ats* (*Musannaf Ibn Abi Shayba* 2:110),

and the narration of *Daraqutni* contains the following words:

> Anas 🌸 narrates that a person from the Qays tribe entered while the Messenger 🌸 was delivering the sermon. The Messenger 🌸 told him to stand up and perform two *rak'ats* and discontinued the sermon until the person completed his prayer (*Sunan al-Daraqutni* 2:15 U).

This means that the Companion had completed his *salat* and was no longer engaged in it while the Messenger 🌸 was delivering his sermon.

(e) Yet another explanation for this incident is that, since the Messenger 🌸 had interrupted his sermon and begun to converse with him, the prohibition of talking or praying was lifted and Sulayk had to no longer adhere to the command "remain silent and listen."

Therefore, for him to perform two *rak'ats* while the Messenger 🌳 remained silent (and waited for him) was permissible. Ibn al-'Arabi has offered this explanation and considered it most accurate.

(f) It has been already mentioned that the Messenger 🌳 ordered Sulayk 🌼 to rise and perform the prayer so as to expose his poverty-stricken state in front of the Companions. In this regard, a narration in *Sunan al-Tirmidhi* and *al-Nasa'i* from Abu Sa'id 🌼 states:

> A person entered the *masjid* in a shabby state (*Sunan al-Tirmidhi* 1:93 U, *al-Nasa'i* 1:208 U).

(g) Another point that should not be overlooked here is that for the two *rak'ats* to be considered *tahiyyat al-masjid,* they must be offered immediately upon entering the *masjid* and prior to sitting down. However, we find in some versions of this narration that Sulayk 🌼 had sat down upon his arrival, after which the Messenger 🌳 had instructed him to stand and pray. The narration in *Sahih Muslim* states: "Stand up and pray," (*Sahih Muslim* 1:287) and another narration states:

> Sulayk sat down without praying, and the Messenger 🌳 asked him if he had performed two *rak'ats?* He replied that he had not, so the Messenger 🌳 ordered him to stand up and perform two *rak'ats* (*Sahih Muslim* 1:287).

This proves that he was ordered to stand up and pray in order to reveal his condition to the other Companions.

When the above points are taken into consideration, it makes it quite difficult to claim that *tahiyyat al-masjid* was permitted at the time of the sermon. The incident of Sulayk 🌼 was a unique and isolated one, and not one instructing the whole *Umma* to pray at that time, especially when there are other narrations that clearly prohibit its performance.

2. Another seemingly contradictory narration is as follows:

> Jabir 🌼 narrates that once while the Messenger of Allah 🌳 was delivering the sermon he said, "When you [enter the *masjid*] and find the *imam*

delivering the sermon..." or [he said] "[...] and find that the *imam* has arrived [for the sermon], you should perform two *rak'ats*" (*Sahih al-Bukhari* 1:156).

This is another narration that is used to establish the desirability of *tahiyyat al-masjid* at the time of the sermon. The same words are narrated by Imam Muslim in his *Sahih* as part of the narration of Sulayk al-Ghatafani ﷺ (*Sahih Muslim* 1:287).

It can be said that this narration is in contradiction with the command of the Holy Qur'an and many other rigorously authenticated hadiths that have already been mentioned above. Many explanations have been offered in order to remove the conflict between this hadith and the hadiths of prohibition. One explanation is that the phrase, "delivering his sermon," in the narration, actually means, "about to begin the sermon" (i.e. the *imam* was sitting waiting to begin the sermon). This is one way of reconciling the narrations so that no contradiction remains.

Otherwise, the second way to deal with this issue is to leave it as an independent rigorously authenticated narration in conflict with the other rigorously authenticated narrations of prohibition; and determine, in the light of the principles of hadith [*usul al-hadith*], which of the narrations are more superior and stronger. The result of such an analysis would be that the hadiths of prohibition presented by the Hanafis are stronger for a number of reasons:

(a) The narrations used by the Hanafis are of a prohibitive nature (i.e. they prohibit the prayer at a particular time), whereas this narration (hadith 2) is of a permissive nature. One of the principles of hadith [*usul al-hadith*] is that when there is a conflict between hadiths, a hadith prohibiting something is considered superior to one that permits it. Therefore, since the hadiths presented by the Hanafis are of a prohibitive nature, they are considered superior to those hadiths which are of a permissive nature (i.e. hadith 2).

(b) The narrations of prohibition presented by the Hanafis are more in harmony with the implications of the above mentioned Qur'anic verses, which prohibit anything that would distract a person from listening to the sermon.

(c) The narrations presented by the Hanafis are substantiated by the practice of many of the Companions and Followers (may Allah be pleased with them all), as has been previously detailed; whereas this narration, if taken as an independent narration, is only supported by the lone narration of Sulayk 🙵.

(e) There is greater caution in acting upon the hadiths prohibiting *tahiyyat al-masjid* at the time of the sermon than upon those permitting it, since *tahiyyat al-masjid* is not considered an obligatory prayer in any opinion. While holding it permissible, neglecting it would not be considered a sin. However, if one were to pray during the sermon while holding the view that it is prohibited, he would be considered sinful for going against what is believed to be a prohibition.

CONCLUSION

Many narrations state that the Messenger 🙵 had discontinued his sermon while Sulayk 🙵 performed his prayer. What would happen today if many people began to arrive late, and worse still, all at different times (as is to be observed nowadays in the *masjids*)? How many times and for how long would the *imam* remain silent, and when would he be able to complete the sermon?

The Hanafis have taken all these aspects into consideration in forming their opinion. They have adhered to the hadiths of prohibition and have answered and explained all the seemingly conflicting narrations. Their view has also been fully substantiated by the statements of various Companions and Followers. Therefore, we can safely conclude that after taking all the above points into consideration, it will be prohibited to perform two *rak'ats* of *tahiyyat al-masjid* after the *imam* has started his sermon.

11

The Number of *Rak'ats* in *Tarawih*

FOR ABOUT twelve hundred and fifty years, until the 20thcentury, there was little controversy surrounding the issue of how many *rak'ats* are to be performed for *tarawih*. There was a general consensus among Muslim scholars that *tarawih* is no less than twenty *rak'ats*, and some scholars were even of the opinion that it was more than twenty *rak'ats*. Until recently, there was also no mention of any *masjid* in which less than twenty *rak'ats* were performed or of any scholar holding such a view. It has only been in the last hundred years that some people have begun insisting that the *tarawih* prayer consists of only eight *rak'ats*. The practice of the Companions [*sahaba*], Followers [*tabi'in*], and other scholars (may Allah be pleased with them) who proceeded them has always been of performing twenty *rak'ats*.

A consensus [*ijma'*] was reached among the Companions at the time of the Leader of the Faithful [*Amir al-mu'minin*] 'Umar ibn al-Khattab ⚜ that *tarawih* was twenty *rak'ats*. He had appointed Ubay ibn Ka'b ⚜ to lead the people in twenty *rak'ats,* as is understood from authentic reports. He was not met with any refutation or argument concerning this agreement; neither from the Companions who had performed *tarawih* with the Messenger 🌸, nor from any of the wives of the Messenger 🌸. If it had been a practice he had innovated himself, it would have most certainly been rejected and refuted by the Companions and household of the Messenger 🌸. This chapter

discusses the issue in detail, and establishes that the correct number
of *rak'ats* for *tarawih* is indeed twenty.

Opinions of the Scholars

Imam Abu Hanifa, Imam Shafiʿi, and Imam Ahmad are unanimous
that twenty *rak'ats* are to be performed for *tarawih* during Ramadan.
There are different opinions recorded from Imam Malik: one states
twenty *rak'ats;* another is of thirty-six *rak'ats,* about which Imam Malik
said, "This is our former opinion;" and a third view is of thirty-eight
rak'ats. There is also an opinion which states forty-one *rak'ats* (*Bidayat
al-mujtahid* 1:210). ʿAllama ʿAyni has mentioned the second view of
thirty-six *rak'ats* to be Imam Malik's more popular opinion.

What becomes clear at this point is that none of the four prominent
imams held a view of *tarawih* being less than twenty *rak'ats.* Twenty is
the minimum number mentioned, and the reason for Imam Malik's
view of thirty six *rak'ats* is that it was the practice of the people of
the noble city of Makka to perform *tawaf* [circumambulation] of the
Kaʿba after every four *rak'ats* of *tarawih.* During the pause between
each four *rak'ats* of *tarawih,* the people of the illuminated city of
Madina would observe an extra four *rak'ats* of prayer in place of the
tawaf [see *al-Mughni* 2:167].

Therefore, since *tarawih* was performed as twenty *rak'ats,* consisting of five sets of four *rak'ats* (each set called a *"tarwiha"*), the people
of Madina would perform an extra four *rak'ats* after every *tarwiha,*
bringing the total number of extra *rak'ats* to sixteen. Sixteen extra
rak'ats plus the twenty *rak'ats* of *tarawih* make thirty-six *rak'ats.* Hence,
the actual number of *rak'ats* of *tarawih* was twenty even according
to Imam Malik.

Tarawih During the First Generations

For centuries, ever since *tarawih* came to be observed in congregation,
no less than twenty *rak'ats* were performed by the Muslims throughout
the Islamic world. Nafiʿ, a prominent *tabiʿi* states, "I never found

any one performing less than thirty-nine *rakʿats* (three of which were *witr*)." Nafiʿ remained in Madina for most of his life and passed away in 117 A.H. (*Fath al-Bari* 4:254 U). At that time, the number of *rakʿats* observed for *tarawih* in Madina were thirty six (twenty *rakʿats tarawih* and sixteen supererogatory [*nafl*] *rakʿats*).

Thereafter, Imam Shafiʿi states, "I observed the people performing thirty-nine *rakʿats* in Madina [which include three *witr*], and twenty three *rakʿats* in Makka." Imam Shafiʿi was born in 150 A.H. and passed away in 204 A.H. Hence, this report accounts for the second century of Islam. Furthermore, Ibn ʿAbd al-Barr states, "Twenty *rakʿats* was the opinion followed by the majority of scholars, including those of Kufa, Imam Shafiʿi, and most other jurists." This specifies that, throughout the earlier period of Islam, the minimum number of *rakʿats* performed in *tarawih* was twenty.

Sufyan al-Thawri (died 161 A.H.) and Imam Abu Hanifa (died 150 A.H.) of Kufa both held the opinion of twenty *rakʿats*. Imam Ahmad ibn Hanbal of Baghdad (died 235 A.H.) held the same opinion as did Dawud al-Zahiri (died 270 A.H.). ʿAbdullah ibn al-Mubarak (died 181 A.H.), one of the prominent scholars of Khurasan, also held the view of twenty *rakʿats* (*Bidayat al-mujtahid* 1:210).

From the above, one can comfortably conclude that the predominant view of the scholars from Makka to Khurasan and beyond was of *tarawih* being twenty *rakʿats*. There is not a single opinion of eight *rakʿats* to be found during this extensive period, neither from the great Imams nor from any other jurist.

The mass of people who follow the Hanafi, Shafiʿi, Maliki, and Hanbali schools of thought, and who constitute the majority of the *Umma*, have until today adopted the view of twenty *rakʿats* for *tarawih*. In the two sanctified sites of Islam—Makka and Madina—twenty *rakʿats* are performed in congregation for *tarawih* until today. It was not until approximately a century and a half ago, that the first arguments were made, after the consensus reached by ʿUmar ﷺ; claiming that *tarawih* was only eight *rakʿats* and not twenty.

FIQH AL-IMAM

Imam Tirmidhi, well known for recording in his *Sunan* the various opinions held by different scholars in jurisprudential [*fiqhi*] issues, does not mention so much as even a weak opinion of *tarawih* being eight *rak'ats* when discussing the issue. If there had been an opinion of eight *rak'ats* concurrent among the earlier scholars, he would not have failed to mention it. [*See Sunan al-Tirmidhi* 1:166]

ABSENCE OF AUTHENTIC NARRATIONS CONCERNING THE NUMBER OF *RAK'ATS* IN *TARAWIH*

Another point to be taken into consideration in this issue is that many scholars state that there are no authentic [*sahih*] and direct [*marfu'*] chains of narration (from the Messenger 🕮) mentioning the exact number of *rak'ats* performed by him in *tarawih*.

1. Shaykh al-Islam Ibn Taymiya writes:

   Whoever assumes that there is a fixed number of *rak'ats* reported from the Messenger of Allah 🕮 concerning *tarawih,* and does not accept any greater or lesser number, has erred (*Majmu' al-fatawa* 46 U, *Mirqat al-mafatih* 3:381).

2. 'Allama Subki writes:

   Let it be known that it has not been narrated as to how many *rak'ats* the Messenger of Allah 🕮 performed during those nights [in congregation], whether they were twenty or less (*Tuhfat al-akhyar* 116 U).

3. 'Allama Suyuti says,

   The scholars have differed on the number of *rak'ats* [in *tarawih*]. If it [the number] had been established through the practice of the Messenger of Allah 🕮, they would not have differed [regarding it] (*al-Masabih* 42 U).

4. 'Allama Shawkani writes:

   What has been understood from the hadiths in this chapter is the validity of the nightly prayers of Ramadan, and that they can be performed either in congregation or individually. However, to confine the prayer known

182

as *tarawih* to a stipulated number of *rak'ats*... is not understood from the Sunna (*Nayl al-awtar* 3:53 U).

5. Mawlana Wahid al-Zaman states:

There is no fixed number [of *rak'ats*] for the prayer in the nights of Ramadan, i.e. *tarawih* (*Nazl al-abrar* 1:126 U).

The scholarly statements mentioned above clearly establish that there are no authentic narrations stating that Allah's Messenger 🌸 performed a fixed number of *rak'ats* for *tarawih*. Hence, this strikes down the claim that the Messenger 🌸 only performed eight *rak'ats* and that to perform anything besides eight is a "reprehensible innovation" [*bid'a*], as claimed by some.

There are however a handful of weak reports which inform us of the number of *rak'ats* performed by the Messenger 🌸 in *tarawih*. For instance, there is a narration of Ibn 'Abbas 🌸 which states that the Messenger 🌸 performed twenty *rak'ats*. Although the hadith scholars have classified this narration to be weak, it could still be used as evidence, because it is supported by the consensus of Companions and the practice of the whole *Umma*, generation after generation, for more than twelve hundred years.

Other weak reports from the Messenger 🌸 on this issue that are not substantially supported by the practice and statements of the pious predecessors, will be rejected. One must understand though that even if the narration of Ibn 'Abbas 🌸 is rejected, the scholarly consensus [*ijma'*] reached by 'Umar 🌸—which established that *tarawih* was twenty *rak'ats*—would be sufficient evidence to prove that *tarawih* is indeed twenty *rak'ats*.

The reason why there are no authentic and direct reports from the Messenger 🌸 concerning the number of *rak'ats* in *tarawih*, is that the Messenger 🌸 performed the prayer in congregation for a few days only, after which he performed *tarawih* in the confines of his home. Hence, many of the Companions did not observe him performing the prayer. Thereafter, the prayer continued to be performed individually or in small groups until the time of 'Umar ﷺ, when he appointed an *imam* to lead everyone in twenty *rak'ats*. Thus, it came to be performed as twenty *rak'ats* in a large congregation. The few Companions fortunate enough to have observed it with Allah's Messenger ﷺ in congregation did not voice any objection to the decision of 'Umar ﷺ. If the Messenger ﷺ had performed more or less than twenty *rak'ats* on any of the nights during Ramadan, these Companions would surely have refuted 'Umar's ﷺ decision for establishing *tarawih* as twenty *rak'ats*.

The Hadiths on This Issue

Since it has been established that there are no authenticated hadiths from the Messenger ﷺ regarding the number of *rak'ats* in *tarawih*, all that remains in terms of proof for *tarawih* being twenty *rak'ats* is the agreement of scholars with 'Umar's ﷺ decision; for once this is established, the *Umma* must follow it wholeheartedly as it is incumbent on Muslims to follow the rulings of the Companions ﷺ.

1. 'Irbad ibn Sariya ﷺ narrates [that the Messenger ﷺ said]:

> Keep to my Sunna and the Sunna of the guided Caliphs who followed the right way [*al-khulafa' al-rashidin al-mahdiyyin*]. Hold fast to it, and cleave onto it with your teeth (*Sunan Abi Dawud* 2:287, *al-Tirmidhi* 2:97, *Ibn Maja* 5).

First, the Messenger of Allah ﷺ very strongly instructed, "Keep to my Sunna and the Sunna of the guided Caliphs who followed the right way." This means that the rightly guided Caliphs must also be followed in their rulings, just as the Messenger ﷺ is to be followed. 'Umar ﷺ, being the second rightly guided Caliph, is the one who put forth the verdict that *tarawih* was to be performed as twenty *rak'ats*, which the Companions unanimously agreed upon. Due to the above hadith, his decisions will have to be accepted just as if it had come from the Messenger ﷺ himself.

Second, it should also be remembered that the amount of *rak'ats* stipulated by 'Umar 🟤 could have only been acquired from the Messenger 🟤 himself. This is obviously assumed because the number of *rak'ats* for any prayer cannot be determined through one's own preference, but rather must be set by Allah 🟤 through His Messenger 🟤. For 'Umar 🟤 to have ruled on this matter and not have received any objections from the Companion regarding it, indicates that the number of *rak'ats* performed by the Messenger 🟤 in *tarawih* was twenty. Ibn 'Abbas's 🟤 narration (mentioned earlier) confirms that the Messenger 🟤 performed twenty *rak'ats*.

'Umar 🟤 determined the number of *rak'ats* of *tarawih* to be twenty and appointed Ubay ibn Ka'b 🟤 to lead the people in congregation. This then remained the practice of the Muslim *Umma* throughout the caliphate of 'Uthman and 'Ali 🟤, and then on and on for twelve hundred years. Hence, it will be necessary to follow suit. Some of the following hadiths mention this in more detail.

2. 'Abd al-Rahman ibn 'Abd al-Qari relates:

> One night during Ramadan, he went out to the *masjid* with 'Umar ibn al-Khattab 🟤. People were scattered around in groups. One person was praying alone, whereas another was leading a group of people in prayer. 'Umar 🟤 remarked, "If I could have them all congregate behind one *imam* it would be better." He then made a firm commitment to do so and had them all pray behind Ubay ibn Ka'b 🟤.
>
> 'Abd al-Rahman states that he went out with him again on another night and found the people congregated behind their *imam*. Upon seeing this, 'Umar 🟤 remarked, "How great an innovation this is" [*ni'mat al-bid'atu hadhihi*, i.e. a practice that has been revived]" (*Sahih al-Bukhari* 1:269, *Muwatta Imam Malik* 42).

The Messenger 🟤 had performed the *tarawih* in congregation for a few days and then discontinued it for fear of it turning into an obligation on the *Umma*. It then remained like this throughout the caliphate of Abu Bakr 🟤, who remained occupied with the many issues that arose in his time. Thereafter, 'Umar 🟤 revived the practice and had everyone perform twenty *rak'ats tarawih* behind one *imam*.

He called it a good practice saying that if it was an innovation, that it was indeed a good one. This practice was then continued throughout the generations.

Hadith 1 above makes it clear that a reprehensible innovation cannot be attributed to 'Umar ﷺ or any of the other three Caliphs. Regarding 'Umar's ﷺ statement of the practice being such a "wonderful innovation," 'Allama Tibi writes:

> 'Umar ﷺ was referring to the praiseworthy deed of encouraging the prayer and reestablishing the congregation after it had not been observed during the caliphate of Abu Bakr ﷺ, even though it had been observed for a few days in the time of the Messenger ﷺ in this manner. However, the Messenger ﷺ had discontinued it for fear of it becoming an obligation [*fard*] on his *Umma*. 'Umar ﷺ was aware of this and established this procedure as a *sunna* for time to come [i.e. as a *sunna mu'akkada*, not a *fard*]. Hence, for him is the reward of this tradition and the reward of all who observe it until the Day of Judgment. (*Fath al-Mulhim* 2:319)

This clarifies that 'Umar's ﷺ practice was in line with that of the Messenger of Allah ﷺ. Because Abu Bakr ﷺ, for most of his caliphate, remained occupied with the important task of dealing with the apostates and those who either claimed prophethood after the Messenger's ﷺ death or demanded certain radical changes in the religion, many issues that were under debate in his time were clarified during the time of 'Umar ﷺ.

3. Yazid ibn Khusayfa narrates Sa'ib ibn Yazid as saying:

> They would perform twenty *rak'ats tarawih* during the month of Ramadan in the time of 'Umar ﷺ, and they would recite the chapters containing a hundred or so verses [*mi'in*]; and during the time of 'Uthman ibn 'Affan ﷺ they would lean on their staffs from standing [for so long]" (*Sunan al-Bayhaqi* 2:496).

The narrators of this hadith have all been rigorously approved as 'Allama Nimawi confirms in his *Athar al-sunan*. This hadith is clear evidence that twenty *rak'ats* were observed during the time of 'Umar ﷺ as well as during the time of 'Uthman ﷺ.

4. Yazid ibn Ruman relates:

> The people would perform twenty-three *rak'ats* during Ramadan in the time of 'Umar ﷺ. (*Sunan al-Bayhaqi* 2:496, *Muwatta Imam Malik* 1:71)

Although this is a rigorously authenticated hadith, it is *mursal,* or one with a broken chain. However, this does not alter its effectiveness for a number of reasons:

(a) By consensus of the hadith scholars, *mursal* narrations can be used as evidence.

(b) This is a hadith narrated by Imam Malik, and it is an established fact that the *mursal* narrations of Imam Malik in his *Muwatta* rank alongside his *mawsul* narrations [i.e. those with unbroken chains].

(c) There are many other *mursal* and *mawsul* narrations which strengthen this one; for instance, hadith 2 above.

(d) Shah Waliyullah writes that Imam Shafi'i said:

> The most authentic book after the Qur'an is the *Muwatta* of Imam Malik, and the hadith scholars are unanimous that all its narrations are authentic according to the judgment of [Imam] Malik, and all its *mursal* narrations reach the Messenger ﷺ in some way or another (*Hujjatullah al-baligha* 1:106 U).

5. Yahya ibn Sa'id narrates that

> 'Umar ibn al-Khattab ﷺ appointed an *imam* to lead them in twenty *rak'ats* (*Musannaf Ibn Abi Shayba* 2:393).

6. 'Abd al-'Aziz ibn Rafi' narrates that

> Ubay ibn Ka'b ﷺ would lead the congregation in twenty *rak'ats tarawih* in Madina during Ramadan, followed by three [*rak'ats*] *witr* (*Musannaf Ibn Abi Shayba* 2:393).

7. 'Ata' reports:

> I found the people observing twenty-three *rak'ats,* which included *witr* (*Musannaf Ibn Abi Shayba* 2:393).

8. Abu Khusayb narrates:

> Suwayd ibn Ghafala would lead them in prayer during the month of Ramadan. He would perform five *tarwihas* [sets of four *rak'ats*]—twenty *rak'ats* [in all] (*Sunan al-Bayhaqi* 2:496).

9. Nafi' ibn 'Umar narrates that

> Ibn Abi Mulayka would lead them in twenty *rak'ats* prayer during Ramadan (*Musannaf Ibn Abi Shayba* 2:393).

10. Sa'id ibn 'Ubayd narrates that

> 'Ali ibn Rabi'a would lead them in five *tarwihas* [i.e. twenty *rak'ats*] and three *witr* during Ramadan. (*Musannaf Ibn Abi Shayba* 2:393)

11. Ibn 'Abbas ⬥ relates:

> The Messenger ⬥ would perform twenty *rak'ats* during Ramadan and three *rak'ats witr*. (*Musannaf Ibn Abi Shayba* 2:394)

This hadith may be weak since a narrator in its chain, Abu Shayba Ibrahim ibn 'Uthman, has received some criticism. However, as mentioned earlier, since the *Umma* has adopted the same number of *rak'ats* for the greater part of history, it will not be totally rejected but rather used as supplementary evidence.

12. It has been narrated from Shutayr ibn Shakl (a companion of 'Ali ⬥) that

> he would lead them during the month of Ramadan in twenty *rak'ats* [*tarawih*] and three *rak'ats witr*. (*Sunan al-Bayhaqi* 4:496)

13. Muhammad ibn Ka'b al-Qurazi says,

> The people would perform twenty *rak'ats* in the month of Ramadan during the caliphate of 'Umar ⬥. They would lengthen the recitation and perform three *rak'ats witr* (*Qiyam al-layl* 91 U).

14. A'mash reports that 'Abdullah ibn Mas'ud ⬥ would perform twenty *rak'ats* [*tarawih*] and three *rak'ats witr* (*Qiyam al-layl* 91 U).

All of these reports mention the *rak'ats* of *tarawih* as being twenty and no less.

THE OPINIONS OF VARIOUS JURISTS AND SCHOLARS

1. The author of *Bidayat al-mujtahid,* Ibn Rushd, writes:

> Imam Malik (in one of his opinions), along with Imam Abu Hanifa, Shafi'i, Ahmad, and Dawud al-Zahiri, has preferred that the *tarawih* performed in the month of Ramadan be twenty *rak'ats* excluding *witr.* Ibn al-Qasim reports from Malik that he preferred thirty-six *rak'ats* with three *rak'ats witr* [according to another of his opinions] (*Bidayat al-mujtahid* 210).

2. The great hadith master Imam Tirmidhi presents a detailed report on the various opinions surrounding this issue:

> The knowledgeable people have disputed over the number of *rak'ats* to be performed for *tarawih* during Ramadan. Some say forty-one *rak'ats* including *witr:* this is the opinion of the people of Madina and such is their practice. However, the opinion of the majority is that *tarawih* is twenty *rak'ats,* and this opinion is more in agreement with the narrations of 'Ali, 'Umar ◈, and the other Companions of the Messenger ◈, and it is also the opinion of Sufyan al-Thawri, 'Abdullah ibn al-Mubarak, and Imam Shafi'i. In fact, Imam Shafi'i states, "I found the people of my city, Makka, performing twenty *rak'ats.* "Imam Ahmad states, "There are various reports to be found concerning *tarawih,* but no exact number is confirmed." Ishaq states, "We prefer forty-one *rak'ats,* according to what has been narrated from Ubay ibn Ka'b ◈." (*Sunan al-Tirmidhi* 1:166)

In such a detailed analysis of the opinions, there is not even a mention of *tarawih* being eight *rak'ats,* even as a weak opinion.

3. In his commentary on *Sahih al-Bukhari,* 'Allama Qastalani writes:

> Imam Bayhaqi has reconciled the various narrations and concluded that initially the Companions performed eleven *rak'ats* for *tarawih,* after which they performed twenty with three *rak'ats witr.* The scholars accepted the agreement on twenty *rak'ats* during the time of 'Umar ◈ as a consensus.

4. In the Maliki *fiqh* text, *al-Anwar al-sati'a,* it states:

We say that twenty *rak'ats* of *tarawih* following the 'Isha prayer is an emphasized [*mu'akkada*] *sunna* during the month of Ramadan, with *salams* to be made on every second *rak'a* [i.e. to be performed in two *rak'a* units].

5. Ibn Qudama writes:

   It is reported from 'Ali that he appointed an *imam* to lead the people in twenty *rak'ats tarawih* during Ramadan (*al-Mughni*).

This narration proves that the practice of twenty *rak'ats* continued on into the time of 'Ali.

6. The great Shafi'i scholar Imam Nawawi writes:

   The number of *rak'ats* in *tarawih* remained twenty, since this was constantly accepted century after century.

7. It is reported in the *Mirqat al-mafatih* that Hafiz Ibn Hajar said:

   The Companions reached a unanimous verdict that *tarawih* was twenty *rak'ats* (*Mirqat al-mafatih* 3:382).

8. Ibn Taymiya states:

   This is the opinion most Muslims follow [i.e. of *tarawih* being twenty *rak'ats*] (A'zami in his *Rak'ate tarawih* 92).

9. Shaykh Mansur ibn Idris al-Hanbali writes:

   Tarawih is twenty *rak'ats* during Ramadan.

10. Asad ibn 'Amr reports that Imam Abu Yusuf said:

    I asked Abu Hanifa regarding *tarawih* and concerning 'Umar's role in it. He informed me that *tarawih* is an emphasized *sunna*. It is not something 'Umar established through his own preference or innovated, but he established it based on some evidence or information he possessed from the Messenger (*I'la' al-sunan* 46 U).

11. Imam Ghazali writes:

    Tarawih is twenty *rak'ats,* its method is well known, and it is an emphasized *sunna* (*Ihya' 'ulum al-din* 1:139).

12. Sayyid 'Abd al-Qadir Jilani writes:

Tarawih is a *sunna* of the Messenger of Allah ﷺ and is twenty *rak'ats* (*Ghunyat al-talibin* 567 U).

13. Imam Nawawi says,

Let it be known that *tarawih* is a *sunna* by agreement of all the Muslims, and it is twenty *rak'ats* (*Kitab al-Adhkar* 83).

14. Ibn Taymiya says,

It has been established that Ubay ibn Ka'b ﷺ would lead the people in twenty *rak'ats* of *tarawih* throughout the month of Ramadan, after which he would perform three *rak'ats* of *witr*. Hence, most scholars have taken twenty *rak'ats* to be *sunna,* as Ubay ibn Ka'b ﷺ performed this number of *rak'ats* amidst the Emigrants [*muhajirin*] and Helpers [*ansar*] and none refuted him (*Fatawa Ibn Taymiya* 23:112 U).

Other Important Points to be Noted

First, it has to be fully comprehended that the amount of *rak'ats* for any prayer is not something which can be made up and established through one's own intellect and reasoning. It has to come from Allah ﷻ and His Messenger ﷺ. Hence, the scholars state that whenever anything of this nature (i.e. that which is not established through human reasoning alone) is reported by a Companion, it will be considered as being directly acquired from Allah's Messenger ﷺ.

According to the agreement of the hadith scholars, all the Companions are considered trustworthy and legally upright [*'adul*]. It cannot be believed that they would introduce a new concept into the religion which is contrary to the principles of the *Shari'a*. Hence, even though there are no *marfu'* [directly related from the Messenger ﷺ] hadiths to be found concerning the number of *rak'ats* in *tarawih*, the decision of 'Umar ﷺ of *tarawih* being twenty *rak'ats* is accepted. It is believed, as explained by Imam Abu Hanifa [*see* hadith 10 above], that the number was acquired from the Messenger of Allah ﷺ and not something 'Umar ﷺ established through his own desire.

191

Second, once the unanimous agreement concerning the number of *rak'ats* was reached, not a single Companion of the Messenger 🌸 was reported to have refuted it. The Companions who had performed *tarawih* with the Messenger 🌸 (during the few days he performed it in congregation) and who were present at the time of 'Umar 🌸, also did not refute his decision.

'Umar 🌸 did not even receive criticism from the wives of the Messenger 🌸, who constantly observed the Messenger's 🌸 *tarawih* prayer at home after he had abandoned performing it in congregation. This indicates that the Messenger 🌸 must have performed twenty *rak'ats*, and it was because of this fact that the Companions supported 'Umar's 🌸 decision to set the *tarawih* prayer at twenty *rak'ats*.

Third, 'Allama Halabi has made a very noteworthy point as to why the number of *rak'ats* of *tarawih* may have been set at twenty. He states:

> The *sunna* and *nawafil* [supererogatory] prayers are supplementary prayers which make up for any deficiencies that may have been left in the obligatory [*fard*] prayers. The obligatory prayers of the day, along with three *rak'ats* of *witr*, total to twenty *rak'ats*. Hence, it is appropriate to have twenty *rak'ats* of *tarawih*, so that there is a balance between the two types of prayers, i.e. between the *rak'ats* of the obligatory prayers and the *rak'ats* of the supplementary *nafl* or *sunna* prayers.

Analyzing the Narrations Concerning Eight *Rak'ats*

Those who claim the *tarawih* to be eight *rak'ats* try to establish this opinion in two ways. One way is by claiming that the Messenger 🌸 only performed eight *rak'ats*, and the other is by claiming that 'Umar 🌸 also ordered only eight *rak'ats* to be performed; hence, their rejection of 'Umar's 🌸 decision establishing twenty *rak'ats*. We will now look at the narrations which they have used to substantiate these two claims.

1. It is reported from Abu Salama that

he asked 'A'isha ❀ regarding the prayer of the Messenger ❀ during Ramadan. She explained, "The Messenger of Allah ❀ would not perform more than eleven *rak'ats,* neither in Ramadan nor out of it. He would perform four *rak'ats,* and do not ask of their beauty and length, followed by another four, and do not ask of their beauty and length, after which he would perform three [*witr*]." 'A'isha ❀ continued, "I asked, 'O Messenger of Allah, do you sleep before you perform the *witr.*' He replied, 'O 'A'isha, my eyes sleep, but my heart does not'" (*Sahih al-Bukhari* 1:154).

This hadith is probably the most widely used in claiming that *tarawih* is only eight *rak'ats.* However, there are a number of reasons why this hadith cannot stand as evidence:

(a) The prayer mentioned in the hadith is clearly not *tarawih* but rather the *tahajjud* [night-vigil] prayer. Abu Salama's inquiry was regarding whether or not the Messenger ❀ performed any extra *rak'ats* of *tahajjud* during Ramadan. 'A'isha ❀ answered by stating that the Messenger ❀ would perform no more than eight *rak'ats* (*tahajjud*) throughout the year, regardless of what month it was.

Hence, 'A'isha ❀ was speaking of a prayer that was performed by the Messenger ❀ both in and out of Ramadan, which is why she used the words "neither in Ramadan nor out of it." She could not have been speaking about *tarawih* since *tarawih* is not performed out of Ramadan. The question of Abu Salama therefore had to be about *tahajjud* (which is performed throughout the year) and not about *tarawih.*

What further supports this explanation is that there are some narrations of 'A'isha ❀ which speak of the Messenger ❀ increasing his worship during the month of Ramadan. She states:

The Messenger of Allah ❀ would exert himself [in worship] during the last ten days of Ramadan more than at any other time (*Sahih Muslim* 1:372).

This narration and many others like it indicate that the Messenger ❀ would perform more prayer in Ramadan than in any other month, even though the *rak'ats* of *tahajjud* performed by him would remain constant throughout the year. This means that the increase in worship by him during Ramadan was through the performance of *tarawih* and other supererogatory prayers. Hence, the narration of 'A'isha 🙵 above is concerning *tahajjud*, since the *rak'ats* of his *tahajjud* prayer remained constant in all the months of the year.

(b) Imam Muhammad ibn al-Nasr al-Marwazi, in his book, *Qiyam al-layl*, has compiled many narrations under a chapter entitled, "Chapter on the *Rak'ats* Performed by the *Imam* in Ramadan for *Tarawih*." However, he does not mention the above hadith of Abu Salama in that chapter despite it being a rigorously authenticated hadith of *Sahih al-Bukhari*. Like al-Marwazi, there are many other authors who, in their works, have not mentioned this hadith to be concerning *tarawih*.

(c) Many compilers of hadith, such as Imam Muslim, Nasa'i, Abu Dawud, Tirmidhi, Ibn Maja, Ibn Khuzayma, and Imam Malik, have also not included this hadith in their chapters on *tarawih*, despite it being such a rigorously authenticated hadith. Instead, they mention it in their chapters on *tahajjud* or *witr*. Indeed, had this narration been in regards to *tarawih*, they would have surely included it in their chapters on *tarawih*.

(d) Furthermore, if this hadith was concerning *tarawih*, then why did 'A'isha 🙵, the narrator, not reject the consensus [*ijma'*] reached by 'Umar 🙵? She could have informed him in some way or the other that the correct number of *rak'ats* for *tarawih* was eight. Thus, the prayer she describes in the above hadith can be none other than *tahajjud*.

Another narration popularly used to claim that the Messenger 🙵 performed only eight *rak'ats* for *tarawih* is the following:

2. Jabir 🙵 narrates that

> the Messenger 🙵 led them in prayer during Ramadan. He 🙵 performed eight *rak'ats* followed by *witr* (*Sahih Ibn Hibban, Ibn Khuzayma, I'la' al-sunan* 7:60:7).

The following explanations have been given for this hadith:

(a) This hadith furnishes details of only one night in which the Messenger ﷽ led the congregation in *tarawih* prayer. The following narration is actually more detailed in this regard:

> Jabir ﷺ narrates that the Messenger ﷽ performed eight *rak'ats* during one night of Ramadan followed by *witr*. The following night, we gathered together in the *masjid* hoping that he would come out to us. We remained waiting for him until morning, when he [came out and] said, "I did not desire…" or [he said], "I was afraid that the *witr* would be made obligatory [*yuktabu*] upon you (*Qiyam al-layl* 91 U).

There are many narrations which mention that the Messenger ﷽ performed the *tarawih* in congregation for three nights then failed to appear on the fourth night [*see* the narrations of 'A'isha in *Sahih al-Bukhari* and *Muslim*]. However, the above narration indicates that the congregation took place for one night only and that the Messenger ﷽ did not turn up on the second night; which means that both are concerning two different occasions.

Other differences between it and 'A'isha's ﷺ other narrations is that 'A'isha's other narrations do not mention the number of *rak'ats* performed for *tarawih* (despite those narrations being so widely transmitted) whereas this one does. Also, the other narrations of 'A'isha mention that Allah's Messenger ﷽ was fearful of *tarawih* becoming obligatory on the *Umma* whereas the hadith of Jabir ﷺ mentions he was fearful of *witr* becoming obligatory. Hence, Hafiz Ibn Hajar al-'Asqalani has hesitated in accepting this narration to be concerning the same incident mentioned in the other narrations (*Fath al-Bari* 2:12 U).

(b) The other point Mawlana Habib al-Rahman A'zami makes about this narration is that there is only one person relating it from Jabir ﷺ. This single narrator, 'Isa ibn Jariya, has been strongly criticized by the scholars of hadith. Hafiz Dhahabi and Ibn Hajar al-'Asqalani have recorded much criticism about him, and Yahya ibn Ma'in states that "he is not strong" [*laysa bi dhaka*]. Likewise Imam Nasa'i, Abu Dawud, 'Uqayli, Saji, and Ibn 'Adi all have grave statements to make about him, either rejecting his narrations outright or labelling him as weak. Only Ibn Hibban and Abu Zur'a have not criticized him. However, since the criticism of the former group is very severe, it will take precedence over the opinions of the latter in determining his status as a narrator.

Hence, his narrations are weak and cannot be accepted as evidence for the claim of *tarawih* being eight *rak'ats;* even more so, in that no one else has reported that the Messenger 🌸 performed eight *rak'ats* in congregation during those nights he performed it in congregation (A'zami in *Rak'ate tarawih* 28).

(c) Some scholars have explained that even if the hadith were to be accepted, it would only inform as to the number of *rak'ats* the Messenger 🌸 performed in congregation, and does not negate the possibility that the Messenger 🌸 could have performed the remaining twelve *rak'ats* at home. Jabir 🕸 does not negate this possibility either, but merely informs us of the number of *rak'ats* that the Messenger 🌸 performed in congregation with the Companions, before retiring to the confines of his home.

There are also other narrations of Jabir 🕸 on this issue which mention that the Messenger of Allah 🌸 performed eight *rak'ats* in congregation; however, since they are all narrated through 'Isa ibn Jariya, they are all to be classified as weak and not to be used or related as evidence.

3. Sa'ib ibn Yazid relates:

> 'Umar 🕸 appointed Ubay ibn Ka'b and Tamim al-Dari 🕸 to lead the people in eleven *rak'ats* (*Muwatta Imam Malik* 1:71).

This is the narration presented to substantiate their second claim that 'Umar 🕸 ordered only eight *rak'ats* to be performed for *tarawih* and that there was never a consensus on twenty. However, this claim is even weaker than the first due to the following reasons:

(a) This hadith has been related from Sa'ib ibn Yazid ﷺ by two people—Muhammad ibn Yusuf and Yazid ibn Khusayfa. Five people have then related it from Muhammad ibn Yusuf. However, all five reports are different from one another, even though each one relates it from the same person. Due to its inconsistency and conflicting nature, this narration cannot stand as evidence to prove that *tarawih* is eight *rak'ats*. The different reports from Muhammad ibn Yusuf are as follows:

(1) The version mentioned above, transmitted by Imam Malik, mentions eleven *rak'ats,* but does not mention Ramadan.

(2) Yahya ibn Qattan's version mentions that 'Umar ﷺ brought the people together behind Tamim al-Dari ﷺ and they would perform eleven *rak'ats*. It does not mention 'Umar ﷺ issuing any specific command on the number of *rak'ats*, nor does it mention the month of Ramadan.

(3) The version narrated by 'Abd al-'Aziz ibn Muhammad simply mentions that they performed eleven *rak'ats* during the caliphate of 'Umar ﷺ. There is no mention of any specific command or of Ubay ibn Ka'b ﷺ, Tamim al-Dari ﷺ, or Ramadan.

(4) Ibn Ishaq's report mentions that they would perform thirteen *rak'ats* in Ramadan during the period of 'Umar ﷺ. It does not speak of 'Umar's ﷺ instructions, Ubay ibn Ka'b, or Tamim al-Dari ﷺ.

(5) Lastly, 'Abd al-Razzaq's version describes 'Umar ﷺ commanding that twenty-one *rak'ats* be performed instead of eleven.

Some versions of this narration mention eleven *rak'ats*, others thirteen *rak'ats*, and one also mentions twenty-one. So what is the reason for choosing the version of eleven *rak'ats* over the rest? In fact, the great Maliki jurist Ibn 'Abd al-Barr has given preference to the narration of twenty-one *rak'ats* and called the narrations of eleven to be an "erroneous assumption" [*wahm*] (*Rak'ate tarawih* 39). Hence, the version of twenty *rak'ats* has been adopted in light of these and other similar factors that only serve to strengthen its authenticity.

(b) The other narrator of this hadith from Sa'ib ibn Yazid ☙ is Yazid ibn Khusayfa, and Yazid's two students, Ibn Abi Dhi'b and Muhammad ibn Ja'far, relate this narration from him [*see* hadith 3 in "The Hadiths on This Issue" above]. All versions of this narration through Yazid ibn Khusayfa are unanimous in mentioning twenty *rak'ats;* and Imam Nawawi, 'Iraqi, Suyuti, and others have judged its chains [*asnad*] to be strong and reliable.

Hence, the question is: Why would the version of Muhammad ibn Yusuf mentioning eight *rak'ats* be adopted, despite it being so confusing and inconsistent in its mention of the number of *rak'ats,* and the version of Yazid ibn Khusayfa be abandoned despite it being consistent? Justice would demand that the narrations of Sa'ib ibn Yazid ☙ through Yazid ibn Khusayfa be accepted since they are consistent and have been classified as rigorously authenticated by many scholars; and that the narrations through Muhammad ibn Yusuf, because of their confusing nature, be interpreted and reconciled with those of Yazid ibn Khusayfa.

(c) Some scholars have reconciled the various versions of Sa'ib ibn Yazid's ☙ narration by stating that 'Umar ☙ initially ordered eleven *rak'ats* to be performed but then changed his decision to twenty after learning that it was the more correct view. Nobody refuted his decision, and twenty *rak'ats* continued to be performed for the most part of Islamic history.

Imam Bayhaqi, after mentioning the eleven and twenty *rak'ats* narrations, states:

> It is possible to reconcile the two types of narrations because the Companions would [initially] perform eleven *rak'ats* in congregation after which they began to perform twenty *rak'ats* and three *witr* (*Sunan al-kubra li 'l-Bayhaqi* 2:496).

Imam Bayhaqi makes the same point at another place in his *Sunan al-kubra*. Many other scholars have also provided similar explanations. Ibn Habib Maliki writes:

> It was initially [performed as] eleven *rak'ats,* but they would prolong the recitation in them, which proved difficult on the people, so they increased the number of *rak'ats* and shortened the recitation. They would perform twenty *rak'ats* excluding *witr* (*Tuhfat al-akhyar* 192 U).

CONCLUSION

It is only recently that some people have emerged with the opinion of only eight *rak'ats* being *sunna* for *tarawih*. Some have even gone as far as saying that performing any more than eight *rak'ats* would be considered a "reprehensible innovation" [*bid'a*] (may Allah forbid).

None of them have been able to produce a single example of any *masjid* in the world in which a *tarawih* congregation of less than twenty *rak'ats* was held during the first twelve hundred years or more of Islam. Likewise, not a single scholar from among the pious predecessors [*salaf salihin*] held an opinion of eight *rak'ats*. Can the opinions of contemporary men be preferred over the scholarship and opinions of those who enjoyed a greater proximity to the fountain of Prophethood?

Also, how does one overlook the fact that over a period of twelve hundred long years, nobody had any dispute with regards to the *rak'ats* of *tarawih* being twenty? How absurd it is to call it a reprehensible innovation in religion when 'Umar ﷺ himself reached an agreement with the Companions on that amount, and his decision was made through what he must have acquired from the Messenger ﷺ himself. Neither the Companions nor the household of the Messenger ﷺ refuted him. He then remarked as to "how wonderful a practice he had revived" [*ni'mat al-bid'atu hadhihi*], since people had not performed it in a large congregation during the time of Abu Bakr ﷺ.

It can therefore be concluded quite easily that since there has been an agreement among the four Imams and the overwhelming majority of scholars of this *Umma* concerning *tarawih* being twenty *rak'ats*, it is considered the *sunna* amount.

12

Combining Two Prayers

THERE ARE HADITHS which state that the Messenger of Allah ﷺ would combine two obligatory [*fard*] prayers together while travelling. The hadiths explain how he would alight from the back of the animal and perform Maghrib followed by 'Isha, and then resume his journey. There is a difference of opinion regarding the interpretation of these hadiths, i.e. exactly how he performed the two prayers together.

The Hanafis offer the following explanation. Although the Messenger of Allah ﷺ performed the prayers one after another, he actually performed each prayer in its own time. For example, when combining Maghrib and 'Isha, he would stop a short time prior to the end of Maghrib and would perform the prayer. Then as soon as the time of 'Isha would enter, he would perform 'Isha and then resume his journey.

Other scholars offer the explanation that the Messenger of Allah ﷺ would perform both Maghrib and 'Isha in the time of 'Isha (i.e. after Maghrib had expired).

The method offered by the Hanafi school of performing the first prayer toward the end of its time and the second prayer immediately after, at the beginning of its time, is known as *jam' al-suri* or "apparent combining" in the terminology of the jurists [*fuqaha'*]. The method of performing two obligatory [*fard*] prayers in one prayer time is known as *jam' al-haqiqi* or "real combining."

There are many hadiths which describe combining two prayers. According to Hanafi scholars, the most suitable explanation is that of *jam' al-suri,* wherein each prayer is performed in its own time. The Hanafi approach in explaining this issue is in total agreement with the Qur'an and hadiths, both of which emphasize each prayer being performed in its own stipulated time. On the contrary, the *jam' al-haqiqi* approach leads to great conflicts between the Qur'an and hadiths.

By the end of the chapter, it will become evident that the Messenger ﷺ never combined two prayers together by actually moving one into the time of the other. It is also important to remember that performing Maghrib and 'Isha in the time of Maghrib, and Zuhr and 'Asr in the time of Zuhr, is known as *jam' al-taqdim* or "advanced combining," since one of the prayers is performed before its time. Combining them at the time of the later prayer is known as *jam' al-ta'khir* or "delayed combining," because one of the prayers is delayed from its specific time.

THE VARIOUS OPINIONS

One opinion is that it is permissible to perform *jam' al-haqiqi* if one is undertaking a hurried journey. The second opinion is that *jam' al-haqiqi* is permissible when undertaking any type of journey; whether it be hurried or relaxed. For some, it is also permissible in the event of heavy rainfall, and some state that is also permissible in the event of illness.

The view of Imam Abu Hanifa is quite simple. According to him, the *jam' al-haqiqi* method is not permissible except at 'Arafat (during the pilgrimage), where advanced combining takes place between Zuhr and 'Asr, and at Muzdalifa, where the pilgrims perform delayed combining between Maghrib and 'Isha. The practice of advanced and delayed combining at these two places is established through the consensus of the scholars. Hence, the Hanafis do not permit *jam' al-haqiqi* except in these two instances. They have interpreted the hadiths which mention the combining of two prayers to be *jam'* *al-suri*. This type of combining is permissible at all times, as there can be no doubt concerning the permissibility of two prayers performed in their own times.

THE QUR'AN ON THIS ISSUE

1. Allah ﷻ says,

"Verily the prayer is enjoined on the believers at fixed hours [times]" (*al-Qur'an* 4:103).

This means every prayer has an appointed time with a beginning, prior to which the prayer is not valid, and an ending, after which the prayer is not to be delayed; otherwise it will become a *qada'* or missed prayer. Hence, this verse indicates the importance of performing each prayer in its own time.

2. Allah ﷻ says,

"Guard strictly the [five obligatory] prayers" (*al-Qur'an* 2:238).

This verse is also quite clear about performing prayers at their appointed times and not delaying them.

3. Allah ﷻ says,

"So woe unto those worshippers [hypocrites] who are negligent in regards to their prayer" (*al-Qur'an* 107:5).

A group of scholars state that this verse is admonition for those who delay the prayers beyond their appointed times.

4. Allah ﷻ says,

"Then, there succeeded them a posterity who gave up prayers" (*al-Qur'an* 19:59).

According to a group of scholars, the words, "who gave up prayers," mean those who delay the prayers beyond their stipulated times.

In short, these verses of the Qur'an verify that delaying any prayer is undesirable and extremely disliked. Delaying the prayer has been portrayed as a trait of the hypocrites [*munafiqin*]. For this reason, the hadiths, which seem to inform that the Messenger ﷺ delayed prayer, must be interpreted in a way that corroborates these verses, in order to remove the notion of undesirability from the Messenger's ﷺ practice. The only way this can be achieved is by taking the *combining* mentioned in them to mean "apparent combining." Now we will look at a few hadiths which are quite explicit in their prohibition of taking a prayer out of its time.

The Hadiths on This Issue

1. Abu Musa ﷺ narrates that the Messenger ﷺ said:

   Combining two prayers together without any valid reason is from the major sins [*kaba'ir*] (*Musannaf Ibn Abi Shayba* 2:459, *al-Ta'liq al-sabih* 2:124).

Thus, combining prayers would not be permissible even in the event of a journey or rain, just as other major sins are not made permissible in such circumstances.

2. It is narrated from 'Umar ﷺ that

   he wrote to the people [around the Islamic world] prohibiting them from combining two prayers together. He informed them that combining two prayers together was a major sin (*al-Ta'liq al-sabih* 2:124).

3. 'Abdullah ibn Mas'ud ﷺ narrates:

   I never observed the Messenger of Allah ﷺ perform any prayer out of its time except at Muzdalifa. He combined Maghrib and 'Isha at Muzdalifa (*Sahih al-Bukhari* 1:227, *Sahih Muslim* 1:417, *Sharh Ma'ani 'l-athar* 1:164).

4. In another narration Ibn Mas'ud ﷺ states:

   The Messenger of Allah ﷺ combined two prayers while on a journey. He would combine Maghrib and 'Isha by delaying Maghrib until just before its expiry time and performing 'Isha immediately as its time entered (*Musannaf Ibn Abi Shayba* 2:458).

5. 'A'isha ﷺ narrates:

The Messenger of Allah ﷺ, while on a journey, would delay Zuhr and perform 'Asr early and would delay Maghrib and perform 'Isha early [i.e. perform each prayer in its own time] (*Sharh Ma'ani 'l-athar* 1:164, *Musannaf Ibn Abi Shayba* 2:457).

6. It is related that Ibn 'Abbas ﷺ said:

I performed eight *rak'ats* together [four of Zuhr and four of 'Asr] and seven *rak'ats* together [three of Maghrib and four of 'Isha] with the Messenger of Allah ﷺ. [One of the narrators says,] "I asked Abu 'l-Sha'tha', "I assume he delayed Zuhr [to the end of its time] and performed 'Asr as soon as it entered, and delayed Maghrib [likewise] and performed 'Isha early." He replied, "I also think the same" (*Sahih Muslim* 1:246, *Musannaf Ibn Abi Shayba* 2: 456).

This hadith from *Sahih Muslim* is very precise in its description of combining two prayers. The method described by the narrator is *jam' al-suri*.

7. Imam Abu Dawud has transmitted the following report:

The muezzin of 'Abdullah ibn 'Umar ﷺ informed him it was time for prayer. Ibn 'Umar ﷺ instructed him to continue on the journey. When the red of sunset [*shafaq ahmar*] had nearly disappeared, he got off from his mount and performed Maghrib. Then he waited until the red had completely disappeared and performed 'Isha. He then said, "Whenever the Messenger of Allah ﷺ was in a hurry for some reason, he would do just as I have done" (*Sunan Abi Dawud* 1:178).

As we can see, the method of *combining* mentioned in the above hadiths is none other than that of *jam' al-suri*. It is an agreed upon method which no one disputes. How can there be an objection to two prayers being performed together in a way that does not cause them to be performed either before their stipulated time or after it? Undoubtedly, this is not only the safest method of combining two prayers, but it is also the most suitable way to explain the hadiths on the subject of combining.

It is also common knowledge that the Fajr prayer should not be performed before its time or intentionally delayed beyond it. Similarly, other prayers should not be performed out of their stipulated times either, especially not while considering it to be *sunna*. This indicates that the *sunna* method of combining two prayers is *jam' al-suri,* as has also been substantiated through the Qur'an and hadiths. This is the Hanafi opinion in this issue.

If it were permissible to practice *jam' al-haqiqi* in the event of travel or illness, then why is it confined to some prayers only? Why is it not permissible to perform all the prayers of the day together in the morning before departing on a journey? The reason for this is quite simple. The practice of combining mentioned in the hadiths is not to be taken as *jam' al-haqiqi* but as *jam' al-suri,* wherein each prayer remains in its own time, but all prayers are performed one after another.

THE HADITHS ON COMBINING PRAYERS

In the following, we will analyze some hadiths that are normally presented to establish the permissibility of *jam' al-haqiqi.*

1. Ibn 'Umar ﷺ narrates:

> Whenever the Messenger of Allah ﷺ would undertake a hurried journey, he would combine Maghrib and 'Isha (*Sahih Muslim* 1:245).

This narration is sometimes used to prove the permissibility of "real combining," whereas it just mentions that the Messenger of Allah ﷺ combined two prayers and does not mention that *jam' al-haqiqi* was performed. The Hanafis have explained that the Messenger ﷺ performed "apparent combining" and not "real combining," since the former is a method agreed upon by all scholars.

In this hadith, since Ibn 'Umar ﷺ does not mention the actual method of combining, we turn to hadith 7 above—also a narration of Ibn 'Umar ☙—where he expounds on the method of combining prayers. The method he describes in that narration is none other than *jam' al-suri,* so it will be taken as a commentary for this narration.

2. Nafi' reports:

> Whenever 'Abdullah ibn 'Umar ☙ had to travel in a hurry, he would com-bine Maghrib and 'Isha after the red twilight of sunset disappeared. Ibn 'Umar ☙ stated that whenever the Messenger ﷺ was forced to travel in a hurry, he would also combine Maghrib and 'Isha (*Sahih Muslim* 1:245).

3. 'Abdullah ibn 'Umar ☙ narrates:

> Once the Messenger ﷺ had to travel quickly due to some emergency in his family. He delayed Maghrib until the red twilight had disappeared, then got off his animal and combined the two prayers. Thereafter, 'Abdullah ibn 'Umar ☙ informed everyone that this was the practice of the Messenger ﷺ whenever he had to travel in a hurry (*Sunan al-Tirmidhi* 1:124).

These two hadiths seem to be in apparent conflict with the opinion of the Hanafis. However, in reality, if they are understood correctly, they would be found to be in total agreement. This is due to the following reasons:

(a) Firstly, there are two types of *shafaq* or "twilight:" one is the redness [*ahmar*] seen in the sky after sunset, and the second is the whiteness [*abyad*] that remains for a short while after the redness disappears. 'Allama 'Ayni states:

> It is possible that the twilight referred to in the narrations is the red one. [In the Hanafi school] there are two views regarding the expiry of Maghrib time. Some say it ends when the redness disappears, and others say it ends when the whiteness disappears. Therefore, if the Messenger ﷺ performed both prayers immediately after the redness had disappeared, it means he performed Maghrib during the whiteness, i.e. within its stipu-lated time (according to the view that Maghrib ends after the whiteness has disappeared), and he also performed 'Isha within its stipulated time (according to the view that Maghrib ends with the disappearance of the redness after which 'Isha begins) [(*'Umdat al-qari* 3:568)].

(b) Another explanation, mentioned in *al-Ta'liq al-sabih,* is that these hadiths have been narrated with various differences. Some contain the addition, "the redness was close to disappearing." This indicates that one of the narrators may have become slightly confused regarding the exact wording due to the various reports, so he finally reported it in the words, "after the redness had disappeared," according to his speculation. This means that in reality it was just prior to the ending of the red twilight that the Messenger ﷺ performed Maghrib, which means it was *jam' al-suri.*

(c) Another reason for preferring *jam' al-suri* is that since the hadiths of Ibn 'Umar ؓ on this issue are inconsistent and do not maintain a fixed expression, it would be more preferable to regard hadith 7 above (also narrated by him) as the commentary for the various transmissions of his report. That hadith makes it clear that the method of combining used by the Messenger ﷺ was "apparent combining." Hence, the combining mentioned in the remaining hadiths of 'Abdullah ibn 'Umar will also be considered to be "apparent combining."

4. Mu'adh ؓ narrates that

> during the expedition of Tabuk, whenever the Messenger ﷺ would set out before the sun declined from its meridian, he would delay Zuhr and perform it [just prior to its expiry time] with 'Asr, and when he would depart after noon he would perform 'Asr early by combining it with Zuhr [i.e. Zuhr at the end of its time and 'Asr as soon as it entered], then he would continue his journey. Whenever he would depart before Maghrib, he would delay it and perform it with 'Isha [i.e. in their respective times], and if he set out after Maghrib he would perform 'Isha early by combining it with Maghrib (*Sunan al-Tirmidhi* 1:124, *Sunan Abi Dawud* 1:178).

The following points have been made about this narration:

(a) 'Allama 'Ayni states regarding this narration:

> This hadith was rejected by Imam Abu Dawud, and it is also reported from him that there is no clear hadith to be found concerning the performance of a prayer before its stipulated time.

(b) Another problem is the strong criticism of Husayn ibn 'Abdillah, a narrator in this hadith's chain, by the hadith experts [*muhaddithin*]. Ibn al-Madini says, "I have abandoned his reports." Imam Ahmad states, "He has defects." Ibn Ma'in calls him weak [*da'if*]; and Nasa'i says, "His narrations have been rejected."

(c) Even if the hadith were accepted for a moment to be authentic, it would still be considered as describing *jam' al-suri* for various reasons. It is indicated in the hadith that the Messenger 🕌 would delay the first prayer to the end of its time and perform the second one immediately thereafter in its own time. The following two narrations of Ibn 'Abbas 🕳 suggests the same explanation:

> The Messenger 🕌 performed Zuhr and 'Asr together and Maghrib and 'Isha together without [being in the state of] fear or travel.

> The Messenger 🕌 combined Zuhr and 'Asr together and Maghrib and 'Isha together in Madina without [being in the state of] fear or rain (*Sahih Muslim* 1:246).

These narrations speak of the Messenger 🕌 combining the prayers even though the circumstances were not of fear, rain, or travel. These are the main three circumstances under which one can perform *jam' al-haqiqi* according to many scholars besides the Hanafis.

So was he performing *jam' al-haqiqi,* as some like to say, even though none of the valid reasons for doing so were present? The correct explanation we could offer here is that these narrations of Ibn 'Abbas 🕳, as well as the other narrations on this issue, do not speak of the Messenger 🕌 performing *jam' al-haqiqi* at all; but rather to his performance of *jam' al-suri.*

CONCLUSION

It could be safely concluded that the Hanafis have followed a safe path in explaining the hadiths in this issue. Their explanation does not contradict the hadiths or Qur'anic verses that strictly enjoin that prayer be performed in their own times. They interpret the hadiths of *combining* to be based on *jamʿ al-suri,* wherein two prayers are performed one after another—the first prayer at the end of its time and the second prayer immediately thereafter, at the beginning of its time. This seems to be the safest and most uncontroversial approach to adopt in light of the many narrations on this issue.

On the other hand, taking the various narrations to be based on *jamʿ al-haqiqi*—wherein one prayer is intentionally delayed and performed in the time of the other, or the later prayer is performed in advance during the time of the earlier prayer—will cause these hadiths to contradict the verses and hadiths that encourage prayers to be performed in their own times. Furthermore, those who allow *jamʿ al-haqiqi* have also stated that it is superior not to combine the two prayers but to perform them separately in their own respective times.

Glossary

A'IMMAT AL-RIJAL. Leading authorities and experts in the scrutiny of hadith narrators.

'ALLAMA. Great learned scholar.

'ARAFA. Ninth day of Dhu 'l-Hijja [last month in the Islamic calendar].

'ARAFAT. Expansive plain approximately thirteen miles from Makka. Here pilgrims remain standing in prayer to Allah ﷻ for some time. Zuhr and 'Asr prayers are combined here with the condition that the Imam of the Muslims is present. The *masjid* located in this plain is called Masjid al-Namira.

'ASR. Late afternoon prayer, performed after an object's shadow (minus the length of its shadow at the sun's zenith) is twice as long as the object.

BAYTULLAH. The Ka'ba, House of Allah ﷻ in the Sacred Precinct (*Haram*) in Makka.

BINT. Daughter.

DA'IF. Weak, a hadith in which there is some defect; either in the chain of transmission; or in the proper understanding of the narrator; or its contents; or because it is not in perfect agreement with Islamic beliefs and practices. It is a hadith of less reliable authority.

DIN. Religion (Islam).

FAJR. Prayer performed between true dawn and sunrise.

FAQIH (pl. *fuqaha'*). Islamic jurist.

FARD. Obligatory divine command that is established through decisive proof [*dalil qat'i*]. One who neglects a *fard* injunction without any valid excuse is termed a transgressor [*fasiq*] in Islamic *Shari'a*, and one who rejects a *fard* injunction is considered an unbeliever [*kafir*].

FIQH AL-IMAM

FATWA (pl. *fatawa*). Formal legal ruling issued by a competent jurist.

FIQH. Islamic law or jurisprudence.

HADITH. Literally, a piece of news, a story or a report relating to a present or past event. In the technical sense, it refers to the reports of the words, deeds, and approvals or disapprovals of the Messenger of Allah ﷺ.

HAFIZ. Hadith master, one who has memorized one hundred thousand hadiths by heart. Also used for one who has memorized the entire Qur'an.

HANAFI. Follower of the Hanafi school of Islamic law.

HANBALI. Follower of the Hanbali school of Islamic law.

HARAM. Forbidden, prohibited, unlawful. The status of something being completely unlawful under Islamic law and established through decisive [*qat'i*] proof. *See also MAKRUH.*

HASAN. Approved or sound, similar to a rigorously authenticated hadith [*sahih*] but of a slightly lower degree.

IBN. Son.

IJMA'. Consensus. Often used to refer to the complete agreement among the Companions or the jurists regarding a particular juridical issue.

IJTIHAD. An ability of the intellectual understanding by which the subtleties, implications, finer points, mysteries, wisdom, and causes of the laws [*ahkam*] of Islam are ascertained.

'Ilm. Sacred Knowledge.

IMAM. Derived from the Arabic word "to lead," Imam is widely used for the leader of the prayer or the leader of a school of thought in Islamic law.

'ISHA. The night prayer, performed after the redness of sunset disappears.

JAHRI PRAYER. Prayer in which the Qur'an is recited aloud (e.g. Fajr, Maghrib and 'Isha).

JAM' AL-HAQIQI. Real combining—combining two *fard* prayers in the time of one.

JAM' AL-SURI. Apparent combining—combining two prayers by performing the first prayer at the end of its time and the second prayer at the beginning of its time.

JAM' AL-TA'KHIR. Delayed combining—combining Maghrib and 'Isha together in the time of 'Isha and combining Zuhr and 'Asr together in the time of 'Asr.

JAM' AL-TAQDIM. Advanced combining—combining Maghrib and 'Isha together in the time of Maghrib and combining Zuhr and 'Asr at the time of Zuhr.

JUMU'A. Friday.

KUFA. An important city of Iraq founded by 'Umar ﷺ.

MA'LUL. Defective narration.

MADHHAB (pl. *madhahib*). School of Islamic religious law.

MADINA MUNAWWARA. Illuminated city of the Messenger of Allah ﷺ and second holiest city of Islam (located in Arabia, today known as Saudi Arabia).

MAGHRIB. Evening prayer performed after sunset.

MAKKA. Holiest city of Islam and home to the Masjid al-Haram and the Ka'ba (located in Arabia, today known as Saudi Arabia).

MAKRUH. Disliked. Status of something that is undesirable [*tanzihi*], and sometimes reproachable [*tahrimi*], under Islamic law but not to degree of being unlawful [*haram*] (due to being established through speculative [*dhanni*] proof). *See also* HARAM.

MALIKI. Follower of the Maliki school of Islamic law.

MARFU'. Chain of transmission that reaches to the Messenger ﷺ.

MASHHUR. Hadith which is handed down by at least three reliable authorities; or, according to another view, a hadith which, although widely disseminated later, was originally transmitted by one person in the first generation.

MAWDU'. Fabricated and spurious hadith attributed to the Messenger of Allah ﷺ.

MAWQUF. Chain of transmission that does not reach the Messenger ﷺ but ends at a Companion.

MAWSUL. Unbroken chain leading to the narrating authority.

MUFASSIR. Exegete or elucidator of the Holy Qur'an.

FIQH AL-IMAM

MUHADDITH. Hadith scholar.

MUNFARID. Person performing prayer alone.

MUNKAR. Disowned or denied hadith.

MUQTADI. Person performing prayer behind an *imam* in congregation.

MURSAL. Hadith narrated by a Follower [*tabi'i*] or someone after him directly from the Messenger 🌸 without mentioning the authority in between.

MUSALLI. Person performing prayer.

MUSTAHAB. Preferred practice.

MUTAWATIR. Event or statement reported by such a vast number of people in every generation that it is impossible for it to contain any falsehood.

MUZDALIFA. Place near Makka between the plains of 'Arafat and Mina—also known as *al-Mash'ar al-Haram.* Pilgrims camp there for the night on their return from 'Arafat.

NAFL. Supererogatory practice.

QADA. Missed prayer that must be made up.

QIBLA. The direction of the Ka'ba in Makka towards which Muslims face in prayer.

QIRA'A. Recitation (normally of the Holy Qur'an).

QIYAM. Standing posture of prayer.

QA'DA. Sitting posture of prayer.

RAK'A. Unit of prayer consisting of a standing and bowing posture and two prostrations.

RUKU'. Bowing posture of prayer.

SAHIH. Hadith rigorously authenticated in its text [*matn*] and transmission.

SAJDAT AL-TILAWA. Prostration performed after reciting a verse of prostration.

SHAFAQ AHMAR. Red evening twilight appearing in the sky after sunset.

SHAFAQ ABYAD. Soft white light appearing after the red evening twilight disappears.

SHAFI'I. Follower of the Shafi'i school of Islamic law.

SHARI'A. Islamic Sacred Law.

SIRRI PRAYER. Prayer in which the Qur'an is recited silently (e.g. Zuhr and 'Asr prayers).

SIWAK. Toothstick from the branches or roots of shrubs having known anti-bacterial properties.

SUJUD AL-SAHW. Prostrations of forgetfulness—performance of two additional prostrations after completing the *tashahhud* in the final *rak'a,* done to compensate for certain defects in the performance of prayer.

SUNNA. Precedent and custom; the actions and practices of Allah's Messenger 🌿. The second source of Islamic sacred knowledge called hadiths. Also used for acts of the category between *wajib* and *mustahab. See also* HADITH, *WAJIB* and *MUSTAHAB.*

SUNNA MATRUKA. Early practice of the Messenger of Allah 🌿 that he later abandoned.

SUNNA MU'AKKADA. Emphasized practice of the Messenger of Allah 🌿 or his Companions that cannot be left out without valid reason.

SUNNA MUSTAMIRRA. Permanent or continuous practice of the Messenger 🌿.

SURAT AL-FATIHA. Opening chapter of the Qur'an; also known as Umm al-Qur'an.

SUTRA. Stick or similar object placed in front of a person performing prayer, so that a passerby may pass outside the object and not directly in front of the worshipper.

TABI'I. Follower or Successor—one who saw the Companions [*sahaba*] while in the state of faith (*iman*) and then died in that state.

TAB'AL-TABI'IN. Follower of the Followers—one who saw the Followers during their lifetimes in the state of faith.

TAFSIR. Explanation, commentary, or exegesis of the Holy Qur'an.

TAHIYYAT AL-MASJID. Welcoming-the-*masjid* prayer—two *rak'ats* performed upon entry into the *masjid* prior to sitting down.

TAKBIR TAHRIMA. Opening *takbir* of prayer (e.g. *Allahu akbar*).

TAQLID. Following reliable authority in the affairs of Islamic law (esp. one of the four Imams). *See also* MADHHAB.

FIQH AL-IMAM

TARAWIH. Twenty *rak'ats* of *sunna* prayer performed after the *fard* of 'Isha during the month of Ramadan.

TARWIHA. Brief interval observed after every four *rak'ats* of *tarawih.*

'ULAMA (sing. *'alim*). Islamic scholars well-versed with Islamic sciences.

UMMA. Community.

UMM al-QUR'AN. Opening chapter of the Qur'an known as al-Fatiha.

USUL al-FIQH. Principles or roots of jurisprudence.

USUL al-HADITH. Principles or roots of hadith.

WAJIB. Divine command established through proof that, although very strong [*dalil zanni*], is of a lower category than absolute proof [*dalil qat'i*]. One who neglects or rejects a *wajib* injunction is termed a transgressor [*fasiq*].

WUDU'. Ritual ablution for prayer.

ZUHR. Noon prayer performed just after the sun has left its zenith.

Bibliography

Abu 'l-Hasan, Muhammad. *Tanzim al-ashtat*. Karachi, Pakistan: Darul Ishaat.

al-Asbahi, Malik ibn Anas. *al-Muwatta*. Multan, Pakistan: Maktaba Faruqiyya.

al-'Asqalani, Ahmad ibn Hajar. *Fath al-Bari bi sharh Sahih al-Bukhari*. Cairo, Egypt: Dar al-Rayyan.

A'zami, Habib al-Rahman Abu 'l-Ma'athir. *Rak'ate Tarawih*. Gujranwala, Pakistan: Qadri Kutub Khana.

al-Bayhaqi, Abu Bakr Ahmad ibn al-Husayn. *al-Sunan al-kubra*. First edition. Makka Mukarrama: Dar al-Baz.

Binnori, Muhammad Yusuf. *Ma'arif al-sunan*. Karachi, Pakistan: Maktaba Rashidiyya.

al-Bukhari, Muhammad ibn Isma'il. *al-Jami' al-Sahih*. Karachi, Pakistan: Qadimi Kutub Khana.

al-Daraqutni, Abu 'l-Hasan 'Ali ibn 'Umar. *al-Sunan*. Cairo, Egypt: Dar al-Mahasin.

al-Dhahabi, Abu Abdillah. *Mizan al-i'tidal*. First edition. Beirut, Lebanon, Dar Ihya' al-Kutub al-'Arabiyya, 1964.

al-Gujrati, Muhammad Tahir al-Pattani. *Majma' bihar al-anwar*. Third edition. Madina Munawwara, Saudi Arabia: Maktaba Dar al-Iman, 1415/1994.

———. *al-Mughni fi dabti asma' al-rijal*. Lahore, Karachi, Pakistan: Idara Islamiyyat.

al-Hakim al-Naysaburi, Muhammad ibn 'Abdillah. *al-Mustadrak 'ala 'l-Sahihayn*. Beirut, Lebanon: Dar al-Ma'rifa.

FIQH AL-IMAM

al-Haythami, Nur al-Din. *Majma' al-zawa'id wa manba' al-fawa'id.* Beirut, Lebanon: Dar al-Kitab.

al-Hilali, Muhammad Taqi al-Din and Muhammad Muhsin Khan. *Interpretation of the meaning of The Noble Qur'an in the English Language.* Riyadh, Kingdom of Saudi Arabia: Maktaba Dar al-Salam, 1993.

al-Humaydi, 'Abdullah ibn al-Zubayr. *al-Musnad.* Makka Mukarrama, Saudi Arabia: Dar al-Baz.

Ibn Abi Shayba, 'Abdullah. *al-Kitab al-Musannaf fi 'l-hadithi wa 'l-athar.* Second edition. Bombay, India: Dar al-Salafiyya, 1399/1979.

Ibn Kathir, 'Imad al-Din. *al-Bidaya wa 'l-nihaya.* Beirut, Lebanon: Maktabat al-Ma'arif.

Ibn Qudama al-Maqdisi. Ahmad ibn 'Abd al-Rahman. *al-Mughni.* Beirut, Lebanon: Dar al-Kitab al-'Arabi.

Ibn Taymiya, Ahmad ibn 'Abd al-Halim. *Majmu' al-Fatawa.* Saudi Arabia: Published by the Custodian of the Haramayn.

Jalandhry, Khayr Muhammad. *Bis tarawih ka thubut.* Karachi, Pakistan: Idara Da'wate Islam and Maktaba Sharifa.

Khandelwi, Muhammad Zakariyya. *Awjaz al-Masalik ila Muwatta Malik.* Saharanpur, India: al-Maktabat al-'Ilmiyya.

Khandelwi, Muhammad Idris. *al-Ta'liq al-sabih.* Deoband, India: al-Maktaba al-Fakhriyya.

al-Khazraji, Safi al-Din Ahmad ibn 'Abdillah al-Ansari al-Yamani. *Khulasa Tadhhib Tahdhib al-Kamal fi asma' al-rijal wa 'alayhi Ithaf al-khassa bi tashih al-Khulasa.* Halab, Syria: Maktabat al-Matbu'at al-Islamiyya.

Lane, E. W. *Arabic-English Lexicon.* Cambridge, England: Islamic Text Society.

Ludhyanwi, Muhammad Yusuf. *Ikhtilafe ummat awr sirate mustaqim.* Deoband, India: Maktaba Thanawiyya.

al-Manbaji, Abu Muhammad 'Ali ibn Zakariyya. *al-Lubab fi 'l-jam' bayn al-Sunnati wa 'l-Kitab.* Damascus, Syria: Dar al-Qalam and Beirut, Lebanon: al-Dar al-Shamiyya.

Mirathi, Muhammad Faruq. *Raf'e yadayn awr qira'ate Fatiha khalf al-imam.* Mirath, India: Maktaba Mahmudiyya.

al-Nasa'i, Abu Abd al-Rahman Ahmad ibn Shu'ayb. *al-Sunan al-Sugra (al-Mujtaba)*. Karachi, Pakistan: Qadimi Kutub Khana.

al-Nawawi, Abu Zakariyya Yahya ibn Sharaf. *al-Adhkar al-muntakhab min kalami Sayyid al-abrar*. First edition. Beirut, Lebanon: Dar al-Khayr, 1411/1990.

al-Naysaburi, Muslim ibn al-Hajjaj. *al-Sahih*. Karachi, Pakistan: Qadimi Kutub Khana.

Nazir, Muhammad. *Ashraf al-tawdih*. Third edition. Faisalabad, Pakistan: Maktabat al-'Arifi, 1414.

al-Nimawi, Muhammad ibn 'Ali. *Athar al-sunan*. Multan, Pakistan: Maktaba Imdadiyya.

Qala'ji, Muhammad Rawwas and Hamid Sadiq Qa'nabi. *Mu'jam Lughat al-fuqaha'*. Karachi, Pakistan: Idarat al-Qur'an wa 'l-'ulum al-Islamiyya.

al-Qari, Mulla 'Ali. *Mirqat al-mafatih sharh Mishkat al-masabih*. First edition. Lebanon, Beirut: Dar al-Fikr, 1412/1992.

al-Qazwini, Abu Abdillah Muhammad ibn Yazid ibn Maja. *al-Sunan*. Karachi, Pakistan: Qadimi Kutub Khana.

al-Qurtubi, Ibn Rushd. *Bidayat al-mujtahid*. Beirut, Lebanon: Dar al-Ma'rifa.

al-San'ani, 'Abd al-Razzaq. *al-Musannaf*. First edition. Beirut, Lebanon: al-Majlis al-'Ilmi, 1390/1970.

al-Shawkani, Muhammad ibn 'Ali. *Durr al-Sahaba*.

———. *Nayl al-awtar min ahadithi Sayyid al-akhyar*. Beirut, Lebanon: Dar al-Jil and Dar al-Fikr.

al-Shaybani, Muhammad ibn al-Hasan. *al-Muwatta*. Karachi, Pakistan: Qadimi Kutub Khana.

Siddiqi, 'Abd al-Hamid. *Sahih Muslim. An English Translation*. Lahore, Pakistan: S. H. Muhammad Ashraf.

al-Sijistani, Abu Dawud Sulayman ibn al-Ash'ath. *al-Sunan*. Multan, Pakistan: Maktaba Haqqaniyya.

al-Tibrizi, Wali al-Din Muhammad ibn 'Abdillah al-Khatib. *Mishkat al-Masabih*. Karachi, Pakistan, Qadimi Kutub Khana.

FIQH AL-IMAM

al-Tahawi, Abu Ja'far. *Sharh Ma'ani 'l-athar.* Second edition. Beirut, Lebanon: Dar al-Kutub al-'Ilmiyya, 1408/1987.

al-Tirmidhi, Abu 'Isa Muhammad ibn 'Isa. *al-Sunan [al-Jami'].* Karachi, Pakistan: Sa'id Company Limited.

'Uthmani, Shabbir Ahmad. *Fath al-Mulhim sharh Sahih Muslim.* Deoband, India: al-Maktabat al-Ashrafiyya.

'Uthmani, Muhammad Shafi'. *Kashkol.* Karachi, Pakistan: Darul Ishaat.

'Uthmani, Muhammad Taqi. *Darse Tirmidhi.* Ninth edition. Karachi, Pakistan: Maktaba Dar al-'Ulum, 1413/1992.

'Uthmani, Muhammad Zafar Ahmad Thanawi. *I'la' al-sunan.* Karachi, Pakistan: Idarat al-Qur'an wa 'ulum al-Islamiyya.

Wehr, Hans. *A Dictionary of Modern Written Arabic.* Edited by J. Milton Cowan. Beirut, Lebanon: Librarie Du Liban.

al-Zabidi, Muhammad ibn Muhammad al-Husayni. *Ithaf al-sadat al-muttaqin bi sharh Ihya' 'ulum al-din.* Beirut, Lebanon: Dar al-Fikr.

al-Zayla'i, Jamal al-Din Abu Muhammad. *Nasb al-raya li ahadith al-Hidaya.* First edition. Cairo, Egypt: Dar al-Hadith, 1415/1995.

Index of Persons

FIQH AL-IMAM

161, 169, 180–181, 189, 209
Ahmad Muhammad Shakir 104
'A'isha 119, 121, 127, 135–137, 141–147,
 154–160, 162, 193, 194, 195, 205
'A'isha bint 'l-Ajrad 23
'Ali ibn Abi Talib 37, 38, 60, 61, 77, 93, 96,
 99, 105, 109, 111, 138, 141, 143, 162, 171,
 185, 188–190
'Ali ibn Rabi'a 188
'Alqama 36, 104–105, 110, 111, 114, 115,
 140–141, 170
'Alqama ibn Wa'il 91
A'mash 28, 30, 188
'Ammar ibn Yasir 38
'Amr ibn 'Abasa 161
'Amr ibn al-'As 38
'Amr ibn Dinar 28, 29
'Amra bint 'Abd al-Rahman 137
Anas ibn Malik 22–23, 51, 62, 89, 138,
 140–141, 143, 172, 174
al-Ansari, Abu 'Uthman 128
al-Ansari, Abu Mas'ud 28
Asad ibn 'Amr 31, 190
Asad ibn al-Furat 31
'Asim ibn Kulayb 109
Aswad 109, 110, 111, 114
Aswad ibn Yazid 6
'Ata' ibn Yasar 76
'Ata ibn Abi Rabah 29, 89, 140, 171, 187
Awza'i (Imam) 25, 69
'Ayni 161, 180, 207–208
al-'Ayni, Badr al-din xvii, 63, 75
Ayyub ibn al-Nahik 167
A'zami, Habib al-Rahman 195

al-Baghdadi, Khatib 23, 31, 134
Bara' ibn 'Azib 108
Bayhaqi 27, 60, 61, 69, 189, 198–199
Binnori, Yusuf xix, 47
Bishr ibn Rafi' 94
Bukhari 24, 58, 59, 84, 89, 94, 110, 136,
 137, 156
al-Bunani, Thabit 138

Daraqutni 23, 27, 83, 134, 174

al-Dari, Tamim 196, 197
Dhahabi 22–23, 25, 27, 30, 40, 58, 59,
 114, 136, 137, 143, 195
al-Dulabi, Abu Bishr 95, 96

Fudayl ibn 'Iyad 31

al-Ghatafani, Sulayk 171, 173–177
Ghazali, Abu Hamid 190

al-Hadhdha', Khalid 170
Hafiz Ibn Hajar al-'Asqalani 22, 39, 51,
 58, 89, 142, 149, 150, 156, 157, 190, 195
Hafs ibn Ghiyath 31
Hakim 22, 27
Hakim (Imam) 136–137
Halabi 192
al-Hanbali, Mansur ibn Idris 190
Harith 29
Haritha ibn Mudrib 129
Harun (Prophet) 89
Hasan al-Basri 129, 130, 139, 140–141, 144
Hasan ibn Ziyad 27
Haskafi ('Allama) 46–47
Haythami 161, 169
Hibban ibn 'Ali 31
al-Himmani, Yahya 29
Hisham 83
al-Hudhali, Nubaysha 169
Hudhayfa 28, 35, 38, 39, 128
Hudhayfa ibn al-Yaman 143
Hulb 59
Humaydi 105
Husayn ibn 'Abdillah 209

Ibn 'Abbas, 'Abdullah 60, 71, 76, 77, 95,
 106, 108, 128, 137, 140–143, 147,
 154, 156, 157, 161, 162, 169, 183,
 185, 188, 205, 209
Ibn 'Abd al-Barr, Abu 'Umar 23, 56, 83,
 181, 197
Ibn 'Abidin, Abu Amin 46
Ibn Abi 'l-'Awam 41
Ibn Abi Dhi'b 198
Ibn Abi Hatim 69

222

Subject Index

FIQH AL-IMAM

FIQH AL-IMAM

About the Author

THE AUTHOR, MUFTI ABDUR-RAHMAN IBN YUSUF MANGERA, has been studying the traditional Islamic sciences and writing scholarly works for most of his life. He completed the bulk of his studies at Darul Uloom Bury, North England, where he memorized the Qur'an by age fifteen and thereafter went on to complete a rigorous, six-year *Shari'a* program. He graduated from this program with authentic certifications [*ijaza*] in numerous Islamic disciplines, including Arabic, Islamic jurisprudence, and hadith (with particular emphasis on the six authentic books of hadith [*Sihah Sitta*] and the *Muwattas* of Imam Malik and Imam Muhammad). His teachers at Darul Uloom Bury included Shaykh Yusuf Motala and other students of Shaykh al-Hadith Mawlana Muhammad Zakariyya Kandhelwi.

After graduating, the author traveled to South Africa, where he attended Madrasah Zakariyyah part-time to gain specialized training in answering legal questions [*ifta*] under Mufti Rada al-Haq. While in South Africa, he also completed a B.A. with honors in Islamic studies at Rand Afrikaans University, Johannesburg, under Professor Abdur-Rahman Doi, Ph.D.

He then traveled to Syria, where he received a second certification in Qur'anic recitation and memorization, this time from Shaykh 'Abd al-Razzaq al-Halabi, who possessed a short, unbroken chain of transmission [*sanad*] to the Messenger of Allah ﷺ in this subject. He also received a certification from Shaykh Adib Kallas after reading Mulla 'Ali al-Qari's *Sharh al-Fiqh al-Akbar* and attending lectures on other classical texts of Islamic creed ['*aqida*].

He spent the following year in Saharanpur, India, where he received

FIQH AL-IMAM

formal authorization to issue legal rulings [*fatawa*], which required a close study of part or all of a number of classical jurisprudential texts, including, among others, Ibn Nujaym's *Al-Ashbah wa 'l-naza'ir* and 'Allama Haskafi's *Al-Durr al-mukhtar* (along with its commentary, *Radd al-muhtar*, by 'Allama Ibn 'Abidin al-Shami). During this time, Mufti Abdur-Rahman also attended classes on the principles of hadith [*usul al-hadith*], studying 'Allama Lakhnawi's *Al-Raf' wa 'l-takmil fi 'l-jarh wa 'l-ta'dil* and parts of Imam Suyuti's *Tadrib al-rawi*.

The author acquired additional certifications in hadith from such great scholars as Shaykh Muhaddith Habib al-Rahman al-A'zami (through his student Shaykh Mufti Zayn al-'Abidin), Shaykh Abu 'l-Hasan 'Ali Nadwi, and Shaykh Muhammad al-'Awwama. May Allah continue to bless those of his teachers who are still alive and have mercy on those who have passed on to the next life.

To date, Mufti Abdur-Rahman has written *Fiqh al-Imam: Key Proofs in Hanafi Fiqh* (1996) and co-authored *Reflections of Pearls* (1995). He also published *Provisions for the Seekers* (1996), a translation and commentary of the Arabic work *Zad al-Talibin*, a small collection of short hadiths compiled by Mawlana Ashiq Ilahi from 'Allama Tibrizi's *Mishkat al-Masabih*. He is currently working on a revised, second edition of this work, which is set for release later this year. His latest published work is *Prayers for Forgiveness: Seeking Spiritual Enlightenment through Sincere Supplication* (2004), a translation of *Al-Istighfarat al-Munqidha min al-Nar*, a collection of seventy prayers for forgiveness by 'Allama Qutb al-Din al-Hanafi transmitted from Imam Hasan al-Basri. Additionally, Mufti Abdur-Rahman has completed an unpublished translation of Imam Abu Hanifa's *Al-Fiqh al-Akbar*, along with its commentary, written by 'Allama Maghnisawi.

He presently serves as Imam of a southern California *masjid* and continues to work on scholarly publications through White Thread Press.

Some of his *fatawa* can be found at *www.whitethreadpress.com* and *www.sunnipath.com* and some of his lectures at *www.zamzamacademy.com* and *www.al-rashad.com*.